Preventing Corruption in Asia

Despite intensified governmental and public efforts at corruption control in recent years, official transgression continues to surface in various ways of abusing the unique power and trust that a government holds.

Preventing Corruption in Asia addresses a number of crucial questions:

- What institutional arrangements are necessary to ensure a clean and honest government?
- What self-regulatory capabilities must government institutions develop in order to maintain integrity?
- How should a sense of ethical responsibility be instilled in the civil services?
- Do special anti-corruption agencies help keep government clean?
- How will a regulatory framework of official conduct work properly?
- How useful are anti-corruption campaigns in containing corruption?

Focusing on a number of carefully selected countries in the Asia and Pacific region, the book sets as its focal point the choice of institutional design in preventing corruption, rather than treating corruption as a practical or technical problem to be corrected by strong political will and good anti-corruption policy measures. While focusing on institutional designs and policy choices, the book also examines other aspects of clean government such as the social environment, the legal and regulatory framework, the role of the public, and the impact of culture.

Preventing Corruption in Asia will be of interest to those studying Asian politics, Chinese politics, comparative political economy, comparative development studies and Asian cooperation.

Ting Gong is Professor of Political Science at City University of Hong Kong. She has done extensive research on corruption and anti-corruption reform.

Stephen K. Ma is Professor of Political Science at California State University, Los Angeles. He has done extensive research on administrative ethics.

Routledge Contemporary Asia Series

Preventing Corruption in Asia

Institutional Design and Policy Capacity

Edited by
Ting Gong and Stephen K. Ma

Routledge
Taylor & Francis Group

LONDON AND NEW YORK

First published 2009
by Routledge
2 Park Square, Milton Park, Abingdon, Oxon, OX14 4RN

Simultaneously published in the USA and Canada
by Routledge
711 Third Avenue, New York, NY 10017

Routledge is an imprint of the Taylor & Francis Group, an Informa business

First issued in paperback 2011

Typeset in Times New Roman
by Taylor & Francis Books

British Library Cataloguing in Publication Data
A catalogue record for this book is available from the British Library

Library of Congress Cataloging-in-Publication Data
Preventing corruption in Asia : institutional design and policy capacity /
edited by Ting Gong and Stephen K. Ma.
       p. cm. – (Routledge contemporary Asia series ; 15)
     1. Political corruption–China–Prevention. 2. China–Politics and
government–2002- 3. Corruption–Prevention. I. Gong, Ting, 1955- II. Ma,
Stephen K.
     JQ1509.5.C6P74 2009
     364.1'3230951–dc22

                                                          2008043395

ISBN10: 0-415-48408-1 (hbk)
ISBN10: 0-415-66599-X (pbk)
ISBN13: 0-203-87976-7 (ebk)

ISBN13: 978-0-415-48408-4 (hbk)
ISBN13: 978-0-415-66599-5 (pbk)
ISBN13: 978-0-203-87976-4 (ebk)

For
Feng and Sonya
Lee Anne, Royce and Ryan

Contents

Illustrations

Figures

Tables

Contributors

Muhittin Acar is an Associate Professor of Public Administration at Hacettepe University in Turkey. He holds a BA from Ankara University, an MPM from Carnegie Mellon University, and a PhD in public administration from the University of Southern California. His research focuses on accountability, integrity, and collaboration in public governance.

Gerald E. Caiden is a Professor of Public Administration in the School of Policy, Planning and Development at the University of Southern California. He is best known for his research in administrative and public sector reform, corruption and administrative ethics, and administrative culture and organizational diagnosis.

Hon S. Chan is a Professor and Head of the Department of Public and Social Administration, City University of Hong Kong. He received his PhD at the Maxwell School of Syracuse University. His research focuses on civil service reforms, performance management, and the nomenklatura in the People's Republic of China.

Chun-Ming Chen is an Associate Professor in the Department of Public Policy and Management of Shih Hsin University, Taiwan. He has been conducting nation-wide Government Integrity Perception Surveys in Taiwan for six consecutive years since 2003.

O.P. Dwivedi, Order of Canada, PhD, LLD (Hon.), Dr Env. S. (Hon.), Fellow of the Royal Society of Canada, is Professor Emeritus, University of Guelph, Canada. He teaches comparative public policy and administration, and environmental policy and management. He has published 35 books and numerous articles and book chapters.

Uğur Emek has been a senior expert in the State Planning Organization of Turkey since 1989. He holds a BA in business administration and a PhD in economics from Ankara University, and an MS in economics from Northeastern University. His research interests include competition policy; public finance, and Turkish economy.

Jie Gao holds a PhD from City University of Hong Kong and is an instructor in the Department of Public and Social Administration, City University of Hong Kong. Her research interests focus on performance management in the public sector, and cadre evaluation system in the People's Republic of China.

Ting Gong is a Professor of Political Science at the City University of Hong Kong. She is the author of the first English book-length study of China's corruption, *The Politics of Corruption in Contemporary China: An Analysis of Policy Outcomes*, and has published in various academic journals on corruption-related issues.

Lung-Teng Hu is an Assistant Professor in the Department of Public Policy and Management at Shih Hsin University, Taiwan. He currently serves as the Director of Knowledge Management of the Transparency International's chapter in Taiwan.

Michael Johnston is the Charles A. Dana Professor of Political Science and Division Director for the Social Sciences at Colgate University in Hamilton, New York. His most recent book is *Syndromes of Corruption: Wealth, Power, and Democracy* (Cambridge University Press, 2005). He has written extensively on corruption, reform, and other development and globalization themes.

Wen-Jong Juang is an Assistant Professor in the Department of Public Policy and Management of Shih Hsin University, Taiwan. He has been participating in nationwide and local Government Integrity Perception Surveys in Taiwan since 2004.

Peter Larmour is a Reader at the Australian National University and teaches a course on corruption and anticorruption with the New South Wales ICAC. His recent book *Foreign Flowers* dealt with the international transfer of policies, and he is currently working on a book on corruption in the Pacific Islands.

Stephen K. Ma, Fulbright Senior Specialist in comparative politics/public administration, is Professor of Political Science and Director of the Institute for Executive Leadership at California State University, Los Angeles. His latest book is *Administrative Ethics in the US: Theories and Practices* (Fudan University Press, 2006).

Melanie Manion is a Professor of Political Science and Public Affairs at the University of Wisconsin–Madison. Her research focuses on institutions and institutionalization in Chinese politics. Publications include work on the Chinese bureaucracy, grassroots democratization, and the political economy of corruption and good governance.

D.S. Mishra, BTech, MBA, is an Indian Administrative Service officer. He has served 24 years in the government and is currently Chief Vigilance

Officer in the Airports Authority of India. He has published several articles/ research papers in Indian and international journals.

Meera Mishra, MA International Development and MA Social Work, has eighteen years' experience in the social development sector. She worked as Senior Policy Specialist with UNDP in Asia Pacific and is currently working as Senior Advisor Policy and Programmes with Constella Futures.

Tak-Wing Ngo teaches Chinese politics at Leiden University and is concurrently IIAS Professor of Asian History at Erasmus University, Rotterdam, the Netherlands. His most recent publications include *Rent Seeking in China* (Routledge 2008) and *China in Verandering: Balans en Toekomst van de Hervormingen* (Parthenon 2008).

Jon S.T. Quah, a former Professor of Political Science at the National University of Singapore, has published extensively on corruption in Asian countries. His major publications include: *Curbing Corruption in Asia: A Comparative Study of Six Countries* (2003) and *Combating Corruption Singapore-Style: Lessons for Other Asian Countries* (2007).

David H. Rosenbloom is Distinguished Professor of Public Administration at American University and Chair Professor of Public Management at City University of Hong Kong. Author or co-author of over 300 professional publications, including 26 books, he received the Gaus and Waldo Awards for lifetime contributions to political science and public administration. His research focuses on public administration and democratic constitutionalism.

Yan Sun is a professor of political science at the Graduate Center and Queens College, City University of New York. Her most recent book is *Corruption and Market in Contemporary China* (Cornell University Press, 2004). She has also published numerous articles on China's post-Mao economic transition, corruption, and comparative studies of corruption in China, Russia and India.

Andrew Wedeman is an Associate Professor of Political Science at the University of Nebraska, Lincoln. His recent publications include *From Mao to Market: Rent Seeking, Local Protectionism, and Marketization in China* (Cambridge University Press, 2003) and articles in *China Quarterly, Journal of Contemporary China*, and *China Review*.

Chilik Yu is a Professor in the Department of Public Policy and Management and Vice President (Academic Affairs) of the Shih Hsin University, Taiwan. He has been serving as Executive Director of Transparency International–Taiwan since January, 2003.

Foreword

A few years ago, a doctoral student in one of my public administration seminars asked, "What's wrong with political corruption?" She read some of the law and economics theories on the subject and repeated their contention that corruption, like markets, can enhance distributive efficiency by setting prices for scarce public services. Her question is answered easily, as the chapters in this book make clear. A price does not always capture the costs, as in the case of externalities. Corruption is contagious. It spreads on the rationale that "everybody does it." Corruption also weakens the rule of law, which is already fragile in many nations. Absent strict adherence to the rule of law, temptation grows greater and the enforcement of anticorruption measures lags. Additionally, corruption can sap economic development and political stability by diverting funds from productive investment into individuals' pockets and by moving wealth off-shore. Corruption in the form of nepotism and political patronage may reduce government's administrative capacity. Corruption promotes public cynicism, distrust, and resentment, undermining the legitimacy of political leaders and governments. And, of course, it is rarely, if ever, moral.

Had the student framed the question as "What are the impacts of political corruption?" the answer, as this book also demonstrates, would have been far more complex. Corruption can have beneficial effects, regardless of whether these outweigh the costs. For instance, during the nineteenth century, the US used a so-called spoils system to fill positions in public bureaucracies. The system rewarded partisanship rather than merit and was widely condemned as

> unsound in principle, dangerous in practice, demoralizing ... and calculated to encourage and perpetuate the official ignorance, inefficiency and corruption which, perverting the powers of Government to personal and party ends, have burdened the country with debt and taxes, and assisted to prostrate the trade and industry of the nation.[1]

However, the same system is credited with contributing to the development of strong mass-based national political parties and electoral competition that continue to vitalize US democracy. As Robert Merton explained,[2] political practices that are widely condemned as corrupt may have beneficial "latent" functions. Corruption can also be instrumental in producing infrastructure, public goods, and the private wealth that funds museums, public libraries, and valuable research. Consequently, from functional and normative perspectives, corruption can be a mixed bag for a political system. This immensely complicates the social scientific study of political corruption and the prescription of viable anticorruption strategies.

Analyzing political corruption

Among the many challenges to analyzing political corruption is the problem of definition. As Peter Larmour contends in Chapter 13, culture can be central to defining corruption as well as an excuse for it. Practices that are standard operating procedure in one culture may be viewed as corrupt in another. The scope of a practice and the size of an exchange are also relevant in defining corruption. In a gift-giving culture, when does a gift to or from a political official or bureaucrat constitute a bribe? By extrapolation, in a modern mass democracy, when is a contribution to a political candidate's electoral campaign good citizenship, and when is it an effort to buy access or specific public policy initiatives?

However defined, measuring corruption may also be challenging. In Chapter 12, Chilik Yu, Chun-Ming Chen, Lung-Teng Hu, and Wen-Jong Juang employ a variety of approaches for measuring perceptions of corruption. But following Stephen K. Ma in Chapter 6, we normally assume that by its nature, much corruption is hidden. Perceptions may be affected by media accounts of spectacular cases of corruption and highly public "show trials" of perpetrators. Yu, Chen, Hu and Juang's data suggest that despite a widespread perception of political and business corruption in Taiwan, few people are engaged in bribery and a minority—though a substantial one at 38 percent—believe that corruption extensively affects their "personal and family life."

Measurement is also complicated by the degree of transparency in a political system. How well do freedom of information, proactive governmental dissemination of information, open meetings, and whistleblowing work? What about anticorruption agencies, inspectors general offices, and legislative and other investigatory committees? Does greater political competition promote transparency? What is the relationship between transparency, corruption, and perceptions of corruption? Presumably, transparency reduces the opportunity to engage in corruption and by increasing the probability of getting caught, creates an incentive to refrain from it. But in uncovering corruption, transparency can generate greater perceptions of it. This might partly account for Yu, Chen, Hu and Juang's finding that perceptions of greater political corruption have accompanied Taiwan's transformation to democracy. Assuming that transparency reduces the incidence of corruption, how can it be improved? Contemporary public administration places a heavy emphasis on achieving results and for the overwhelming number of government agencies transparency is a diversion to which scarce resources may only begrudgingly be devoted.

Analysis of political corruption is further complicated by the need to gain a better understanding of the role of scarcity in fostering corrupt practices. As Ma notes, scarcity can be an important generator of corruption. Government often controls the means necessary for the advancement of private economic interests, including contracts, permits, licenses, and subsidies. As Tak-Wing Ngo points out in Chapter 3, firms may engage in "rent-seeking" when government fixes prices, imposes trade quotas, and requires licenses to produce goods and services. Consequently, the opportunities and incentives for bribery, kickbacks, and nepotism are many. This may be especially true when government officials receive poor pay and/or expect their tenure to be short. However, rent-seeking may be a pervasive feature of a nation's administrative culture. On a lower scale, "speed money" or its equivalent may be necessary to motivate ordinary government clerks to process one's application for a government benefit in a timely (and favorable) fashion. Here, too, the definitional problem arises. Is favorable tax treatment of industries that make large financial contributions to a political party's electoral campaign corrupt regardless of the public policy rationale? Is the routine intervention by legislators on behalf of their constituents in administrative decision-making the functional equivalent of speed money?

Combating political corruption

Combating political corruption is also complex. In Chapter 8, Michael Johnston notes that there is a consensus that corruption can be reduced by the introduction of a package of reforms that strengthen transparency, public management, civil society, privatization, the rule of law and courts, and liberalize the economy, political system, and treatment of the news media. In her introductory essay, Melanie Manion emphasizes the importance of institutional design in forestalling corruption. She points out that some government programs virtually invite corruption, including those requiring business licenses or outlawing popular forms of gambling. However, as she and other contributors to this book note, there is no one-size-fits-all prescription for reducing political corruption. The efficacy of reforms and strategies will vary from place to place depending on the prevailing political and administrative cultures. Empowering administrators in modern Weberian or post-Weberian bureaucracies as prescribed by the new public management may enhance efficiency; in other administrative systems it is sure to breed greater corruption.

Preventing Corruption in Asia: Institutional Design and Policy Capacity is a particularly welcome addition to analysis of political corruption. Part I focuses on China, Part II on India, Turkey, Taiwan, Singapore, and the Pacific Islands. As editors, Professors Gong and Ma have brought together and integrated the work of highly accomplished experts to produce an outstanding volume that advances analysis of corruption greatly and will be an invaluable resource on the subject for years to come.

David H. Rosenbloom
American University
Washington, DC
City University of Hong Kong
Kowloon, Hong Kong SAR

Notes

1 US Congress, House, Executive Document 8, 45th Congress, 1st Session, p. 15 (25 October 1877).
2 R.K. Merton, "Latent functions of the machine," in A.B. Callow (ed.) (1973) *American Urban History: An Interpretative Reader with Commentaries*, New York: Oxford University Press, 220–29.

Acknowledgments

This project has taken a long time in coming to fruition. It began in the middle of 2006 when Ting took the initiative to prepare for an exchange of ideas on corruption studies, which led to a workshop held at City University of Hong Kong in May 2007. Originally the title was "Building Clean Government in China: Institutional Design and Policy Capacity." As we moved on with the project after the meeting, we changed the title in order to extend our focus beyond China, to include other parts of Asia. As a result, the final product has become a comparative study of corruption in China and other Asian and Pacific countries.

We would like to thank the authors of various chapters. Without their contribution and cooperation, it would have been impossible to put the volume together. We are most grateful to Gerald Caiden, Michael Johnston and David Rosenbloom. Gerald, though still recovering from several surgeries, not only wrote concluding remarks for the book but also shared with us his insightful views on different aspects of the issue of corruption. Michael, in addition to contributing a chapter, carefully ushered us through the initial conception of the project with considerable patience and professional expertise. David kindly took the time out of his busy schedule to write the Foreword. He also gave us a great deal of invaluable advice and encouragement. All their efforts on behalf of this volume were of immeasurable value to us.

We also owe our thanks to a number of other scholars whose input and inspiration were indispensable: Wenhao Cheng, Anthony Cheung, Yong Guo, Philip J. Ivanhoe, Linda Chelan Li, Jun Ma, Xing Ni, Jianming Ren, Julia Tao, Xiaoqi Wang, Linda Wong, Ray Yep, Baishun Yuan, Qianwei Zhu. They offered first-hand information and important observations on corruption and anticorruption reform in China and helped with the project in many other ways.

We've been fortunate to have generous institutional support from City University of Hong Kong, which sponsored the May 2007 workshop and made all logistic arrangements to ensure the success of the event. At the final stage of this project, CityU again graciously provided editorial support and covered other project-related costs. A special debt of gratitude is due to Hon

S. Chan, Head of Department of Public and Social Administration, CityU, who provided us with well-informed guidance, creating a productive and pleasant research environment for us throughout the entire process of this project.

We are greatly indebted to Desdemona Cardosa, Provost and Vice President for Academic Affairs at California State University, Los Angeles, who has been tremendously supportive of Stephen's research and international academic exchange. We also thank Peter Quan, Vice President and Chief Technology Officer, CSULA, who made extra efforts so that Stephen could obtain all necessary computer assistance, and Jose Galvan, Dean of Graduate Studies and Research, CSULA, a colleague and friend, who, while on business trips to China with Stephen, was unsparing in opening opportunities for Stephen to learn about the latest development in different parts of the nation.

This book could not have been completed without the assistance of Sonja van Leeuwen, Acting Editor of Asian Studies, and Leanne Hinves, Editorial Assistant at Routledge. We appreciate the care with which they reviewed our manuscript, and the competence they demonstrated in guiding us through the many stages of revision, editing, and production. We acknowledge the notable contribution of Huangao Shi, our research assistant. Thanks also go to the two anonymous academic reviewers whose constructive comments and suggestions have improved the initial manuscript remarkably.

Parts of this volume draw to varying degrees on our contributors' previously published articles in *Crime, Law, and Social Change* (2008), 49(1–3). We are grateful to Springer Science + Business Media for permission to use copyrighted materials.

This book is dedicated to our families, who, throughout the tedious and time-consuming process of research, writing, editing, and collaborating, have never failed to understand the importance of our project nor faltered in their sincere support. We hope that the book serves as a minor yet meaningful return on the sacrifices they made during the entire period of this journey.

Ting Gong
Stephen K. Ma
September 2008

Abbreviations

ACB	Anticorruption Branch
ADB	Asian Development Bank
AID	Association for India's Development
AKP	Justice and Development Party
BEEPS	Business Environment and Enterprise Performance Survey
CBI	Central Bureau of Investigation
CCP	Chinese Communist Party
CCPDIC	Chinese Communist Party Discipline Inspection Commission
CCW	Coalition for Citizen Watch
CDIC	Central Discipline Inspection Commission
CID	Criminal Investigation Department
CPI	Corruption Perception Index
CPIB	Corrupt Practices Investigation Bureau
CVC	Central Vigilance Commission
DARPG	Department of Administrative Reforms and Public Grievances
DIC	Discipline Inspection Commission
DPP	Democratic Progress Party
EBRD	European Bank for Reconstruction and Development
FSM	Federated States of Micronesia
GCB	Global Corruption Barometer
GI	Governance Indicators
IAS	Indian Administrative Service
IRMA	International Ramen Manufacturers Association
KMT	Chinese Nationalist Party
LDP	Liberal Democratic Party
NBCP	National Bureau of Corruption Prevention
OECD	Organization for Economic Co-operation and Development
PAP	People's Action Party
PERC	Political and Economic Risk Consultancy
PNG	Papua New Guinea
POCA	Prevention of Corruption Act
POCO	Prevention of Corruption Ordinance
PPA	Public Procurement Agency

PPL	Public Procurement Law
PRC	People's Republic of China
PRI	Institutional Revolutionary Party
PS21	Public Service for the 21st Century
PSC	Public Service Commission
SPF	Singapore Police Force
TGNA	Turkish Grand National Assembly
TI	Transparency International
TIS	Taiwan Integrity Survey

1 Beyond enforcement

Anticorruption reform as a problem of institutional design*

Melanie Manion

Corruption, defined here as the abuse of public office for private gain, is at the core of the study of governance and political economy. In her early analysis of the political economy of corruption, Rose-Ackerman (1978) observes that all theories of the state implicitly or explicitly draw a normative line between market and nonmarket mechanisms of allocating scarce resources. Legislative decisions are not supposed to be for sale to the highest bidder in a liberal democracy, for example, even though democracy coexists with markets for many goods. A generic research problem is to describe and explain the microfoundations of exactly how market forces undermine whatever normative line has been drawn. A practical policy problem is to design measures so that widespread corruption does not become institutionalized as its own "informal political system" (Scott 1972), with the attendant social, political, and economic costs.

The organizing impetus of this volume is a policy perspective on corruption, with a particular focus on institutional sources and remedies. It draws together the perspectives of a diverse range of scholars with expertise on corruption and good governance. Individual chapters investigate policy efforts to reduce, control, and especially prevent widespread corruption across a number of Asian countries. This is not to suggest, however, anything distinctively Asian about the corruption targeted by these efforts. Indeed, where the chapters address this issue, they reject the notion of Asian exceptionalism.

Part I of the volume is an intensive study of the past quarter-century of anticorruption efforts in mainland China, which features what Johnston identifies in this volume as one of the most "disruptive syndromes" of corruption—yet is nonetheless emerging as an economic superpower. Part II extends the study to anticorruption efforts, both highly successful and less successful, in other Asian contexts. The purpose of this introduction is to illuminate the institutional perspective, to provide some background for the focus on Chinese anticorruption reform, and to preview the chapters to follow.

An institutional perspective

Telling a plausible causal story about choices to engage in corruption often seems trivial compared to the formidable task of telling such a story about forbearance from venality. This is especially the case where corruption is already widespread. Yet, it is precisely in contexts of widespread corruption that a story about clean officials or pockets of clean government becomes really interesting and important. The most interesting and important stories, of course, are about change: transformations from widespread corruption to clean government, especially. In such stories, governments are typically the key players just as they are key obstacles in the many stories that highlight the stickiness of corruption. Although grassroots players in society are also crucial to successful transformation, the story is usually one of anticorruption reform initiated by governments. Such reform requires governments to change corrupt payoffs and the "folklore of corruption" (Myrdal 1968)—commonly shared beliefs, among public officials and ordinary citizens alike, about the ubiquity of corruption and the unreliability of government as anticorruption enforcer.

What are the prospects for success in anticorruption reform? There is no shortage of policy prescriptions in the growing literature on good governance. Here I focus on two of the most commonly recognized broad policy instruments: enforcement and institutional design. Anticorruption experts generally agree on the importance of enforcement, just as they agree that an exclusive role for enforcement is a losing strategy. Building appropriate institutions has become part of nearly every clean government policy bundle. It was at the center of the major shift in the World Bank strategy in the mid-1990s. Institution building is not necessarily the same as institutional design, however, a distinction I clarify below.

Enforcement strategies reduce corrupt payoffs by increasing the likelihood that corrupt players are detected and then punished with a severity commensurate to the corrupt act. Both features are important (see Di Tella and Schargrodsky 2003). Enforcement strategies increase resources for monitoring and detection, increase punishments for corruption, or both. The Singapore and Hong Kong experiences, which prominently feature independent anticorruption agencies, have been emulated in many other countries, often unsuccessfully (Johnston 1999; Meagher 2005). A major reason is that generous resources and the reliable political support that ensures their supply, which are key features of the Singapore and Hong Kong models, are often not found in other contexts, especially in developing countries.

As to increasing punishments, this is not as trivial as it may seem. In China and Vietnam, for example, officials can be executed for corruption—but in both countries, enforcement is by no means certain. Even extraordinary penalties must be accompanied by a reasonable likelihood of detection and punishment to be effective. A less extreme way to increase punishments is to alter the legal structure of penalties. For example, in many countries it is illegal for officials to solicit or accept bribes, but not for private citizens to offer or pay bribes.

Policy interventions that enhance anticorruption enforcement but leave unchanged the basic conditions that encourage corruption are unlikely to

[handwritten at top: enforcement unlikely to yield lasting results unless paired w/ institutional design]

yield lasting results. Changing corrupt payoffs must take into account the incentives that promote corruption in particular contexts. Anticorruption reform through *institutional design* restructures transactions to lessen incentives and opportunities to transact corruptly. Clearly, the most drastic institutional reform is program elimination. It may be warranted for programs with no sound policy justification that operate mainly to generate bribes (Rose-Ackerman 1999). Examples of such programs include many of the licenses and permissions required to set up businesses in developing countries. Similarly, a study of corruption in post-communist countries considered whether or not traffic police serve any useful purpose there: "Far fewer traffic police and rather more speed cameras might produce more revenue for the state as well as both tighter and fairer control of traffic" (Miller et al. 2001: 338). Legalizing activities that generate corruption is another way to redesign incentives. For example, when off-track betting in Hong Kong was legalized, payoffs for police protection were no longer necessary, which helped to reduce syndicated police corruption.

Another institutional design to reduce corruption is the "competitive" reorganization of bureaucracies, so that several officials supply the same government service. When officials lack monopoly power, bribes are driven down as clients seek the least corrupt officials (Rose-Ackerman 1978, 1999), unless the situation offers a possibility of corrupt collusion between clients and officials to deprive the state of revenue (Shleifer and Vishny 1993). Multiple veto points in government—such as separation of executive and legislative powers, legislative supermajority requirements, and constitutional courts—similarly limit the power of any single government institution, making it difficult to exert influence to obtain illegal benefits, as every decision point must be purchased. *[handwritten margin: ← not sure?]* In government procurement, sealed competitive bidding requirements and the use of private market prices as benchmarks can also reduce corruption. Statutes that provide rewards and protection for whistleblowers can supply incentives for officials to come forward to reveal corruption (Rose-Ackerman 1999).

The decline of electoral corruption, such as treating and money bribes, from a usual practice in mid-nineteenth century England to a rare and generally disparaged practice by the end of that century reflects the distinct impacts of enforcement and institutional design in anticorruption reform (see Gwyn 1962, 1970; O'Leary 1962; King 1970: Nossiter 1975; Cox 1987).

An enforcement perspective is represented in the 1854 Corrupt Practices Prevention Act, 1867 Second Reform Act, and 1883 Corrupt and Illegal Practices Act, all of which were designed to reduce corrupt payoffs by improving monitoring and increasing punishments. These statutes created an election auditor in each district to record money spent by candidates, established a practice of decisions by independent judges on petitions protesting electoral corruption, increased penalties for bribery to disqualify candidates from holding office for seven years, and introduced candidate liability for bribery practiced by election agents. The statutes prescribed standards for elections and

*[handwritten notes at bottom:
* Program elimination
* Legalisation of activities that generate corr.
* Reorganisation of bureaucracies
* Multiple veto points in gov't
* Rewards/protection for whistleblowers]*

made more salient the illegality of electoral corruption, thereby also playing a role in educating the mass public about what was appropriate.

Other legal changes reduced corrupt payoffs through institutional design, effectively changing the structure of incentives for electoral corruption. The 1872 Ballot Act introduced the secret ballot, which created uncertainty about the return on particular payments for votes. It also made it difficult to judge the closeness of an election until the end and, therefore, difficult to judge whether bribery was a worthwhile investment. While scholars generally agree that the Ballot Act contributed to the decline of electoral corruption, they view it as only one of a number of structural influences. The persistence of widespread vote-buying in the 1880 election is widely acknowledged.[1] The 1884 Third Reform Act and 1885 Redistribution of Seats Act reduced corruption by increasing the size of voting districts. Larger voting districts required extensive vote-buying for it to be efficient at all, especially with the uncertainty introduced by the secret ballot. At the same time, extensive vote-buying was also more easily detected, raising the probability of winning the election but losing the seat as a punishment for corruption.

Considering the magnitude of change required when corruption is commonplace, policy interventions that reduce corrupt payoffs are likely to take years to produce clean government. In such a setting, modest interventions that target certain sectors for change may be more successful, although success may be unsustainable without continuous attention. The notoriously corrupt Marcos regime in the Philippines targeted its Bureau of Internal Revenue for reform in an effort to stem declining revenues due to collusive tax evasion and outright embezzlement by bureau officials (Klitgaard 1988). Under new bureau leadership, grossly corrupt officials were dismissed, strict regulations were introduced, work procedures were reorganized, controls were enhanced, and discretionary authority was reduced. Within a few years, impressive results were achieved. Collected revenues notably increased and corruption in the bureau apparently decreased. Yet, these results were quickly reversed after the bureau experienced another change in leadership.

Where corruption is widespread, which is where such strategies are most needed, implementing anticorruption strategies such as enforcement and institutional design is inherently problematic, however. Consider enforcement. Enforcement to detect a higher proportion of officials engaging in corrupt practices strains limited resources. Most important, enforcement strategies assume clean enforcers—a fantastic assumption, especially (but not only) when corruption is widespread. This is especially relevant when the enforcement strategy focuses on increasing the probability of detection and punishment. In Argentina, for example, Ocampo (2000) points out that increasing the likelihood of punishment requires reversing a history of no legal precedent of conviction for bribery, although the law carries a sentence of up to six years for private agents who give or offer gifts to officials and a similar sentence for officials who receive gifts to do (or not do) something relating to official duties. Focusing on the other component of the calculus by introducing draconian punishments is not necessarily a feasible alternative if many officials are corrupt. Even in China and Vietnam, notable for high levels of corruption and extreme penalties for corrupt acts, the government can only execute so many.

Institutional design presents a different sort of problem. Restructuring procedures to reduce incentives and opportunities for corrupt activities must take into account the near irrelevance of rules, which practically defines situations of widespread corruption. The problem here is not that some officials are bound to discover loopholes in redesigned procedures and take advantage. Rather, officials do not need to search for loopholes. It is taken for granted that rules, organizations, and procedures pose few obstacles because they are quite unimportant to actual practice. Put differently, many institutional design interventions assume that formal institutions matter in guiding actions, but this correspondence is itself an "informal institution." That is, if institutions are the "rules of the game" that constrain the actions of individuals (North 1990; Calvert 1995), then the emergence of the underlying constraining relationship may be preliminary (or at least integral) to any tinkering with design to reduce corrupt payoffs. This problem of weak institutionalization is also pertinent to enforcement strategies that essentially involve new rules, prohibiting certain activities as corrupt acts—which should not be confused with changes in institutional design. It goes without saying that the relevance of rules cannot be mandated. Obviously, many institutional design strategies, such as the introduction of competition as a substitute for regulation, do not depend so much on rules that matter. These sorts of strategies may be better suited to contexts with weak institutions (Broadman and Recanatini 2002).

At some point, tinkering with institutions to create incentive structures that guard against corruption may come up against lines set by constitutional design. Indeed, this is the crux of the problem identified in many of this volume's chapters on anticorruption agencies' corruption in mainland China. Is effective institutional design to reduce and prevent corruption possible in the context of the constitutional design of single-party authoritarianism?

Anticorruption reform in mainland China

Anticorruption reform in mainland China began in earnest with an explosion of corruption in the early 1980s. Despite serious (if seriously flawed) efforts, the country still ranks among the more corrupt in the world.[2] For about the first two decades of the war on corruption, the Chinese mainly implemented an enforcement strategy, buttressed by fairly ineffectual moral education, but neglecting institutional design (see Manion 2004). In a document issued in late 2004, the Central Committee announced a major policy shift, introducing a set of comprehensive guidelines to govern anticorruption reform for the next five years (Xinhua, 16 January 2005). The guidelines called on different agencies in the party and government to come up with

[handwritten: 2004 Central Cttee major policy shift]

institutional innovations to prevent corruption at its roots. The document was the culmination of an incremental shift that began in the late 1990s and became especially prominent in this century. The Chinese essentially rejected campaign-style enforcement for an approach emphasizing institutional change and corruption prevention.

Preview

[handwritten: authors are skeptical if A-C efforts have been at all useful]

The six chapters that make up Part I of this volume mainly investigate the institutional reforms aimed at anticorruption in mainland China. The broad consensus of the authors as to the status and direction of these reforms is skeptical, if not always completely pessimistic. They find institutional tinkering, not changes in institutional design. The incentives remain essentially the same in the government–business relationship, anticorruption coordination, and mechanisms governing official careers. Moreover, although the authors see a number of possibilities for improving the institutions they investigate, the suggested improvements often cross the line into changes in constitutional design, which makes them unlikely if not entirely unimaginable.

Wedeman asks whether the Communist Party is winning its war on corruption, now entering its 25th year. In recent years, judging from anticorruption enforcement statistics and corruption perception measures, the corruption rate appears to have leveled off. Yet, as Wedeman recognizes, such measures are problematic. Both sorts of data are imperfect reflections of actual volume and severity of corruption. Wedeman focuses instead on another measure, which reflects risk of corrupt actions—the lag time between corrupt action and apprehension, with a shorter lag time reflecting higher risk. He compares lag times for large numbers of corruption cases in 1993–96 and 2005–06 and finds much longer lag times for cases in the most recent period.

Ngo examines government–business collusion in rent creation and rent seeking, one of the most common sources of corruption in mainland China since the inception of market reform. In recent years, Chinese anticorruption enforcement has focused on the government–business relationship, but the effort has failed to address the root causes of collusive corruption. The creation, allocation, and pursuit of economic rents have become institutionalized in the state licensing system. Ngo demonstrates that rent production under the prevailing framework of state licensing is a fertile ground for corruption because of significant policy discretion in allocation of rents. Effective measures to reduce this common and costly form of corruption require basic changes in the licensing state.

Sun considers the surge in revealed corruption by local Communist Party and government leaders in recent years, despite efforts to reform the means by which leading officials are appointed and promoted. She finds that the reforms have not fundamentally transformed the incentive mechanisms of leading officials. Even in the more broadly consultative process, the Communist Party committees and their powerful organization departments dominate. This institutional deficit is aggravated by implementation gaps of varying degrees. This is reflected in manipulation, superficial compliance, non-compliance, and even fraud by those with the power to appoint and promote. At the same time, the intermediate accountability measures introduced in the reforms may be a promising bridge to deeper and broader procedural changes.

Gong analyzes the structure of the key anticorruption agencies in mainland China, the party's discipline inspection committees. She demonstrates that the discipline inspection system has gone through continuous institutional conversion, structurally and functionally, as the party has adapted it to changes in the policy environment. At the same time, the basic goal of discipline inspection has remained unchanged: it aims to improve the moral conduct of party members through disciplinary measures imposed from the top down. Yet, as Gong points out, discipline inspection committees are constrained by generalist party committees, which exercise leadership over them but are ostensibly the objects of their moral scrutiny. Freeing the discipline inspection committees from their party committee bosses is not necessarily a solution. In the current political context, without functioning channels for public surveillance, who would inspect the inspectors?

Ma takes up the question on which Gong concludes. He widens the focus to consider the entire set of anticorruption agencies—in the party, government, and criminal justice system. None of the anticorruption agencies is well designed to meet the challenges of policing others and policing themselves. Ma points to a combination of weak supervision over the agencies and weak agency autonomy to police others. The crux of the problem is similar to the one identified by Gong: a multiplicity of measures, including public surveillance, to supervise anticorruption agencies would effectively terminate the party's control over the agencies.

Chan and Gao analyze the target-based performance responsibility system which clarifies responsibilities of local leaders in performance contracts that become the basis for penalties and rewards affecting official careers. Evaluation against performance measures does not seem to have prevented local networks of corrupt leaders across organizations. Chan and Gao argue that the system can in principle serve as an effective means to control corruption. They investigate why in practice it has not played this role and point to the concentration of power. An effective solution is not simply to separate and share powers to increase participation in decisions. Rather, this must be combined with effective oversight and review of decisions. In the absence of this fundamental change in governance institutions, the mechanisms of the performance responsibility system cannot be expected to check local corruption.

The six chapters in Part II look beyond mainland China to other Asian experiences with anticorruption reform. Just as the authors agree that there is no single variant of Asian corruption, they also agree that there is no single anticorruption strategy that can be effective everywhere. Instead, while they recognize that reducing and preventing corruption depends on building institutions and are skeptical of strategies that devalue institutions, they also recognize that corruption comes in a variety of forms and that strategies must be suited to the distinct configurations of corruption in different societies, economies, and polities. This is not to say that the institutional mechanisms proposed in the chapters below cannot be effective in other contexts, but only that getting the context right is preliminary to getting the institutions right.

Johnston points to variation across countries in how people pursue, use, and exchange wealth and power and in the political and social institutions that restrain and sustain these processes. This variation is the source of what he identifies as four fundamentally different syndromes of corruption. In short, there is no distinctive Asian corruption. Mainland China experiences "official mogul" corruption, the most disruptive form. What China shares with the economically successful Asian countries in the other categories, however, is a durable institutional framework. Appropriately identifying corruption syndromes has implications for anticorruption reform: successful reform requires institution building that takes account of this context.

Quah considers lessons from Singapore, the most successful Asian anticorruption experience. Singapore is a particularly interesting example because a single party has dominated politics and society for five decades, presiding over unusually clean government without the robust institutions of democratic pluralism and civil liberties associated with most clean government designs. Quah attributes Singapore's success to a combination of factors. A strong legal framework, a single powerful anticorruption agency, and strong support from the ruling party and its main leaders provide an effective institutional framework for enforcement. Competitive salaries for politicians and senior civil servants reduce temptation to engage in corrupt actions. Relatively little bureaucratic intervention in the economy and the reliance on methods such as e-government to improve transparency reduce opportunities for corruption. Not least of all, Quah points to clean government as one of the dominant party's most valuable assets in retaining confidence of voters and investors alike.

Dwivedi, Mishra, and Mishra reflect on the corruption that threatens to jeopardize a robust Indian democracy, despite impressive economic growth. Rejecting colonial legacy as a factor in Indian corruption today, they find the sources of corruption deeply entrenched in society (religion, socialization, ascription) and perpetuated by a dizzying variety of governance institutions, both electoral and bureaucratic. Their proposed countermeasures take into account the distinct sources of Indian corruption. As might be expected, considering the overdetermined character of corruption, the measures are multipronged. They range from the obvious (but obviously not implemented) institutional changes to transformation of social norms through moral education at early ages.

Acar and Emek analyze the widespread, serious, and enduring corruption in Turkey, using it as a reference point to consider the elements of a successful anticorruption effort. They identify political financing, public personnel, and public expenditure and procurement as the institutional core of robust clean government. Good prospects for clean government can best be found in a coalition of the players (politicians, bureaucrats, and businesspeople) with key interests in these institutions. Most important, these players must commit to creating the conditions for "free and fair competition" in the institutional core. Such competition requires strong institutions. The good news is that there is no dearth of experience and expertise (in and outside Turkey) in creating and implementing them.

Yu, Chen, Hu, and Juang ask whether democratization in Taiwan and specifically the end of one-party dominance in 2000 has produced clean government. Data from a variety of sources, including the Taiwan Integrity Survey, suggest that people in Taiwan doubt the probity of their public officials, especially elected politicians and political appointees. These and other indicators lead them to conclude that the democratic transformation has damaged government integrity. Further, studying the newest regime's anticorruption agenda, they find no effort to leverage grassroots power, including civil society organizations, to combat corruption. This is a serious flaw: without the involvement of ordinary citizens, the anticorruption effort cannot succeed, even with electoral democratization.

Larmour addresses the relationship between culture and corruption—an issue that has a long history in the study of corruption and typically serves as the foil to an institutional perspective on corruption. He finds that statements about the impact of culture regularly emerge in a series of local reports on corruption in the Pacific Islands, even though the template for the reports did not facilitate discussions of culture. Larmour argues that routine practices around which common understandings and expectations have developed constitute cultural institutions. He points to the institution of gift-giving in the Pacific Islands and other societies as an example. Such institutions, which are the products of societies not governments, must be taken seriously if corruption is to be prevented.

Caiden concludes the volume, picking up Larmour's theme of culture and corruption. A central problem of anticorruption reform is the sheer variety of corrupt forms, with patterns distinctive to different societies and deeply embedded in different cultures. As to political systems, authoritarian polities such as mainland China's present a special problem: universalistic standards enshrined in rule of law are not well-established; leaders can ignore their own measures at will, especially when corruption enriches them. Social norms, especially in localized contexts, can reduce corruption—but just as anticorruption reform must take norms into account, it cannot depend on the spontaneous emergence of norms. This leaves the major work in an anticorruption strategy to institution building in public office: monitoring integrity, strengthening professionalism, increasing transparency, enhancing accountability, and enforcing the respect for human dignity that corruption undermines. At the same time, there is no single blueprint for the specific institutional mechanisms to realize these values and thereby reduce corruption.

Notes

* Portions of this introduction are excerpted by permission of the publishers from the introduction to Manion (2004). Copyright © 2004 by Melanie Manion.
1 Another effect is theoretically possible. Cox and Kousser (1981) analyze the impact of the secret ballot on voting in upstate New York at the turn of the century and find that it changed the nature of electoral corruption, but not necessarily the scope. Instead of paying voters for votes, parties paid voters to abstain from voting. For some time after the introduction of the secret ballot in 1890, this "deflationary" corruption appears to have significantly replaced "inflationary" vote-buying
2 For example, the 2007 Transparency International poll of polls estimated a corruption perceptions score of 3.5 for mainland China, with 10 signifying no corruption and 0 signifying complete corruption, ranking it 72 of 179 countries. This places China with Mexico and India. This is far worse than Hong Kong (ranked 14, with a score of 8.3) or Taiwan (ranked 34, with a score of 5.7), for example. See Transparency International (26 September 2007).

References

Broadman, H.G., and Recanatini, F. (2002) "Corruption and policy: back to the roots," *Journal of Policy Reform*, 5(1): 37–49.

Calvert, R.L. (1995) "The rational choice theory of social institutions: cooperation, coordination, and communication," in J.S. Banks and E.A. Hanushek (eds) *Modern Political Economy: Old Topics, New Directions*, Cambridge: Cambridge University Press, 216–67.

Cox, G.W. (1987) *The Efficient Secret: The Cabinet and the Development of Political Parties in Victorian England*, Cambridge: Cambridge University Press.

Cox, G.W. and Kousser, J.M. (1981) "Turnout and rural corruption: New York as a test case," *American Journal of Political Science*, 25(4): 646–63.

Di Tella, R. and Schargrodsky, E. (2003) "The role of wages and auditing during a crackdown on corruption in the city of Buenos Aires," *Journal of Law and Economics*, 46: 269–92.

Gwyn, W.B. (1962) *Democracy and the Cost of Politics in Britain*, London: University of London/Athlone Press.

—— (1970) "The nature and decline of corrupt election expenditures in nineteenth-century Britain," in Arnold J. Heidenheimer (ed.) *Political Corruption: Readings in Comparative Analysis*, New York: Holt, Rinehart, and Winston, 391–403.

Johnston, M. (1999) "A brief history of anticorruption agencies," in A. Schedler, L. Diamond, and M.F. Plattner (eds) *The Self-Restraining State: Power and Accountability in New Democracies*, Boulder, CO: Lynne Rienner, 217–26.

King, J.P. (1970) "Socioeconomic development and the incidence of English corrupt campaign practices," in A.J. Heidenheimer (ed.) *Political Corruption: Readings in Comparative Analysis*, New York: Holt, Rinehart, and Winston, 370–90.

Klitgaard, R. (1988) *Controlling Corruption*, Berkeley: University of California Press.

Manion, M. (2004) *Corruption by Design: Building Clean Government in Mainland China and Hong Kong*, Cambridge, MA: Harvard University Press.

Meagher, P. (2005) "Anticorruption agencies: rhetoric versus reality," *Journal of Policy Reform*, 8(1): 69–103.

Miller, W.L., Grodeland, A.B., and Koshechkina, T.Y. (2001) *A Culture of Corruption: Coping with Government in Post-communist Europe*, Budapest: Central European University Press.

Myrdal, G. (1968) *Asian Drama: An Inquiry into the Poverty of Nations*, New York: Twentieth Century Fund.

North, D.C. (1990) *Institutions, Institutional Change, and Economic Performance*, Cambridge: Cambridge University Press.

Nossiter, T.J. (1975) *Influence, Opinion and Political Idioms in Reformed England: Case Studies from the Northeast, 1832–74*, Hassocks, England: Harvester Press.

Ocampo, L.M. (2000) "Structural corruption and normative systems: the role of integrity pacts," in J.S. Tulchin and R.H. Espach (eds) *Combating Corruption in Latin America*, Washington, DC: Woodrow Wilson Center Press, 53–70.

O'Leary, C. (1962) *The Elimination of Corrupt Practices in British Elections, 1868–1911*, Oxford: Clarendon Press.

Rose-Ackerman, S. (1978) *Corruption: A Study in Political Economy*, New York: Academic Press.

—— (1999) *Corruption and Government: Causes, Consequences, and Reform*, Cambridge: Cambridge University Press.

Scott, J.C. (1972) *Comparative Political Corruption*, Englewood Cliffs, NJ: Prentice-Hall.

Shleifer, A. and Vishny, R.W. (1993) "Corruption," *Quarterly Journal of Economics*, 58(3): 599–617.

Transparency International (26 September 2007) "Transparency International 2007 Corruption Perceptions Index," online. Available at www.icgg.org/corruption.cpi_2007. html (accessed 1 August 2008).

Xinhua (16 January 2005) "Jianli jianquan jiaoyu, zhidu, jiandu bingzhong de chengzhi he yufang fubai tixi shishi gangyao" (Implementing guidelines for building and perfecting an integrated system of education, institutions, and monitoring to punish and prevent corruption), online. Available at http://news.xinhuanet.com/ newscenter/2005–01/16/content_2467898.htm (accessed 19 March 2008).

Part I

Anticorruption reform in the People's Republic of China

2 China's war on corruption*

Andrew Wedeman

Introduction

[handwritten: noise + fury of A-C campaign]

For the past twenty-five years the Chinese government has waged a war against corruption. Triggered by a surge in corruption following the adoption of economic reforms in the late 1970s, the war has witnessed alternating periods of feverish crackdowns and less intense routine policing.[1] Yet, despite all the noise and fury that accompany periodic campaigns and the leadership's oft repeated warning that struggle against corruption is a matter of "life and death," it is not clear if the Chinese Communist Party (CCP) is winning or losing the war.

During 2006, for example, a series of high-level officials were sacked for corruption. In September 2006, the party charged Shanghai Party Secretary and Politburo member Chen Liangyu with illegally lending US$ 475 million worth of municipal pension funds to local real-estate developers (*Wall Street Journal*, 6 February 2007). As of mid-2007, the Director of the State Statistical Bureau Qiu Xiaohua and some two dozen other senior officials in Shanghai had been sacked, arrested, or expelled from the party for their involvement in that same scandal (*China Daily*, 14 March 2007). In December, investigators accused Beijing Vice Mayor Liu Zhihua of accepting US $ 10 million in bribes from contractors working on the 2008 Olympics project and maintaining a "pleasure palace" staffed with "concubines" (*New York Times*, 13 June 2006). The following month, prosecutors accused Zheng Xiaoyu, the retired director of the State Food and Drug Administration, of accepting bribes and ignoring wrongdoing by his subordinates (*Associated Press*, 16 May 2007). Zheng was sentenced to death in May 2007 after being convicted on bribery, dereliction of duty, and corruption charges (*CNN*, 29 May 2007). During the past year, senior officials in Tianjin (Chief Procurator Li Baojin), Shanxi (Deputy Party Secretary Hou Wujie), Jiangsu (Deputy Chairman Provincial People's Congress Wang Wulong), Guangdong (Vice Governor Liu Weiming), Shandong (Deputy Party Secretary Du Shicheng) and Anhui (Vice Governor He Minxu) were also charged with corruption, while a senior naval officer (Admiral Wang Shouye) was sacked after his mistress reportedly told authorities he had accepted $15 million in bribes (*South China Morning Post*, 24 January 2006). In early 2006, Hunan Vice-Governor Zheng Maoqing reportedly attempted suicide after he was accused of corruption.[2]

Do these examples mean that high-level corruption has worsened and that the party is losing the war? Or do they mean that the party has decide to stop concentrating on catching the small fry and is now determined to start bagging the "big tigers"? Individual cases or even a set of cases, unfortunately provide few answers to these questions. The Chen Liangyu case, which some have suggested signals a significant shift in the war against corruption, bears an uncanny resemblance to the 1995–96 case of Beijing Party Secretary and Politburo member Chen Xitong (Wedeman 1996: 61–94). At that time, some also suggested—alternatively—that the party was on the verge of degeneration or that the war on corruption was about to shift into high gear (Pei 1999; Root 1996). Similarly, the lengthy list of senior officials charged with corruption cited above notwithstanding, according to the Supreme People's Procuratorate the number of officials at the provincial level charged with corruption actually fell from eight in 2005 to six in 2006, which is just over half the number charged in 2004.[3]

More "systematic" measures of corruption also fail to provide definitive answers to the question of whether the CCP is winning or losing its war on corruption. The number of officials charged with corruption—or what we might call the "revealed rate of corruption" (RRC)—suggest significant increases during the 1980s, followed by a leveling off of the aggregate incidence of corruption (see Figure 2.1) (Wedeman 2004). Surveys of experts designed to measure the "perceived level of corruption" (PLC) also generally point to a leveling off (see Figure 2.2). The number of senior officials[4] charged with corruption, on the other hand, rose significantly in the 1990s, as did the monies "recovered" by prosecutors, which suggests that corruption underwent a qualitative "intensification" even if it remained at roughly the same quantitative level (see Figure 2.3).

Although they suggest that the overall level of corruption has not appreciable worsened in recent years, neither the RCC nor the PLC can be treated as definitive indicators that the war on corruption has reached a stalemate. Neither measures the "actual rate of corruption" (ARC). Both, in fact, imperfectly approximate it. The RRC, for example, represents that faction of the ARC in which corrupt officials are a) caught and b) indicted. The PLC, on the other hand, is ultimately experts' impressions about the ARC. Thus even though the RRC may have leveled off and experts think corruption has remained at about the same level in recent years, we cannot be sure that the RRC is a linear function of the ARC and hence changes in the RRC mirror changes in the ARC. Nor can we be sure whether experts' opinions are based on a valid sense of changes in the ARC or whether they are biased by their reading of movements in the RRC. Moreover, the leveling off of the RRC and PLC seems to be contradicted by evidence that corruption has intensified.

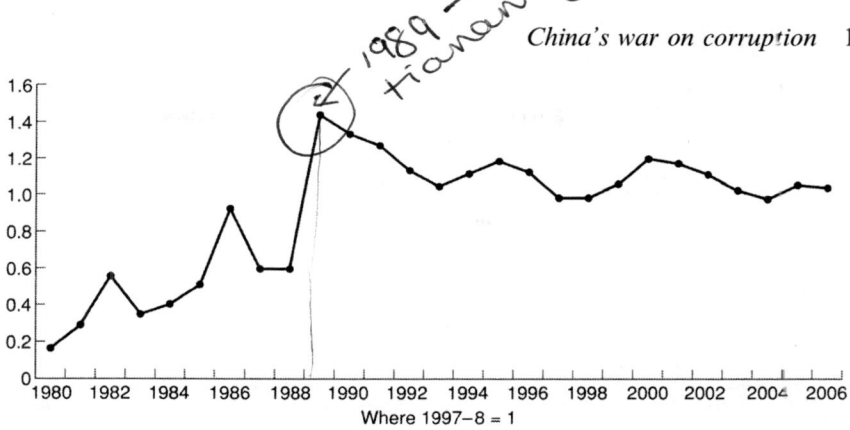

Figure 2.1 Revealed rate of corruption: index of economic crime cases filed.
Source: Based on data in Zhongguo jiancha nianjian (Beijing: Zhongguo jiancha chubanshe, various years) and Zhongguo falü nianjian (Beijing: Zhongguo falü nianjian chubanshe, various years).
Notes: In 1997, a revision of the criminal code led to changes in the legal definition of corruption and the decriminalization of certain offenses. As a result, the number of cases in which the Procuratorate "filed" charges dropped significantly. The number of cases accepted by the Court also fell as a result of the change in the law, but less dramatically. The revision thus served to narrow the gap between the number of cases involving formal charges and the number of criminal cases tried. In this figure, I have assumed that while the change in the law resulted in a change in the number of criminal charges filed, given a uniform definition of corruption for all years, the rate of corruption was not dramatically different in 1997 and 1998. I thus fix these two years as the baseline for the periods 1980–97 and 1998–2006 respectively.

Even though we cannot directly measure the ARC, I believe it is possible to assess if the gap between the ARC and RRC has changed significantly, and in what direction, by examining changes in the odds of getting caught or "risk." Mathematically, the ratio between the RRC and ARC represents risk because the RRC is that fraction of corrupt officials who get caught. Risk will thus vary as the RRC–ARC gap varies. However, because we cannot measure the ARC and thus we cannot directly measure the RRC–ARC gap, we cannot estimate risk using the RRC.

It is possible, though, to approximate risk by examining the lag between when an official first engages in corruption and when he or she gets caught.[5] Intuitively, if enforcement is vigorous, corrupt officials should get caught quickly. In theory, if enforcement was 100 percent effective, for example, malfeasance would be detected immediately and corrupt officials would be caught "in the act." If enforcement is lax, however, they are not only less likely to get caught at all but those who are caught are likely to "get away" with their crimes for some period of time. In other words, a short lag between crime and capture implies high risk while a long crime–capture lag implies low risk. Changes in the crime–capture lag, therefore, presumably reflect changes

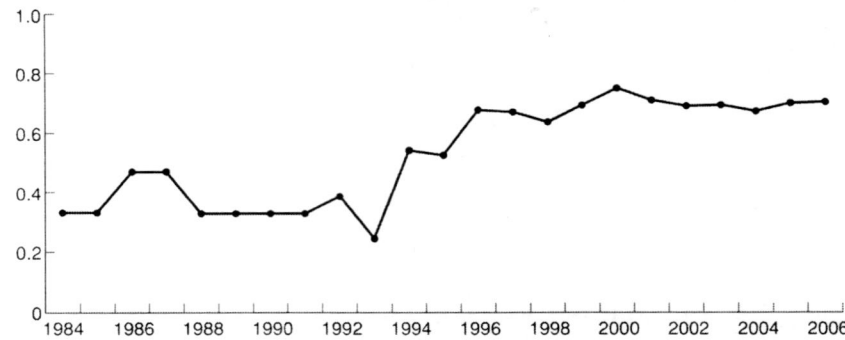

Figure 2.2 Perceived level of corruption (composite index).
Source: Transparency International, "Corruption Perceptions Index," various years, available at www.transparency.org/policy_research/surveys_indices/global/cpi; Political and Economic Risk Consultancy, Ltd (PERC), "Corruption in Asia," available at www.asiarisk.com/; the PRS Group, International Country Risk Guide, 1984–2004; and the World Bank, "Governance Indicators," available at http://info.worldbank. org/governance.

Notes: Composite index based on average scores from Transparency International, International Country Risk, Political and Economic Risk Consultancy, and World Bank Governance Indicators, where raw scores were normalized as a percentage of the worst possible score (i.e. the highest level of corruption).

in risk and, in turn, imply changes in the RRC–ARC gap. Hence, if the lag decreases, this implies that the efficacy of enforcement is rising and that the RRC–ARC gap is decreasing. If the lag increases, this implies enforcement is become less effective and that the RRC–ARC gap is increasing. Comparing crime–capture lag distributions in different periods, therefore, provides a way to assess whether changes in the RRC mirror changing in the underlying ARC or whether the ARC is moving in a different direction.

The purpose of this chapter is, therefore, to determine whether the leveling off of the RRC in recent years reflects a leveling off in the ARC. If the crime–capture lag has decreased significantly while the RRC has remained flat, this implies that the ARC has fallen and a larger percentage of corrupt officials are being brought to justice. In other words, the CCP is winning the war on corruption. If the crime–capture lag has not changed significantly and the RRC has remained flat, this would mean that the RRC–ARC ratio has remained relatively constant, which implies that the flattening out of the RRC reflects a flattening out of the ARC. Such a combination would indicate that the CCP's anticorruption effort has been successful in preventing corruption from increasing but has not been able to significantly reduce it. The war would thus have reached a stalemate. If, finally, the crime–capture lag has increased, the leveling off of the RRC would mask a continued worsening of corruption because while the RRC has remained flat the ARC has continued to rise. That, in turn, would suggest that the CCP is losing the war on corruption.

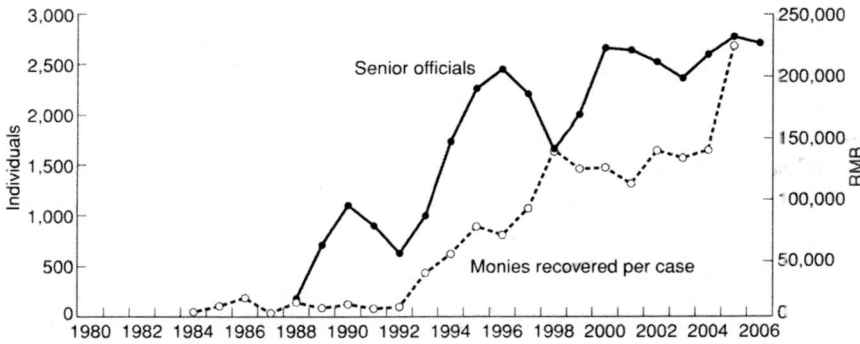

Figure 2.3 Intensity of corruption.
Source: Based on data in Zhongguo jiancha nianjian (Beijing: Zhongguo jiancha chubanshe, various years) and Zhongguo falü nianjian (Beijing: Zhongguo falü nianjian chubanshe, various years).

The chapter begins with a discussion of problems of measuring corruption and estimating risk. It then uses data on crime–capture lags drawn from two samples, each containing data on roughly 875 individuals charged with corruption, to examine changes in risk.[6] One sample includes individuals charged during the period 1993–96. The other includes individuals charged during 2005–06. The final section combines these data on lag structures with data on the RRC to assess the status of China's war on corruption.

Measurement

[handwritten: impossible to measure actual rate of corruption]

As noted previously, the fact that we cannot directly measure the ARC makes it very difficult to determine if the party is winning or losing its fight with corruption. At best the RRC provides a weak alternative measure. To begin with the RRC represents that fraction of the ARC in which illegal acts were a) detected and b) indicted. Because even under the best of circumstances (where prosecutors are vigilant and diligent), some percentage of cases will inevitably go undetected, the RRC remains an imprecise reflection of the ARC. When prosecutors are lax, of course, the gap between the RRC and the ARC may be considerable. Hypothetically, regardless of the overall efficacy of enforcement if the percentage of cases detected and prosecuted remains constant over time, then the RRC would be a simple linear function of the ARC and hence changes in the RRC would reflect changes in the ARC. We cannot assume, however, that the RRC is a constant function of the ARC or a reliable proxy for the ARC.

On the contrary, we need to recognize that the RRC is primarily a measure of the intensity of enforcement and that changes in the RRC largely result from policy-driven shifts between periods of intense and lax enforcement (Gong 1994; Quade 2007). Thus if the RRC rises, we need to assume

*[handwritten: * → revealed rate of corruption actually measures intensity of enforcement]*

that the primary reason it went up is that enforcement was intensified. In most cases, we do not even have to assume sharp increases are the result of more intense enforcement because most campaigns are normally highly publicized events. More intense enforcement should, of course, increase the proportion of the corruption cases that are detected and prosecuted. An increase in prosecutions may, in turn, cause the ARC to drop if it deters officials from engaging in corruption. At a very basic level this is, in fact, what short bursts of "hyper enforcement" are supposed to do and we would not be wrong to assume that most campaigns cause the RRC–ARC gap to narrow. But we cannot be sure how policy-induced increases in the RRC affect the ARC after a campaign ends, and whether once the campaign comes to an end the RRC–ARC gap returns to its previous level. Nor can we tell if the rises in ARC that presumably triggered a campaign will not continue once the campaign ends. As a result, the only way to really know if campaigns actually affect the ARC is to measure changes in the RRC–ARC gap. Yet we cannot measure the gap because the ARC is by definition immeasurable.

We can, however, approximate the RRC–ARC gap, albeit indirectly and incompletely. As noted earlier, mathematically the RRC is the fraction of all cases in which corrupt officials were caught and prosecuted. That proposition also represents the "risk" of getting caught.[7] That is:

$$ARC = \frac{\text{Corrupt Officials}}{\text{Total Officials}}$$

$$RRC = \frac{\text{Officials Prosecuted}}{\text{Total Officials}}$$

$$\frac{RRC}{ARC} = \text{Percentage of corrupt officials prosecuted}$$

$$\frac{RRC}{ARC} \approx \text{Odds of prosecution}$$

Thus, if the RRC is a quarter of the ARC and one in four corrupt officials get caught, then a corrupt official's chance of getting caught is also one in four. Similarly, if 1 in 10 officials is corrupt but only 1 in 50 is prosecuted, the odds of prosecution will be 20 percent. If 5 in 10 are corrupt and 1 in 50 is prosecuted, the odds of prosecution will be 4 percent.

It is important to note that, as used herein, "risk" refers to the aggregate odds of prosecution, not the risk that a specific individual faces.[8] Although individual risk is not unimportant, ultimately individuals' assumptions about risk are subjective and dependent on context. An official's assumptions about risk may thus diverge considerably from aggregate objective risk, which is what the RRC–ARC ratio represents. Since the purpose of this analysis is to assess whether the RRC–ARC gap has changed, individuals' beliefs about risk are exogenous to the analysis.

Because we can restate the RRC–ARC gap in terms of risk, it is possible to shift from aggregate measures of the level of corruption to data on individuals charged with corruption and specifically the length of time between when they become corrupt and when they get caught. To do so we must conceive of corruption as a form of iterated game wherein once an official commits a corrupt act she or he faces a series of "lotteries" (games of chance) in which the official may either evade capture and punishment or may get caught.[9] Each lottery is governed by a set of odds which are determined largely by the RRC–ARC gap—which we cannot determine.

We can, however, posit that if the odds of getting caught are high, then it is likely that corrupt officials will be caught in the first few lotteries.[10] Thus, for example, if the probability of getting caught is 10 percent, in a repeated game of chance a corrupt official would have a greater than 53 percent change of avoiding detection after six rounds and after ten rounds would still have a 38.7 percent chance of getting away with his or her crimes (see Table 2.1).[11] If the odds of getting caught are 50 percent, however, after six rounds, the odds that a corrupt official will be caught are 98.4 percent. In slightly different terms, if we begin with a group of 100 corrupt officials, if the odds of getting caught are 10 percent a total of 47 will be caught in six rounds, whereas 99 will be caught in six rounds if the odds are 50 percent.

Not only do the odds of ultimately getting caught differ based on the one-shot odds, the temporal pattern of when corrupt officials get caught also varies. The pattern can be illustrated by modeling a group of 100 corrupt officials over time. If the odds of getting caught are 50 percent, then half of all those officials who will get caught within six rounds will be caught in the first round and 89 percent of the 99 that will get caught after six rounds will have been caught by the third round. If the odds are 10 percent, on the other hand, less than a quarter of the 47 who will get caught in six rounds will be caught in the first round. By the third round, 57 percent of those who will get caught have been detained.

Hypothetical analysis using comparative statics suggests that we should find significant differences in crime–capture lag distribution depending on whether corrupt officials are repeat or one-time offenders, as well as differences in the risk of getting caught. With repeat offenders, when the odds of capture are high, most corrupt officials are caught soon after they become corrupt. When the odds of getting caught are 50 percent, for instance, 57 percent of those caught in the first six rounds of play will be caught in the same round that they turn corrupt, and by their second go at the lottery nearly 90 percent of those who get caught will have been caught. When the odds are 5 percent, on the other hand, only 21 percent will be caught in their first round and less than half will be caught in the first two rounds. As a result, the lag distribution skews more toward the preliminary rounds and drops

Table 2.1 Effect of differential odds of capture on crime–capture lag (N = 100 corrupt officials)

	Where p(caught) = 10%					Where p(caught) = 50%				
Round	p (caught)	p (not caught)	Number caught	Percent caught	Cum.	p (caught)	p (not caught)	Number caught	Percent caught	Cum.
1	10.0	90.0	10	21.3	21.3	50.0	50.0	50	50.5	50.5
2	19.0	81.0	9	19.1	40.4	75.0	25.0	25	25.3	75.8
3	27.1	72.9	8	17.0	57.4	87.5	12.5	13	13.1	88.9
4	34.4	65.6	7	14.9	72.3	93.7	6.3	6	6.1	95.0
5	41.0	59.0	7	14.9	87.2	96.9	3.1	3	3.0	98.1
6	46.9	53.1	6	12.8	100	98.4	1.6	2	2.0	100
Total caught			47					99		

Notes:

Where: $p(\text{not caught})_{\text{roundx}} = p(\text{not caught})^x$

$p(\text{caught}) - 1\text{-}p(\text{not caught})$

number caught $= 100 * p(\text{caught})_{\text{roundx}}$

percent caught $= \text{caught}_{\text{roundx}}/\text{Total caught}_{\text{rounrnd 1-6}}$.

off rapidly when the odds are high (see Figure 2.4). As the odds decrease, the distribution becomes flatter and the "peak" round shifts from the early round to later rounds.

Data and analysis

$\left(\begin{array}{l} 1992-6 \ \& \\ 2005-6 \end{array} \right)$

To test whether the crime–capture lag distribution has changed over time, I use two set of data on individuals detained or sentenced for corruption. The first contains data on individuals arrested during the period 1992–96. The second contains data on individuals arrested during 2005–06. Both data sets were developed from reports published in the Chinese press, using *Jiancha Ribao*, a daily newspaper published under the auspices of the Supreme People's Procuratorate, as the primary source. For the 1992–96 dataset, data from *Jiancha Ribao* were supplemented by data published in other newspapers, including provincial "legal dailies." For the 2005–06 dataset I used the Internet to search for missing data. I also supplemented the 2005–06 dataset with cases reported in *Renmin Fayuan Bao*, a daily published under the auspices of the People's Court system.

Although both samples are large, they cannot be assumed to be perfectly representative samples because they are based on reported cases and there is a clear bias in reporting that results in the overrepresentation of high-profile cases. Imperfect though they may be, the data provide us with the opportunity to test the intuition embodied in the PLC and the conclusions suggested by the RRC. Based on their "sense" experts polled by various organizations believe that after increasing significantly during the 1980s and early 1990s, the level of corruption has stabilized. At the same time, the RRC, which measures the number of officials charged with corruption, has also leveled off. Because the regime has putatively intensified its

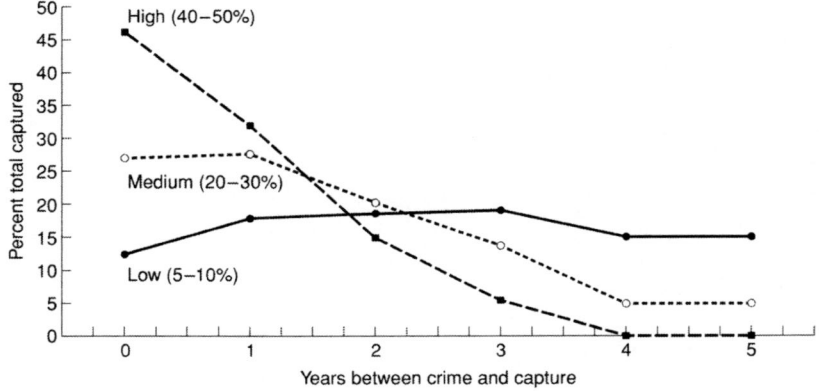

Figure 2.4 Crime–capture lag distribution (repeat offenders).
Source: Hypothetical distribution estimated by author.

anticorruption efforts since the late 1980s, the trends in the PLC and RRC suggest that the war on corruption has been fought to a standstill in which the government's anticorruption efforts have kept corruption under control.

The crime–capture lag distributions for the mid-1990s and mid-2000s, however, show that the distribution 2005–06 was significantly flatter than in 1992–96 (see Figure 2.5). Statistical tests using both chi-squares and analysis of variance (ANOVA) confirm that the distributions are significantly different. (See Table 2.2).

In concrete terms, among those detained in the early 1990s, 11.2 percent were caught in the same year that they become corrupt. Nearly 40 percent had been caught by the second year. Nearly two-thirds were caught within three years. Among those detained in 2005–06, however, 6.1 percent were caught within a year. After three years 23.2 percent had been caught. In all, nearly 90 percent of those caught in 1992–96 had been involved in corruption for six years or less. By contrast, 60 percent of those caught in 2005–06 had been involved in corruption for six years or less. Forty percent, on the other hand, had been involved in corruption for over six years, three and a half times the 12 percent who had been engaged in corruption for more than six years in 1992–95. The data thus suggest that it took prosecutors longer to detect and file charges in 2005–06 than it had in 1992–96. The data, therefore, suggest that risk was considerably lower in the latter period and, in turn, that the gap between the RRC and the ARC widened.

Other data also suggest that the crime–capture lag has increased from around four years to over six years.[12] These data, however, reveal a more complex picture. Until the mid-1990s, the number of officials who turned to corruption was greater each year than the number arrested (see Figure 2.6).

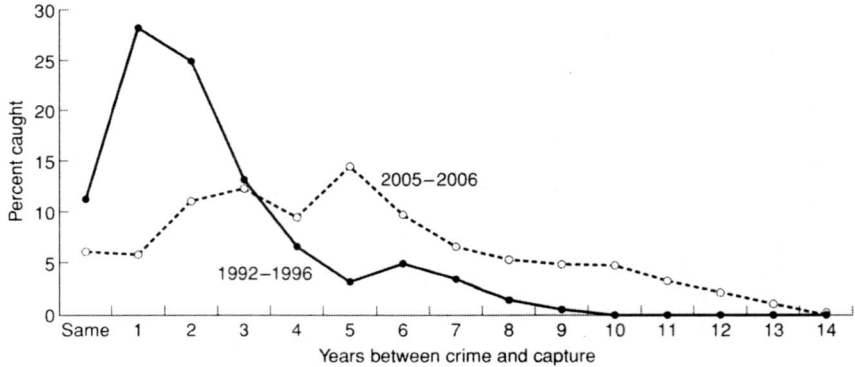

Figure 2.5 Actual crime–capture lag distribution.
Source: Author s database.

Table 2.2 Crime–capture lag

Years	1992–96			2005–06		
	Individuals	*Percent*	*Cumulative*	*Individuals*	*Percent*	*Cumulative*
Same	98	11.16	11.16	54	6.14	6.14
1	247	28.13	39.29	52	5.92	12.06
2	219	24.94	64.24	98	11.15	23.21
3	117	13.33	77.56	109	12.40	35.61
4	59	6.72	84.28	84	9.56	45.16
5	29	3.30	87.59	128	14.56	59.73
6	45	5.13	92.71 ⑤	89	10.13	69.85
7	32	3.64	96.36	60	6.83	76.68
8	14	1.59	97.95	49	5.57	82.25
9	5	0.57	98.52	45	5.12	87.37
10	3	0.34	98.86	43	4.89	92.26 ⑩
11	3	0.34	99.20	32	3.64	95.90
12	1	0.11	99.32	22	2.50	98.41
13	2	0.23	99.54	12	1.37	99.77
14	2	0.23	99.77	0	0.00	99.77
15	2	0.23	100.00	2	0.23	100.00
N	878			879		

[handwritten margin note: suggests takes double amount of time to detect corruption by 2005/6 research.]

Chi-square tests	Value	df	Asymp. sig. (2-sided)
Pearson chi-square	416.7154	15	0.000
Likelihood ratio	458.1245	15	0.000
Linear-by-linear association	322.3430	1	0.000
Valid N	1755		

ANOVA	Sum of squares	df	Mean square	F-stat.	Sign
Between groups	3091.45	1	3081.45	394.695	0.000
Within groups	13685.96	1753	7.81		
Total	16767.41	1754			

Since 1998, the number arrested has exceeded the number of officials turning bad. The lag between crime and capture causes underreporting of the number of newly corrupted officials in the more recent years and thus part of the drop-off is a data artifact. Nevertheless, the divergence implies that even though the crime–capture lag has increased, the regime's anticorruption effort may be making headway.

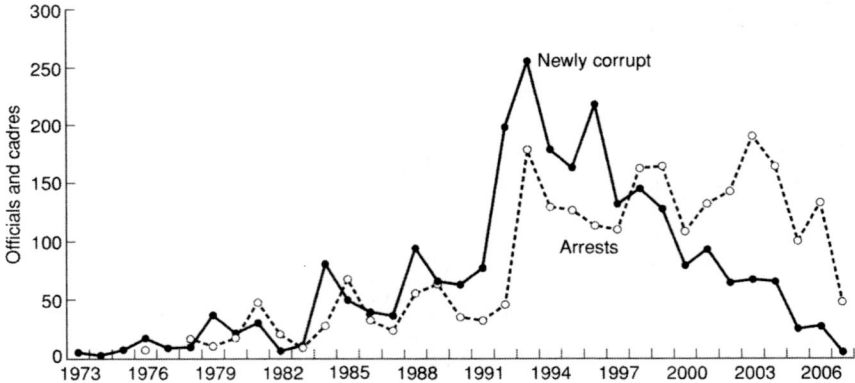

Figure 2.6 Newly corrupt vs arrests.
Source: author's database.

Conclusions

As is invariably true when using hard data to analyze corruption, this attempt
to determine if the CCP is winning the war on corruption suffers from
drawbacks. As a result, conclusions must be taken as tentative and sugges-
tive, rather than definitive. Comparison of the lag between crime and capture
during the periods 1992–96 and 2005–06 appears to show a significant change
in risk. During 2005–06, officials were apparently less likely to get caught
immediately or soon after they first engaged in corruption than during 1992–96.
On average, corrupt officials were caught after 20 months during the earlier
period. During the later period, that average lag between crime and capture
was 63 months. Because a decrease in the odds of getting caught can be
associated with a widening of the ARC–RRC gap, the data suggest that
although the RRC leveled off in the mid-1990s, the ARC likely continued to
rise. Corruption, in other words, worsened rather than stabilized.

Evidence of declining risk is troublesome because analysis using comparative statics implies that a decrease in odds can be associated not only
with a direct decrease in the percentage of corrupt officials caught, but also a
rise in "recidivism." If we assume that the rate at which officials "go bad" is
roughly constant, then as the percentage of corrupt officials who get caught
goes down the number of "repeat offenders" within the ranks of officialdom
will increase year by year. In the simulated models used to assess the impact
of changes in risk on the crime–capture lag distribution, when the probability
of capture was set at 50 percent, after six rounds 531 out of the 608 officials
who became corrupt had been caught. When the probability of capture was
set at 10 percent, however, only 236 out of the 557 officials who became
corrupt had been caught. Thus among the 1,000 officials that would have
entered a hypothetical seventh round, in the former scenario only 77 would

have been prior offenders, while 321 would have been repeat offenders in the latter scenario. The recidivism rate, in other words, would have jumped from 7.7 percent to 32.1 percent, even though the percentage of officials who turned bad each year remained set at the 10 percent rate in both models. If capture rates have in fact fallen, then it is likely that the percentage of Chinese officials tainted by corruption has increased and thus the gap between the RRC and the ARC has widened.[13]   *naïve*

It is important to note, however, that even if the RRC–ARC gap has widened, the regime continues to fight hard against corruption and the RRC has leveled off at a fairly high level. On average, approximately 30,000 public officials have been formally charged with economic crimes each year and over 20,000 have been remanded to the courts for trial. Of these a quarter have been sent to prison for five years or more.[14] The regime has not, therefore, thrown in the towel. Thus, even if we suspect that the party is not winning the war, we also have no evidence that corruption is on the verge of swamping it. The fact that the PLC has remained level would also suggest that even if the incidence and severity of corruption has actually increased, experts do not believe that corruption has become a much more serious problem or threat.

Notes

* This chapter is an abridged version of my article "Win, lose, or draw? China's war on corruption," *Crime, Law and Social Change* (February 2008), 49(1): 7–26, and is based on a paper presented at the Workshop on Toward a Clean Government: Institutional Design and Policy Capacity, City University of Hong Kong, Hong Kong, May 2007. I wish to thank Linda Chelan Li and the other participants for their criticisms and suggestions of my original draft

1 On the party's anticorruption effort see Yao (1997), He (2000), Fan and Grossman (2001), Fabre (2001), and Gong (1997 and 2002).

2 *South China Morning Post*, 3 October 2006. Zheng was one of a number of corruption-related suicides and attempted suicides during 2006. A senior bureaucrat in Zhejiang and a senior official in the anticorruption department of the Liaoning Railway bureau both committed suicide in early 2006 after they were accused of corruption; see *South China Morning Post*, 16 January 2006.

3 Based on data in *Zhongguo jiancha nianjian*, various years.

4 In the parlance of official reports, officials holding positions "at over above the county-department level" (县处级以上) are reported separately as "important cases" (要案). "Monies recovered per case filed" is a crude estimation of the average monetary value of corruption. I calculate this figure by taking the total amount of "losses recovered" by the Procuratorate each year and dividing that sum by the number of cases filed that year. Because it is somewhat unclear how the Procuratorate determines the value of losses and how much it recovers, the reliability of this sum is uncertain. I use this measure for lack of a better means to gauge the changing "value" of corruption.

5 Guo Yong pioneered the analytical use of the lag between crime and capture, which he terms the "latency" period of corruption, and I am in his intellectual debt; see Guo (forthcoming).

6 Both data sets used in this analysis are subsets of larger data sets. Only cases in which crime–capture lags could be calculated were used herein.

7 Although my data plot the RRC based on the number of "cases" in which corrupt officials were indicted on criminal charges, I express the mathematical relationship between the RRC and ARC in terms of individuals, even though there is not a perfect one-to-one correspondence between cases and individuals. The relationship has, however, been relative stable with a ratio of 1 case to 1.12 individuals. The reliance on cases to plot the RRC reflects the fact that data on cases is available for all years since 1980, while data on individuals is only available beginning in 1989.

8 For a discussion of the impact of perceived risk on individual choice, see Wedeman (2005).

9 I treat the game as an iterated lottery because a corrupt official not only faces punishment when he or she commits a crime but also remains liable forever afterward (or until some statute of limitations has been reached). This is true of both officials who engage in "single-shot" corruption (e.g. accepting a single bribe) and those who engage in "serial" corruption.

10 For a more detailed discussion of the methodology for estimating and evaluating lag distributions, see Wedeman (2008).

11 Herein I use a simple chained probability function to estimate odds.

12 Data are from a sample of over 3,000 high-level cases collected by the author from the Lexis Nexis database.

13 Rising recidivism rates, moreover, may disguise the true level of corruption because presumably some of those who were corrupt in the past will "go straight," thus creating a "hidden pool" of dishonesty that auditors and investigators may not notice because they are likely to be preoccupied with finding officials currently engaged in illegal activity.

14 Based on data in *Falü nianjian* (Beijing: Zhongguo falü nianjian chubanshe, various years).

References

Fabre, G. (2001) "State, corruption, and criminalization in China," *International Social Science Journal*, 53(169): 459–66.

Fan, C.S. and Grossman, H.I. (2001) "Incentives and corruption in Chinese economic reform," *Policy Reform*, 4: 195–206.

Gong, T. (1994) *The Politics of Corruption in Contemporary China: An Analysis of Policy Outcomes*, Westport, CN: Praeger.

—— (1997) "Forms and characteristics of China's corruption in the 1990s," *Communist and Post-Communist Studies*, 20(3): 277–91.

—— (2002) "Dangerous collusion: corruption as a collective venture in contemporary China," *Communist and Post-Communist Studies*, 35(1): 84–103.

Guo, Y. (forthcoming) "Corruption in transitional China: an empirical analysis," *China Quarterly*.

He, Z.H. (2000) "Corruption and anticorruption in reform China," *Communist and Post-Communist Studies*, 33(2): 243–70.

Pei, M.X. (1999) "Will China become another Indonesia?" *Foreign Policy*, 116: 94–109.

Quade, E.A. (2007) "The logic of anticorruption enforcement campaigns in contemporary China," *Journal of Contemporary China*, 16(50): 65–77.

Root, H. (1996) "Corruption in China: has it become systemic?" *Asian Survey*, 36(8): 741–57.

Shieh, S. (2005) "The rise of collective corruption in China: the Xiamen smuggling case," *Journal of Contemporary China*, 14(42): 67–91.

Sun, Y. (2008) "Cadre recruitment and corruption: What goes wrong?," *Crime, Law, and Social Change*, 49(1): 61–79.

Wedeman, A. (1996) "Corruption and politics," in H.C. Kuan (ed.) *China Review 1996*, Hong Kong: Chinese University of Hong Kong Press.

—— (2004) "The intensification of corruption in China," *China Quarterly*, 180: 895–921.

—— (2005) "Anticorruption campaigns and the intensification of corruption in China," *Journal of Contemporary China*, 14(41): 93–107.

—— (2008) "Win, lose, or draw? China's war on corruption," *Crime, Law and Social Change*, 49(1): 7–26.

Yao, S.T. (1997) "Corruption and the anticorruption movement: the modeling and analysis of the situation in China," *Australian Economic Papers*, 36(1):156–65.

Yuan, B.S. (2007) "Audit institutions and the building of clean government in mainland China," paper presented at the Workshop on Toward a Clean Government: Institutional Design and Policy Capacity, City University of Hong Kong, Hong Kong, May 2007.

3 Rent seeking under the licensing state

The institutional sources of economic corruption in China

Tak-Wing Ngo

One of the most common sources of corruption in present-day China comes from rent seeking. It originates from government–business collusion seeking to capture the extra profits arising from market regulations. Extra profits, or more specifically economic rents, are generated when production licenses are rationed, when prices are fixed, when trade quotas are imposed by the government, and so on. Typically, bribes are offered by businesses to government officials in exchange for the creation and allocation of rents.

During the market reform, rent seeking has become an almost institutionalized form of practice. Wu Jinglian, an influential economist in China, is one of the earliest and most outspoken critics of the rent-seeking phenomenon in China. He argues that a vicious circle of corruption is fashioned by rent creation and rent seeking in China. Government officials and businesses who benefit from exchanging rents with bribes will try to maintain or expand the existing rent regime, hence leading to more corruption (see Wu's interview in Wei 1999: 13). Wu's idea has been echoed by another influential scholar, Hu Angang. In a series of seminars organized by the Central Disciplinary Inspection Commission, Hu ranked rent seeking as the foremost source of corruption (Hu 2001: 39).

Constraining the creation and the pursuit of economic rents thus constitutes one of the many steps towards controlling rampant corruption in China. In 2006, the central government and the Central Disciplinary Inspection Commission of the Chinese Communist Party made the combat against business bribery a main focus of anticorruption campaigns. Corruption practices relating to rent seeking in six areas have been singled out for special attention. These include government–business collusions in construction works, land sales, property rights transfers, medical and drug supplies, government procurements, and the exploitation of natural resources (Zeng 2007: 15–17). The ostensible goal is to fight corruption, simultaneously its symptoms and root causes.

However, as we argue in this chapter, rent seeking and economic corruption are not just the symptoms of official malfeasance. The root causes go much deeper. They are to a large extent fashioned by a licensing state. Even though market reform has steadily reduced the role of central planning and even when the once-pervasive price control and rationing system has drastically

[handwritten margin notes: "without reform of this, a-c will not succeed in its aims"; "licensing system still govt controlled despite market reforms"]

diminished in its importance, China continues to maintain an elaborate licensing system (Yang 2004). Investors still need numerous official chops to gain market entry. At the same time, the state uses the licensing system to govern industrial planning and set development priorities. Under such a system, rent has been used by the central government as a policy instrument in effecting industrial plans. Local governments have relied on rent allocation to maneuver the development of local economies. Many private businesses have depended upon rents granted by local authorities to compete in the national market.

Under such circumstances, the creation, allocation, and pursuit of economic rents have become institutionalized as part of the state licensing mechanisms. Reducing rent seeking and rent-related corrupt exchanges will require a radical reform of the mode of industrial governance as well as changes in the nature of the licensing state. The following discussion will unveil the complexities involved in such a process.

[handwritten margin notes: "e.g. Rose-Ackerman recommendations"; "reform of mode of industrial governance + nature of licensing"]

The relationship between rent seeking and corruption

To understand the difficulty of combating rent-related corruption, it is essential to distinguish rent seeking from corruption. Although rent seeking and corruption are intimately related, they are not the same thing. They are intimately intertwined because officials can utilize their power of rent creation as a means of bribe seeking. At the same time, economic actors frequently pay bribes to officials as a means of rent seeking. Despite their close relation, rent seeking and corruption belong to different realms of practices. It is such delicate distinctions which make it difficult to control rent seeking during anticorruption campaigns.

In this regard, a clarification of the conceptual distinction between rent seeking and corruption is needed. Corruption is commonly understood as the use of public power for private gain. However, beyond this simple understanding a more precise defining of corruption is anything but straightforward. Generations of scholars have produced competing definitions of corruption, ranging from legalistic, normative, functional, to economistic understandings (Heidenheimer and Johnston 2001). The problem is aggravated in the analysis of China, as Chinese law and official policy consider almost all forms of official malfeasance by state and Party cadres as corruption. These range from crimes with material returns such as embezzlement of public property, fraud, bribery, tax evasion, smuggling, profiteering, and rent seeking to power abuses such as negligence, collusion, sectionalism, and nepotism; to improper behavior of officials such as womanizing, gambling, drinking, stock market speculation, extravagant living, and superstition. In response, some scholars have taken a broad definition of corruption (e.g. Gong 1997). Others prefer a narrower definition confined to the usurpation of public authority for private gains as corruption proper, while leaving aside non-material forms of official malfeasance such as power abuse and misconduct (for instance, Wedeman 2004).

[handwritten margin notes: "defining corr. + distinction from RS."]

Even among those who prefer the narrower definition, many have mistaken rent seeking as a form of corruption. This misconception stands in contrast to the conventional understanding of rent seeking which draws its meaning from public choice economics. Such understanding originates from the concept of rents put forward by Buchanan, Tullock, Tollison, and others. They focus on the extra return above the market clearing price. Rent is the payment made to an owner of resources over and above that which those resources could command in alternative uses (Buchanan 1980: 3). In other words, rent is a return in excess of opportunity cost. In the ideal market system of textbook economics, all economic rents will be eroded or dissipated through time. This is because above-cost payments to any resource owner will attract other profit seekers to engage in identical pursuits. The entry of more and more profit seekers will thus drive the rent down. Eventually, rents will disappear altogether in the long run. Critical to this process is the freedom of entry. If the entry of other profit seekers is blocked, such as in a cartel, monopoly or government regulation, output price will not fall and hence no dissipation of rent can occur. Economists consider this kind of rent as "artificially" contrived. Such artificially contrived rents are subject to competition, or rent seeking. Put differently, the creation of rents by state intervention and the allocation of rents to political supporters invite other social players to engage in rent seeking.

In such conceptions of rents and rent seeking, it is clear that the creation, allocation, and pursuit of economic rents are prone to corruption, but they do not necessarily involve corruption in the form of usurpation of public authority for private gains. A good illustration is the price cartel formed by instant noodle manufacturers in China. The cartel was organized by the China arm of the International Ramen Manufacturers Association, IRMA. Members of IRMA China hold a 95 percent share of the instant noodle market in China. After several meetings, they reached an agreement to raise the price of instant noodles in June 2007, resulting in a nationwide price hike. The jacked-up price thus offers extra profits to the cartel members in the form of rents. The price increase alarmed the China Consumers Association, which filed a complaint to the National Development and Reform Commission. The Commission subsequently ruled that the price cartel contravened the Price Law (State Development and Reform Commission 2007). In this case, the practice is illegal as it hinges upon a conspiracy to manipulate the market price which is punishable under Chinese law (while at the same time IRMA China was not officially registered). However, no public authority was involved in the creation of rents by means of price cartel. It is a clear example of illegal rent seeking without involving corruption.

In the same vein, there is no shortage of corruption cases involving government–business collusion for private gains which at the same time link to rent seeking. The widely reported Yuanhua scandal is a good case in point. In the province of Xiamen, the Yuanhua Corporation set up a dozen companies and smuggled into China an estimated 53 billion yuan worth of goods during a four-year period from 1996 to 1999. The Corporation's founder, Lai Changxing, established a web of personal networks with officials in foreign trade, public security, customs, military, and banks. Lai offered bribes in terms of cash, real estates, gifts, club memberships, mistresses, and so on, to government and Party officials to cover up and maintain his smuggling empire. When the case was eventually investigated by the central government, more than 200 officials were implicated. The Yuanhua case is regarded by observers as an indication of the rise of collective corruption in China (Shieh 2005). It is a case involving government–business collusion in rent seeking. Wank (2009) argues that the huge discount rent derived from the evasion of customs duty and tariffs created the incentive of rent seeking. In the Yuanhua case, discount rents were captured by organized smuggling. Bribes were offered to local authorities to cover up the smuggling.

The preceding examples demonstrate the difference between rent seeking and corruption. Corruption is only one means of seeking rents. There are many other ways of rent seeking such as lobbying and cartel formation. Conversely, whereas bribe is often offered in exchange for rents, bribes can also be used in exchange for votes, official positions, priority treatment, covering up illegal activities, and suchlike. Such kinds of bribery practices as exchanging spoils for school places are outside the realm of rent seeking as they do not involve the pursuit of extra returns above the market price. Certain acts of usurpation of public power for private gains, such as the appropriation of public property, the maintenance of extra-budgetary funds for private usage, local government exactions in the form of arbitrary charges, are also unrelated to rent seeking.

In brief, rent seeking should not be regarded as a form of corruption. It can better be understood as a source of corruption. The distinction is important because, as we will show in the subsequent discussions, it is the dissimilarity between rent seeking and corruption as well as the interrelatedness between the two practices that contribute to the impasse in controlling corruption arising from rent seeking.

Rent creation as legitimate intervention and as a source of corruption

So far scholarly attention on rent seeking has been focused mainly on the demand side, as the word "seeking" indicates. This has grossly overlooked the other equally important rent-related activities. Elsewhere we have proposed the more embracing concept of "rent production," by which we refer to the whole range of activities connected to the fabrication of economic rent, including its creation, allocation, extraction, redistribution, and pursuit (Ngo 2009). In particular, the creation and allocation of rents is closely related to the capacity of the licensing state during market regulation.

Under the state licensing regime, rent creation exhibits dual facets. It can be a legitimate government action or a source of corruption. Specifically,

[handwritten margin note: rent-seeker is a legitimate act of gvt power but in their discretion, agents are prone to bribery]

since the creation of rent involves the manipulation of price and market entry, it can be a perfectly legitimate act of the government (even though many economists argue that it is an undesirable act). In fact, price control and market entry control have been prominent features of the Chinese economy during the market reform. As long as state agents do not profit privately, the rents created from market regulation can be legitimately allocated to specific groups in accordance with government policy. However, in exercising their discretionary power to ration rents, state agents are prone to bribery offers from economic actors who strive to capture the rents. In such circumstances, the creation and allocation of rents become a source of corruption.

We can take two examples to illustrate the dual facets. In the example of the auto industry, the State Council selected three enterprises (First Auto Works in Changchun, Second Auto Works in Shiyan, and Shanghai Automotive Industry Corporation in Shanghai) in 1987 as the key manufacturers of passenger cars. In the following year, another three (Beijing, Tianjin and Guangzhou) were selected as the auxiliary manufacturers. This became the so-called "Big Three and Small Three" strategy which still holds to date (State Council 1988). In an attempt to fence off "random competition," the central government erected strict market entry controls. All manufacturers other than the six selected enterprises were to be excluded from car assembly by state licensing arrangements. At the same time, import restrictions were imposed to protect domestic production. The policy thus created a highly protected market, accruing extra rents to the oligopolies. It is, however, a legitimate arrangement of state licensing using rent creation as a policy instrument.

The second example of highway monopoly offers a typical case of a combination of government exaction, rent seeking, fraud, and corruption. Among the 100 highways of sixteen provinces, 158 unauthorized toll booths have been set up. Until the end of 2005, the National Audit Office discovered 14.9 billion yuan of illicit toll collected from these highways. Another 8.2 billion yuan came from overcharging in seven provinces. Furthermore, 35 commercially operated highways in twelve provinces were given exceptionally long franchises, resulting in a profit return of up to ten times of their endowed investment. Among the 106 franchised highways investigated by the National Audit Office in ten provinces, 60 percent of the franchised projects were found to have been illegally approved by unauthorized local government agencies. Collusions between banks, local governments, and the bidders abound. The value of many highways has been deliberately deflated by local governments. The bidding conditions for the franchise project were tailor-made to a specific bidder. The source of capital investment was also problematic. It was found that in eighteen franchised projects, 17 billion yuan of the total 24.3 billion yuan capital (that is, 70 percent of the investment capital) came from bank loans using the franchised highway itself as the mortgage. An outstanding example is the Hefei–Chaohu–Wuhu Highway. The Anhui government franchised the highway to a private enterprise from Shanghai using invited tender in 2003, and then repurchased it in 2005. Because the selling

[handwritten annotation: makes assumption that opportunity for rent creation evitably encourage rent seeking + corruption]

price was deflated in 2003 and marked up in 2005, the government lost 1.24 billion yuan to benefit the colluder (Li 2007).

Very often, the division between rent creation as a legitimate intervention and as a source of corruption is a thin one. It is such fuzzy boundaries that make it difficult to constrain rent creation. In fact, the extent of rent creation in China is staggering, thus giving rise to enormous incentives for rent seeking and corrupt exchanges. During the early reform period, China maintained a dual-track price system. Price control was applied to a wide range of commodities, including coal, pig iron, steel, aluminum, copper, wood, cement, crude oil, petrol, gasoline, natural gas, chemical fertilizers, pesticides, automobiles, electricity, cotton yarn, paper, televisions, refrigerators, food, and many more. The cheaper-priced commodities had to be rationed to privileged groups (some called this a surplus rent in contrast to monopoly rent, see Hu 2009). One critic gave an estimation of the amounts of rent created in 1988. According to his estimation, rents created by price control in some 30 commodities amounted to 150 billion yuan at that time. Rents created by bank loans under subsidized interest rates amounted to 113.88 billion yuan. The difference in foreign exchange rates between official and black market rates added another 93.04 billion yuan. From this the critic concluded that the dual-track system alone contributed to a total rent value of 356.9 billion yuan, which amounted to 30 percent of the national income in 1988 (Hu 1999). The calculation was updated by another Chinese scholar in 1992 after the price reform. He suggested that the amount of rent arising from the dual-track system had vastly reduced, but still accounted for no less than 76.66 billion yuan in current prices. Rents created by differences in interest rates for bank loans amounted to at least 64.85 billion yuan. Difference in foreign exchange rates created another 115.71 billion yuan (Wan 1999).

With such an extent of rent creation, there existed strong incentives for *[handwritten: PUB. CHOICE]* rent seeking, official profiteering, and corruption. Government officials who control the power of rationing low-interest loans, under-priced commodities, or foreign exchange can either cash the surplus themselves or award the rent to cronies in exchange for parochial or personal returns. Subsequent reforms in the commodities market, capital market, and the foreign exchange market in the 1990s have gradually eliminated price differences and hence eroded much of the rents. However, legacies of the dual-track price system still persist to the present day. Price control still applies to a number of commodities. These include tobacco, salt, chemical fertilizers, certain medical drugs, school textbooks, natural gas, water from cross-provincial reservoirs, electricity, transportation (railways, ports, airports, and air flights), postal services, telecommunication, and a number of professional services such as notary services and surveying (State Development and Planning Commission 2001). In addition to these commodities, rents are still widely created and rationed in a number of crucial areas: when banks extend policy loans to specific industries or enterprises on favorable interest rates; and when local governments offer cheap land to attract investors.

The creation and allocation of rents in industrial planning

Under an elaborate licensing system, the Chinese state has made active use of rent creation and allocation as policy instruments in undertaking industrial planning and assigning development priorities. In essence, the government creates rents by granting subsidies to targeted industries, extending preferential loans to individual businesses, or picking and protecting winners as monopolies. As a matter of fact, the Chinese state is not unique in utilizing rent creation and allocation as an active policy instrument. The so-called developmental states in East Asia are characterized by dirigisme in distorting market mechanisms, or "making the price wrong" as Wade (1990) puts it, for the sake of promoting industrial development. The Japanese state is typical of using state licensing in shaping industrial governance (Sohn 2005). The rents created by state licensing, according to the developmental state theory, are channeled into productive purposes rather than personal gains because of the presence of institutional safeguards such as state autonomy, technocratic insulation, social embeddedness, and collaborative government–business relations (Evans 1995).

During the economic reform in China, state licensing of market activities manifests itself in the central planning over the development of strategic industries. The first comprehensive industrial development policy paper was published in 1989 by the State Council. The paper singled out a number of industries as priority areas of development (State Council 1989). Strict market entry was imposed. This was followed by the promulgation of another policy paper in 1994: *Guideline to National Industrial Policies in the 1990s.* Several pillar industries have been identified, including machine tools, electronics, petrochemicals, automobiles, and construction (State Council 1994). The goal is to raise technological capacity, promote large indigenous enterprises, and enhance international competitiveness. This shares the same rationale behind the policies taken by other East Asian states such as Japan and Korea: to eliminate excessive competition, to prevent duplication of production, and to achieve economies of scale. The goal is to foster a few national giants that are capable of competing in the world market, and to avoid industrial isomorphism that often results in excessive investments and random competition. To realize such goals, a few enterprises are designated by the government as market winners. A series of regulations and preferential policy treatments are then created as the framework of economic governance in coordinating the development of that industrial sector. In doing so, rent creation becomes embedded in the governance structure shaping sectoral developments.

Let us take a close look at the passenger car industry as one typical example. As we have noted earlier, the Big Three and Small Three strategy has been promulgated as the intended development target. Under the strategy, three sets of policy measures have been taken to achieve economic governance: market entry barriers, import restrictions, and preferential allocation of resources. In each of the categories of policy measures, economic rents were created and allocated to specific target groups. It is worth noting the extent of such rent creation.

Entry barrier to sedan production was erected by using administrative directives. The central government demanded that all regions, departments, and enterprises must obtain clearance from the State Council before they could set up car production plants. All existing sedan projects which did not have the State Council's permission had to be brought to an end. A catalogue system was implemented to maintain the entry barrier (Ngo and Chen 2009). A list of enterprises and vehicle models were registered in the catalogue. Only those enterprises appearing in the catalogue were allowed to engage in auto assembling. License plates would only be issued to vehicles that were included in the catalogue.

A second kind of measure was import restrictions. High tariffs were imposed on imported automobiles to protect domestic companies. In 1985, the tariff for automobiles was 120–150 percent and that for parts was 60 percent. In June 1985, 80 percent of adjustment tax was added to it. In 1986, the tariff for cars rose to 180–220 percent in order to restrict the import of sedans. It was not until 1992 that the government began to lower the tariff. The average tariff was reduced from 71.5 percent in 1992 to 39.5 percent in 1997 (Wu 2004). Besides high tariffs, regulations had been tightened to prevent loopholes from being used by local governments for parochial benefits. A series of related protective measures were implemented, including import quotas, foreign exchange control, control of foreign trade licenses, import permits, and control over import categories. Ports were banned from giving clearance to whole-vehicle imports, except for six authorized ports in Dalian, Tianjin, Shanghai, Huangpu, Manzhouli, and Huanggang. The annual quantity and types of auto imports had to be approved by the State Council. No vehicles were allowed to be imported as gifts or donations (Liu et al. 2005: 93).

Finally, rents in the form of state subsidies and contrived surplus were offered to the picked winners. These included tax reduction, low interest loans, priority for foreign investment, and speedy procedure for stock market listing. These measures were mostly outlined in the *Industrial Policy for the Auto Sector* announced in 1994 by the State Planning Commission. To achieve this goal, existing enterprises were encouraged to expand their production capacity, sales volume, and R & D investment. Enterprises that had reached a specified production, sales and R & D target would receive government assistance to double their production capacity (State Planning Commission 1994).

With strict entry barriers in place, the passenger car market was endowed with state-sanctioned rents. To capture this extra profit without delay, all the designated car assemblers chose to form joint ventures with foreign carmakers. Technological and management know-how from foreign carmakers was traded with market entry in the highly protected but growing domestic market, as well as the high profits and rents associated with it. The strategy of joint venture formation proved to be effective in capturing the sedan market within a short period of time. The overall result was the emergence of a few oligopolies with foreign participation. By 1997, the three major groups, the three auxiliary groups, and the official organization China National Automotive Industry Corporation together accounted for 64 percent of China's total vehicle production and 93 percent of its car production (Sit and Liu 2000: 661).

Rent seeking fashioned by state licensing

The passenger car policy offers a remarkable example of enormous rents created legitimately by state licensing in the name of industrial policy and economic governance. Unsurprisingly, the existence of huge extra profits invited rent seeking using lawful as well as illicit means. In this regard, Tullock (1980: 109) argues that one way to reduce rent seeking is to introduce bias into the selection process. By picking only those players who possess certain traits, it discourages those who do not possess those traits from investing in rent seeking because it does not pay. The Big Three and Small Three strategy apparently follows this principle since the bias is clear from the outset. However, it is no secret that during the reform period there are multiple possibilities of getting around state restrictions. It is these possibilities that invite rent seeking in the auto industry.

From the outset, the enterprises being picked as market winners were not necessarily strategic players or outstanding performers. Very often the choices were political rather than economic. The criteria were often fuzzy and because of that much room existed for rent seeking. In the passenger car industry cases, the Big Three were selected partly because of power contentions within bureaucratic politics. Intensive lobbying occurred behind the scenes when the policy was made. While Second Auto Works succeeded in lobbying itself to be designated as one of the Big Three, the enterprise had no prior experience and know-how of sedan production at all (Chen and Ouyang 2005). Later on, special permission was obtained by the China Ordnance Industry Corporation and the Guizhou Aviation Industry Corporation to set up new car factories. Both corporations were formerly engaged in the defense industry and had close relationships with top government leaders (Sit and Liu 2000: 662).

In the meantime, foreign carmakers such as Volkswagen, Peugeot, and Citroën sought rents by forming joint ventures with the designated car assemblers. Much lobbying has been undertaken by these carmakers to obtain state approval in many of the joint projects (see, for example, Harwit 1995). There is no way to tell whether these lobbying efforts involved illicit exchanges. However, later development shows that many of the joint ventures were poorly conceived. For instance, Citroën joined hands with Dongfeng (renamed from Second Auto Works) in the Shenlong project. The project started in 1992 but did not begin actual operation until 1997. The daily production volume was only 30 cars and the factory was running only four days a week. Another foreign carmaker, Panda Motors, a US-based company with a Korean financial background, succeeded in obtaining approval to set up a car assembly despite opposition from the powerful State Planning Commission and China National Automotive Industry Corporation. Yet the project was pulled out before actual production (Harwit 1992: 160).

Some enterprises have exploited a loophole in the licensing system to overcome the entry barrier. State policy required a company and its car models to be listed in the catalogue of auto manufacturers and products before the company could produce for the market. However, it was not until 2004 that the regulations explicitly forbade the buying and selling of production licenses. This had been used by newcomers, especially private enterprises, to break through the protection wall. Some joined the industry by taking over existing state-owned enterprises which had been at the edge of bankruptcy. For instance, Geely took over a bankrupting state-owned automobile factory in Sichuan in 1997, while BYD Auto established itself in 2003 by acquiring the majority shares of an auto factory in Xi'an. Others bought their license from incumbent producers. Chery Automobile is a case in point. The enterprise was a joint investment by enterprises in Anhui Province and Wuhu City. It offered 20 percent of its shares for free to Shanghai Automotive in exchange for its production catalogue. Some enterprises such as the Aux Group simply assembled cars under someone else's license. Aux used to be a well-known manufacturer of air conditioners. It formed a joint venture with Shenyang Shuangma Light Vehicle Manufacturing in 2003 to produce SUV models such as Yuandongli, Langjie and Ruitu. Instead of applying for inclusion in the production catalogue, Aux produced the cars under the licenses of Shenyang Fusang Panther, a company whose 49 percent shares were controlled by Aux's joint venture partner Shenyang Shuangma (Ngo and Chen 2009).

All these cases show the wide range of rent-seeking activities arising in response to the central government's industrial policy. Here the central government itself is a major provider of rents and other particularistic advantages, which indirectly creates massive opportunity for corruption and illicit exchanges in the course of rent seeking. But this is not yet the end of the story. State licensing is not only upheld by the central government in regulating the national market, the system is also replicated at all levels of governments in their application to local economies. It is at the local level of state licensing arrangements that most corrupt exchanges take place.

Rent seeking in local economies

Local authorities in present-day China control large amounts of resources which can be allocated as rents and direct subsidies. These authorities also command regulatory power that can be used to erect market-entry barriers, sponsor price cartels, and create rents. More importantly, under the system of fiscal and economic decentralization, local governments have a strong incentive to utilize these resources not just for private gain but also for the good of local development (and often at the expense of other localities). This phenomenon, commonly referred to as local protectionism, derives from a framework of local economic governance under which local governments are required to balance their own budget, fulfill development targets, raise employment level, and achieve economic growth. The performance of state and Party cadres is judged by the well-being of the local economy under their jurisdiction (Edin 2005). In the words of one observer, local governments assume a double identity both as a state political agent and as a local economic principal (Gong 2006). As state agents, local governments enjoy discretionary power to make and implement public policies. As economic principals, they are responsible for the management and development of their local economies. The problem in the exercise of such dual responsibilities is that one cannot easily distinguish policy discretions undertaken with genuinely developmental or entrepreneurial concerns from policy discretions taken with an agenda for private gains.

Let us illustrate the point with the auto industry. The industry has been designated by 24 provincial governments as a pillar industry. The industry offers high economic and tax returns, affords strong economic linkages to a wide range of local auxiliary sectors, and provides a lot of employment opportunities. It is thus no surprise that local governments pay special attention to its development in their own localities. Given their interests in maximizing economic benefits in their own locality vis-à-vis other regions and other levels of governments, local government agents do not assume a neutral, arbitrator's position. They collaborate with enterprises under their jurisdiction to seek rent from the highly protected auto market. At the same time, they create rents and subsidies through their control of opportunities and exemptions, and distribute the resources to a selected few with specific terms of exchange. They are thus rent creators and seekers at the same time. The situation is self-enforcing: given the multi-layers of protection, rent creation and distribution, enterprises can hardly compete in this kind of market without first seeking ad hoc favoritism from state agents (Lin 2001).

Many auto enterprises have been closely related to local governments in one way or another. Except for First Auto Works and Dongfeng, which are directly under central government supervision, and Chang'an, Hafei, and Changhe, which are under the military system, most of the other automakers are within the jurisdiction of local governments. Major enterprises such as Shanghai Automotive, Tianjin Auto, and Guangzhou Auto are owned by either the provincial or prefecture city governments. There are also private enterprises which disguised themselves as collective enterprises under the consent of local governments, in a practice which is often referred to as "wearing a red hat." Brilliance China Automotive is a case in point. These enterprises have benefited from the support of local authorities, either in terms of preferential provision of resources, granting of regulatory convenience, or protection against non-local competitors. Even for enterprises that are genuinely private, the ability to manipulate official favoritism is a key factor in their survival.

The case of Geely is particularly interesting. Geely is the first private auto company in China based in Taizhou City of Zhejiang Province. One of the most common forms of assistance offered by the local government is the move to overcome entry barriers. To help Geely obtain its listing in the passenger cars catalogue, the Taizhou government sent officials to Beijing to lobby for Geely. The Taizhou government also invited research institutes and central government think tanks to visit Geely and asked these institutes to give positive recommendations to relevant central departments. After Geely succeeded in obtaining an official license to assemble passenger cars in 2001, numerous direct subsidies and rents have been granted by local governments in the name of promoting new and high-tech industrial development.

The estimated value of these policy benefits is startling. In 2002, the Luqiao district government offered Geely an industrial area of 3000 *mu* for its passenger car production. The land was sold by special tender. The tender was tailor-made for Geely, so that no other bidders could fulfill the specific requirements. The selling price was 63,000 yuan per *mu*. Within this total area, the government also allowed 500 *mu* to be used for "labor quarters," an area which in actual fact was used for commercial real-estate development. At that time, the market price for industrial land was around 130,000 yuan per *mu*, while that for real estate was 500,000 yuan per *mu*. The economic rent accrued to Geely in terms of this land sale amounted to 386 million yuan. This is only a conservative calculation. The property market rose sharply shortly after the sale. Before the labor quarter construction was completed, land price had surged to 2 million yuan per *mu*, adding an extra 750 million yuan to Geely's fixed assets (Ngo and Chen 2009).

Other forms of subsidies, administrative privileges and regulatory exemptions offered to Geely have been considerable. It is estimated that the tax relief offered by the Tiazhou government was more than 80 million yuan per year. In 2005, the Taizhou government decided to give Geely 600,000 yuan as a reward for its six new types of car. The Zhejiang provincial government listed the 24 new proposed automobile and key parts projects of Geely as special projects eligible for priority treatment in terms of project and land approval. Special institutions have been established jointly by the Economic and Trade Committee of Zhejiang Province and the municipal government of Taizhou to help Geely overcome any difficulties during its course of expansion.

The local government of Taizhou also helped create monopolistic rents for Geely. The government promised to promote the sale of 10,000 locally made vehicles by means of government purchase and related measures. This is undertaken in the name of supporting local industrial development. In essence it means creating local market protection by discriminating against vehicles produced outside the region.

It should be noted that the rents created by officials in this case fall within the legitimate responsibility of the local government. They do not involve such illegal practices as the tucking away of off-budgetary revenues, embezzlement of public properties, or arbitrary levy of fees and fines. The last-mentioned practices are notoriously common among local governments and led Pei (2006) to label the system of local economic governance as "decentralized predation."

Arguably, the particularistic benefits offered by local governments in Zhejiang to Geely constitute a kind of local developmental policy. Without these benefits it is doubtful whether Geely could compete in a national market dominated by a few oligopolies that have been enjoying central government protection. In this regard, local governments share the same interests as local enterprises because they need investments, tax revenues, job creation, and economic development in their own localities. They need to compete with other cities and regions with respect to their economic and social performance (Montinola et al. 1995). As a result, rents are allocated to selected enterprises with certain terms of exchange. In the case of Geely, the Taizhou government has asked the company to pay extra taxes from time to time in order to fulfill set revenue targets. Besides, the government requires the company to maintain a production volume of at least 300,000 cars per year, and with an annual sales plan of 18 billion yuan. There is an implicit agreement that Geely will not relocate its headquarters elsewhere. Geely will not invest in other regions until its production capacity reaches one million cars per year (in 2006 the capacity was 400,000 cars). Furthermore, Geely has promised to sell two million cars in 2015, of which one million is to be produced in Taizhou (Ngo and Chen 2009).

The case of Geely is typical rather than unique. In Pingyang county of Zhejiang Province, the local government offered land at a favorable price to attract Inbev to invest in a beer plant. The auction price was expected to reach 300,000 yuan per *mu*. To suppress the price, the Pingyang government earmarked the land for a beer plant. Inbev succeeded in bidding for the land at half the market price. In Wenzhou City, the government went so far as to set up road barriers to prevent Hangzhou Beer from reaching the city to compete with the local Yongjia Beer (Wu and Jin 2009).

The problem is that while the power of discretion is by definition a prerequisite for the effect implementation of state-led development, many corruption activities also derive from the allocation of discretionary resources. For instance, the hidden profit accrued to Geely and Inbev during the land sale is an exemplar of grooming market winners through making the price wrong. But similar exercises elsewhere have been plagued with corruption. The most eye-catching case in recent years involves the party secretary of Shanghai, Chen Liangyu, who was also a Politburo member. Chen allegedly sold land at a low price to his own brother and helped his crony businessmen to gain access to some 1 billion yuan from the social security fund. He received huge amounts in bribes from related businesses between 1988 and 2006. Besides Chen, there is no shortage of high-level corruption cases involving people as senior as the governor of Yunan Province, Li Jiating, the governor of Guizhou Province, Liu Fangren, and the Party secretary of Hebei Province, Cheng Weigao. It is reported that from 1998 to 2003, a total of 710,000 cases concerning land deals were investigated for corruption (Gong 2006: 90).

In short, during the allocation of particularistic benefits, the distinction between ad hoc favoritism and developmental discretion is a blurred one. More significantly, the exercise of policy discretion, most notably in the form of rent creation and allocation, has become part and parcel of the regulatory framework constituting the governance mechanism for local development. It has at the same time fueled outstanding economic growth as well as rampant corruption. Unless the whole framework of local economic governance is changed, it is not easy to call a halt to the exercise of such discretionary power without throwing the baby out with the bath water.

Preventing rent seeking: changing the state licensing system?

The prevalence of rent-seeking activities has been attributed by economists to the scope and range of government activities in the economy (Buchanan 1980: 9). In order to reduce rent seeking and to curb opportunities for corruption, it has been argued, the reduction of state intervention in the market is a prerequisite. In Wu Jinglian's words, there should be a two-pronged attack. The first is constraining administrative interference in market exchange, because the use of political power in economic transaction is "the systemic basis of rent seeking." The second is the strengthening of democratic supervision of executive authorities at every level (Wu's interview in Xing 1999: 21–22).

Wu's advocacy is equivalent to a call to change the state licensing practice. While this may seem to be a logical solution, in practice this will require no less ground-breaking effort than the historic open-door policy since it involves changing the power configuration of the licensing state. In this regard, it should be noted that state licensing is not merely a policy practice devised to regulate market activities. It is at the same time a power arrangement among bureaucratic fiefdoms of the party-state (Ngo 2008a).

During the reform, the central government has contracted out its authority to make policy as well as its power to intervene in the economy to various levels of bureaucratic agencies and local governments in order to create coalitional support. Those state agents who are entrusted with such contracted responsibilities become strong supporters of market reform because they now enjoy unprecedented discretionary power. They capitalize this power by creating profits and rents through extensive participation in market activities. Routine mutual accommodation among bureaucratic fiefdoms and between the center and the periphery is often based upon ad hoc compromise and informal defiance, during which rent exchanges play an important part (Ngo 2008b: 40).

While rents created by state intervention may be economically "unproductive" and prone to corruption, they do produce "political goods" in the process of exchanging selective rewards for coalitional support (Ngo 2002).

The price of such political exchange is the institutionalization of rent-seeking politics. At present, there exist a vast number of government departments and agencies with ambivalent jurisdictions and blurred public–private divide. In 2005, there were 5,074 subsidiaries directly under the control of the 31 central ministries. Among them, 2,212 were professional establishments while 2,862 were state-owned enterprises or stock-holding companies. The total number of staff was 1.64 million and the total assets amounted to 447.98 billion yuan. Despite numerous efforts to reduce Party and state overheads and to rectify party–state functionaries, one-third of these units have been set up after 1998. These are the numbers in the central ministries, and are merely the tip of the iceberg if local bureaucracies are taken into account. These government agencies have been involved directly and indirectly in state licensing of market activities. At the same time, they set up economic entities as subsidiaries, which directly participate in various business activities. This has given rise to the phenomenon of state agents as rent seekers, or the "referee as player" problem (Lin 2001). In such rent-seeking politics, the roles played by state actors depend on the position they occupy in the institutional matrix: at all levels the official changes hats easily between a regulator and a market player, and between a rent creator and a rent seeker (Boyd 2009).

Restricting state licensing in such circumstances requires a substantial reorganization of state functionaries, limiting the discretionary power of various levels of bureaucratic administrations, and restraining the political autonomy of local authorities. This will need extraordinary effort and will involve high political risk from the point of view of regime maintenance. It is for this reason that Pei (2006) describes the transition as being "trapped." Further reforms can at best be gradual and incremental. As one observer puts it succinctly, in order to minimize the cost of reform, the government needs to avoid impairing the interests of the status quo actors when putting forward new reform measures. In such a stone-groping approach, every reform measure is the result of compromise. Because of their lack of thoroughness, these reform measures soon become the stumbling blocks for further progress. In consequence, the results of earlier reforms quickly become the targets of the next reform (He 1999).

Conclusion

From the above discussion we can conclude that the production of economic rent is structurally embedded in the state licensing arrangements in contemporary China. Rent production (including the creation, allocation and pursuit of economic rent) is fixated by historical contingencies associated with Deng Xiaoping's stone-groping approach to market reform. Its occurrence has become entwined with coalitional politics, decentralization, and strategies of industrial and regional developments.

Contrary to what economists conceived of as social waste, economic rents can become valuable resources which state agents can create/manufacture by simply using administrative directives. Rent creation and allocation can become a source of state capacity when being used as a policy instrument to guide national and local developments. At the same time, the capacity over rent creation has generated strong incentives among state agents to support the market reform as well as to boost local economic development. Rent production is thus a source of state capacity, political acquiescence, and developmental incentive. Yet it is also a source of dire social problems.

Rent production under the prevailing framework of state licensing has provided a fertile ground for corruption. This is because policy discretions informing the allocation of rents are inevitably ad hoc and arbitrary. In a society characterized by informal relations of patronage, cronyism and nepotism, such official arbitrariness more than often ends up in corrupt exchanges. The combination of extensive state licensing, policy discretions, and profound clientelism thus produces a strong structural nexus between industrial governance, rent seeking, and corruption. In the absence of any basic changes in the licensing state, such structural nexus will defy administrative measures aiming at achieving a clean government in China.

References

Boyd, R. (2009) "The Chinese mode of rent utilization in comparative perspective," in T.W. Ngo and Y. Wu (eds) *Rent Seeking in China*, London: Routledge.

Buchanan, J.M. (1980) "Rent-seeking and profit-seeking," in J.M. Buchanan, R.D. Tollison, and G. Tullock (eds) *Toward a Theory of the Rent-seeking Society*, Texas: A & M University Press.

Chen, Z. and Ouyang, M. (narrator and recorder, respectively) (2005) *Wo de qiche shengya* (My Life in the Auto Sector), Beijing: Renmin Chubanshe.

Edin, M. (2005) "Local state structure and development incentives in China," in R. Boyd and T.W. Ngo (eds) *Asian States: Beyond the Developmental Perspective*, London: RoutledgeCurzon.

Evans, P. (1995) *Embedded Autonomy: States and Industrial Transformation*, Princeton: Princeton University Press.

Gong, T. (1997) "Forms and characteristics of China's corruption in the 1990s: change with continuity," *Communist and Post-Communist Studies*, 30: 277–88.

—— (2006) "Corruption and local governance: the double identity of Chinese local governments in market reform," *Pacific Review*, 19: 85–102.

Guojia fagaiwei (State Development and Reform Commission) (2007) "Guojia fagaiwei dui fangbianmian jiage chuantongan diaocha qingkuang de tongbao" (Report of the State Development and Reform Commission on the investigation of the instant noodles price conspiracy case), *Guojia fazhan gaigewei xun* (Newsletter of the State Development and Reform Commission), 16.

Guojia fazhan jihua weiyuanhui (State Development and Planning Commission) (2001) *Guojia jiwei he guowuyuan youguan bumen dingjia mulu* (Catalogue of Controlled Prices Set by the State Planning Commission and Other State Council Departments), Beijing: Renmin chubanshe.

Guojia jiwei (State Planning Commission) (1994) *Qiche gongye chanye zhengce* (Industrial Policy for the Auto Manufacturing Sector), Beijing: Renmin chubanshe.

Guowuyuan (State Council) (1988) *Guowuyuan guanyu yange kongzhi jiaoche sheng-chandian de tongzhi* (State Council's Notice on Strict Control of Sedan Manu-facturing Locations), Beijing: Renmin chubanshe.

—— (1989) *Guowuyuan guanyu dangqian chanye zhengche yaodian de jueding* (State Council's Decision on the Key Points Concerning Prevailing Industrial Policy), Beijing: Renmin chubanshe.

—— (1994) *Guowuyuan guanyu yinfa "90 niandai guojia chanje zhengche gangyao" de tongzhi"* (State Council's Notice Concerning the Publication of the "Guideline to National Industrial Policies in the 1990s"), Beijing: Renmin chubanshe.

Harwit, E. (1992) "Foreign passenger car ventures and Chinese decision-making," *Australian Journal of Chinese Affairs*, 28: 141–66.

—— (1995) *China's Automobile Industry: Politics, Problems, and Prospects*, New York: M.E. Sharpe.

He, W. (1999) *Xunzu jingjixue* (The Economics of Rent Seeking), Beijing: Zhongguo Fazhan chubanshe.

Heidenheimer, A.J. and Johnston, M. (eds) (2001) *Political Corruption: Concepts and Contexts* (3rd edn), New Brunswick: Transaction Publishers.

Hu, A. (2001) "Fubai: zhongguo zuida de shehui wuran" (Corruption: China's top social pollution), in A. Hu (ed.) *Zhongguo: tiaozhan fubai* (China: Challenging Corruption), Hangzhou: Zhejiang renmin chubanshe.

Hu, H. (1999) "1988 nian woguo zujin jiazhi de gusuan" (Estimation of the value of rents in China in 1988), in Jingji shehui tizhi bijiao bianjibu (ed.) *Fubai xungen* (In Search of the Roots of Corruption), Beijing: Zhongguo jingji chubanshe.

Hu, X. (2009) "The transition from surplus seeking to rent seeking," in T.W. Ngo and Y. Wu (eds) *Rent Seeking in China*, London: Routledge.

Li, J. (2007) *Guanyu 2006 niandu zhongyang yusuan zhixing he qita caizheng shouzhi de shenji gongzuo baogao* (Audit Report on the Implementation of the Central Budget and Other Financial Balances for the Year 2006), Shenjishu Bangongting (National Audit Office), Beijing: Renmin chubanshe.

Lin, Y. (2001) *Between Politics and Markets: Firms, Competition, and Institutional Change in Post-Mao China*, Cambridge: Cambridge University Press.

Liu, Z., Feng, Z., and Dong, X. (2005) *Zhongguo jiaoche chanye fazhan—jiyu chanye zuzhi lilun de yanjiu* (The Development of China's Passenger Car Industry—A Study Based on the Theory of Industrial Organization), Hefei: Hefei gongye daxue chubanshe.

Montinola, G., Qian, Y., and Weingast, B.R. (1995) "Federalism, Chinese style: the political basis for economic success in China," *World Politics*, 48: 50–81.

Ngo, T.W. (2002) "Development imperative and spoliatory politics: a comparative study of mainland China, Taiwan, and Hong Kong," in L. Tomba (ed.) *East Asian Capitalism: Conflicts, Growth and Crisis*, Milan: Feltrinelli Editore.

—— (2008a) "Politieke hervorming: begrensde wederopbouw en vernieuwing," in W. L. Chong and T.W. Ngo (eds) *China in Verandering: Balans en Toekomst van de Hervormingen*, Almere: Parthenon.

—— (2008b) "Rent-seeking and economic governance in the structural nexus of corruption in China," *Crime, Law and Social Change*, 49: 27–44.

—— (2009) "The politics of rent production," in T.W. Ngo and Y. Wu (eds) *Rent Seeking in China*, London: Routledge.

Ngo, T.W. and Chen, Y. (2009) "Rent production and industrial governance in the auto industry," in T.W. Ngo and Y. Wu (eds) *Rent Seeking in China*, London: Routledge.

Pei, M. (2006) *China's Trapped Transition: The Limits of Developmental Autocracy*, Cambridge, MA: Harvard University Press.

Shieh, S. (2005) "The rise of collective corruption in China: the Xiamen smuggling case," *Journal of Contemporary China*, 14: 67–91.

Sit, V.F.S. and Liu, W. (2000) "Restructuring and spatial change of China's auto industry under institutional reform and globalization," *Annals of the Association of American Geographers*, 90: 653–73.

Sohn, Y. (2005) *Japanese Industrial Governance: Protectionism and the Licensing State*, London: RoutledgeCurzon.

Tullock, G. (1980) "Efficient rent seeking," in J.M. Buchanan, R.D. Tollison, and G. Tullock (eds.) *Toward a Theory of the Rent-seeking Society*, Texas: A & M University Press.

Wade, R. (1990) *Governing the Market: Economic Theory and the Role of Government in East Asian Industrialization*, Princeton: Princeton University Press.

Wan, A. (1999) "Zhongguo jingji zhuanxing shiqi de zujin goucheng ji zhuyao tedian fenxi" (An analysis on the composition and major characteristics of rents during the period of economic transformation in China), in Jingji shehui tizhi bijiao bianjibu (ed.) *Fubai xungen* (In Search of the Roots of Corruption), Beijing: Zhongguo jingji chubanshe.

Wank, D.L. (2009) "Local state takeover as multiple rent seeking in private business," in T.W. Ngo and Y. Wu (eds) *Rent Seeking in China*, London: Routledge.

Wedeman, A. (2004) "The intensification of corruption in China," *China Quarterly*, 180: 895–921.

Wei, L. (1999) "Yi quan mou si, genyuan hezai" (The root cause of abusing power to seek personal gain), in Jingji shehui tizhi bijiao bianjibu (ed.) *Fubai xungen* (In Search of the Roots of Corruption), Beijing: Zhongguo jingji chubanshe.

Wu, Y. (2004) "Zhongguo qiche chanye guanzhi shibai yanjiu" (A study on the failure to control China's auto industry), unpublished dissertation, Fudan University.

Wu, Y. and Jin, B. (2009) "Rent seeking and the development of the beer industry," in T.W. Ngo and Y. Wu (eds) *Rent Seeking in China*, London: Routledge.

Xing, X. (1999) "Zaitan genzhi fubai" (Further discussion on an effective cure for corruption), in Jingji shehui tizhi bijiao bianjibu (ed.) *Fubai xungen* (In Search of the Roots of Corruption), Beijing: Zhongguo jingji chubanshe.

Yang, D. (2004) *Remaking the Chinese Leviathan: Market Transition and the Politics of Governance in China*, Stanford: Stanford University Press.

Zeng, Y. (2007) "2006 nian zhongguo fanfu redian zongshu" (A survey of the anti-corruption targets in 2006), *Zhengfu fazhi* (Governmental Legal System), 1: 14–17.

4 Cadre recruitment and corruption

What goes wrong?

Yan Sun

In discussing institutional design and corruption in China, the cadre recruitment system deserves special attention. First, with devolution of economic power and separation of the party and government, cadre management is left as a key area of CCP authority (Bo 2004: 70–100). Second, the surge of corruption cases among local party and government chiefs, especially since the late 1990s, raises the question of how so many of them have managed to get promoted to key positions in the first place. Finally, an assumed link between a non-competitive recruitment system and corruption lies at the core of frequent criticisms about China's political system. A fair question can thus be asked whether cadre recruitment itself is a major source of the country's corruption problem.

Latest scholarship offers disparate assessments. Some scholars suggest that the party has institutionalized the procedures for elite recruitment, helping the party to enhance cadre performance and political resilience (Bo 2004: 70–100; Yang 2004: Chs 5 and 7; Whiting 2004: 101–19). At the top, the institutionalization has ensured a mostly orderly transition of powers (Gilley and Nathan 2003). Others contend that administrative decentralization without horizontal accountability has weakened cadre supervision by superior agencies and thus worsened principal-agent problems, including in cadre management (Pei 2006: Ch. 4; Whiting 2004: 112–15). Both views have grains of truth. As Susan Whiting has argued, even as the new system of cadre evaluation has exacerbated problems in policy implementation, it has simultaneously contributed to the durability of CCP rule (Whiting 2004: 101–19).

The gap between institutional reforms and actual practices, resulting sometimes in corruption, is the topic of this chapter. Cadre recruitment in this chapter refers to the appointment and promotion of cadres to "key party and government posts" above the *ke* rank at sub-national levels and below the chief minister's rank at the national level. These posts include the chief and deputy chief positions at party committees and branches, government agencies, legislative and political consultative bodies, state-owned enterprises, law enforcement agencies and other public institutions.[1]

I attempt to make the following arguments: (1) meaningful reforms have occurred in the *procedures* of formal institutions for cadre recruitment, but they have changed some, rather than fundamentally reshaped, the *incentive mechanisms* for cadres; (2) yet the incentive deficits here are not alone responsible for the many new problems in recruitment, as these also have to do with the realities of China's vast local variance that affects enforcement differently. After tracing the evolution of recent personnel reforms in the first section below, I will highlight how new procedures still leave ample opportunities for idiosyncratic influences, thus residual incentives for manipulation; then, I will discuss how incentives combine with local realities to impact on cadre corruption.

Evolving personnel reforms

The end of the command economy since 1992 has drastically reduced the intimate information and control that higher authorities once had of subordinate agencies and agents. It has also simultaneously increased autonomy and decision power for the latter. In this context, the CCP's personnel reforms, initiated since the mid-1990s, have been earnest efforts to offset its weakened control of local cadre. The crux of the reforms has been to add elements of grassroots feedback, through new recruitment procedures. At least two of the four new procedures (Appendix [1]) aim at increasing input from below. These include "democratic nomination" of candidates from the grassroots and "screening" of nominees by the higher level on the basis of feedback from below. Only then should finalists proceed to the next stage of "deliberation" by local party branches and "submission" to high-level party committees for final approval (Sheng 2001). For candidates who are already chief executives, it is the party organization at the next higher level that conducts the above set of procedures.

A major complaint following initial implementation of the above was that local party branches remained dominant in the recruitment process, as they presided over major proceedings in the recruitment process. This domination engendered the problems of "lobbying for official posts" (*pao guan yao guan*), "buying and selling of office" (*mai guan mai guan*), and "promotion while engaging in corruption" (*bian fu bian sheng*) (Tian 2004: 108–24). Adding the problem of "vote buying and lobbying" (*hui xuan la piao*) in rural elections to the list, these four-letter phrases sum up the major problems since recruitment reforms. In response, the CCP sought further reforms and better implementation, beginning with the so-called 5+1 documents (Appendix [7a] to [7e], [5]) that made up the CCP's blueprint of new recruitment procedures (CCPDIC General Office and Research Office 2005: Ch. 14), and a working conference to hammer out steps to experiment and implement the new procedures.

Nomination of candidates

The "democratic nomination" procedure specifies open selection and competition of candidates (Appendix [3], [7b] and [7c]), including the public announcement of vacant positions, opportunities for job applications and qualifying exams, and final nominees. In practice, the nomination process allows a combination of nomination by oneself as well as by others and the party branch. Open competition may take the form of written exams, interviews, oral presentations, and question and answer sessions. Candidates for the chief executive office, however, are still nominated by the party organization at the next higher level. In other words, open selection and competition apply only to the deputy chief executive position and below, a compromised arrangement.

Screening of candidates

The next step, *kaocha* (screening) of candidates, is primarily conducted by the organization department of the party committee at the next higher level. In principle, the range of screening includes candidates' performance records, political orientation, relations with peers and subordinates, and personal integrity. In reality, economic growth was often valued most, so that a region's GDP growth rates could become direct measures of evaluation. In response, CCP has initiated the development of more "scientific indexes" since spring 2004, such as indexes for social development (training of migrant workers, improvement of workplace safety, and social services), and green GDP indexes (losses from environmental damages and resource depletion). The goal is to create a new index system that emphasizes the balanced strength of the local economy, improvement of life for local residents, social development, social services, environmental protection, and transformation of government functions.

Deliberation of candidates

A key procedural requirement was added in 2004 to address the problem of local party chiefs' domination over the deliberation of candidates: a formal vote by the standing committee of a party committee or at a plenary session, thus limiting the power of the party secretary in the final deliberation (Hu et al. 2005: 97). The voting system was experimented in select provinces and cities from 2001. By 2005, Guangdong had implemented the new system comprehensively across its cities and counties, while a few other provinces, mostly developed regions, implemented the voting system at select ranks.

Together, the above four procedures have added open and grassroots nominations in the candidate selection process, opinion surveys and performance evaluation in the screening processing, and limited voting in the deliberation process. These changes in the ways of doing things should theoretically reorient cadre incentives in the direction of paying more attention to popular support, being responsive to popular grievances, and accepting at least some checks from below.

Incomplete incentive changes

Nevertheless, recent personnel reforms have failed to sufficiently or fundamentally reshape cadre incentives in the intended directions. Structurally this problem appears to stem from a seemingly contradictory arrangement: a constitutional design that predetermines party supremacy and new institutional mechanisms that emphasize popular input and supervision.

Dilemmas of party leadership

Most importantly, incentive mechanisms remain little changed for holders of chief executive offices, especially within the party. To begin with, the continuation of top-down appointment for these offices still channels local chiefs' obligation and loyalty to authorities above, rather than citizens below. Second, differentiated treatment, whereby the appointment of leading positions is from above while that of the rest is by "open selection and competition," creates contradictions in norms and procedures. This official contradiction serves to undermine incentives to take seriously the more democratic procedures. Third, the appointment of leading officials from above perpetuates the classic problem of information asymmetry in the supervision of subordinates by their superiors, a problem already exacerbated by decentralization. Finally, appointment from above, structurally, leaves open opportunities for arbitrariness in the hands of local party chiefs, who are responsible for operating the new recruitment procedures.

For those below the chief executive offices, to whom the procedures aim to apply, incentives for compliance are also insufficiently strong. One reason is the administrative nature of the new procedures and the lack of compliance enforcement. Local party committees are exhorted rather than legally obligated to follow them. Monitoring is weak and is exercised mainly through periodic inspections from above, reports of abuse from the rank and file, and investigations of violations already committed. These fall short of routine oversight. The appointment of chief executive offices from above, in particular, weakens effective monitoring from below. Although reappointment is subject to opinion surveys and voting at party congresses (for party offices) or people's congresses (for state offices), these congresses meet infrequently (every three to five years) so delegates may not know the nominees well (Xu and Guo 2004). All these factors serve to weaken incentives for compliance, notwithstanding incentives encouraged by the new procedures.

New dominance of the organization department

The key function of the organization department of the party is cadre management within the party as well as outside the party where the party still dominates. Since decentralization, local party chiefs began to dominate personnel matters while leaving the organization department on the sideline. As a corrective, the Working Guideline of 2002 (Appendix [4]) elevates the role of the organization department in the recruitment process. The new chain of command is thus structured:

1   The higher-level organization department gathers nominations from various sources.
2   The office of the secretary of the party committee, at the level where the candidates are to be appointed, discusses the nominees.
3   The standing committee of the party committee at this level decides on a proposed list of candidates.
4   This standing committee communicates with the higher-level organization department and decides on a final list of candidates.

Despite the principle of "open selection and open competition," thus, it is the organization department of the higher-level party committee that has the *initial* and *final* say in making up the nominees' list. Herein lie room and incentives for deviance among both personnel staff and office seekers.

After the critical stage of nomination, the higher-level organization department also heads the process to screen the candidates. Yet seldom would these departments find fault with or remove the candidates whose nomination they have already approved. The non-transparent nature of the screening process also engenders plenty of room and incentives for maneuvering, whether it is in the administering of opinion surveys and written exams or in the evaluation of performance records and personal qualities. In the next stage, voting at party plenary sessions or legislative sessions (the latter is required for the re-appointment of key government officials), it is again the organization department that operates the procedures. Since by now the nominees already appear as official candidates, it is hard for others to openly object to their candidacy (Xu and Guo 2004).

Besides its direct role in the new recruitment process, the organization department is also responsible for other matters that affect the quality of recruitment. These include the transfer, relocation and rotation of officials, annual reviews, reward or punishment for officials, training and overseas training, expansion or reduction of official posts, entry and exit of officials, selection and hiring of civil servants, etc. The process of conducting all these matters leaves room for much manipulation.

Overall, incentives for compliance with recruitment procedures are not always stronger than incentives to manipulate them in order to gain office. In other words, the new reform measures do not place sufficient restraints on nefarious incentives. Rather, they still make possible the distortion of incentives. Not surprisingly, personnel matters at all sub-national levels have become the latest "disaster area" for corruption.

Implementation hurdles, abuse and corruption

Since 2002, over half of all violations related to official posts are associated with officials in charge of personnel matters, in contrast to early years when economic-sector officials comprised a majority (Yang 2005). The surge in corruption in personnel matters has coincided with the rise in abuse by the executive chief of local government agencies and party branches since the late 1990s. These officials, previously not directly engaged in economic matters, are finally cashing in on their powers in the marketplace. Personnel reforms, apparently, have not stemmed this latest surge in abuse.

Are the distorted incentives, outlined in the previous section, responsible for the surge? My assessment is mixed, in contrast to the "trapped transition" argument that would place the blame overwhelmingly on institutional limitations. In some areas, I find, the rise of corruption has indeed stemmed from new incentives spurred by the limitations inherent in the new procedures, while in others it has more to do the weakness of central power and regional diversity in enforcing them. In other words, how cadres are picked has to do with why they behave in certain ways, but how they behave also has to do with whether and how the recruitment procedures are enforced.

Plenty of formality, not uniformity

When would officials—both those in charge of promotional matters and those aspiring them—be motivated to follow the new procedures? Obviously, they will be more so when the procedures are implemented and enforced. Here sectoral and regional variance, shaped by varying state strengths and levels of development, makes a difference.

At one end, among higher ranks of the official hierarchy, major cities, more developed regions, and large state enterprises, namely where central strength is strong and levels of development high, the procedures are enforced more seriously, and the incentives for compliance are stronger as a result: for example, the recruitment of deputy positions and the reappointment of the chief and deputy positions in central ministries, provincial governments, major municipal governments and large state enterprises in more developed regions. The provinces of Hainan, Guangdong, Fujian, Sichuan and Zhejiang, as well as the metropolis of Beijing, were the first to implement voting at the standing committee or plenum of party committees. Only Sichuan was a less developed region on the list. Beijing, Zhejiang, Guangdong, Jiangsu, Anhui and Fujian were the first to include green GDP in the calculation of economic data and performance evaluation, again all developed regions except Anhui (Hu et al. 2005: 97–98). Only later did implementation expand to the rest of the country, with varying effects.

At the other end, among less developed provinces, cities and counties, or at lower ranks of the official strata across the board, remote reach of the center and ineffective enforcement help to weaken incentives for compliance. New procedures may be taken just as another set of formalities. In the best of circumstances, the procedures may be followed nominally while, in reality, the dominance of party secretaries or the organization department continues. In the worst circumstances, the new procedures may be utilized to cover up abuse. The party secretary or organization department may set the tone and criteria for "ideal" candidates, then set out to find the "right fit," before going through the formal procedures to legitimize the search. Others may make clever use of the democratic nomination process.

Even when official procedures are earnestly followed, they may still end up being formalities for various, but mostly structural, reasons. For one thing, since the candidates are presented as proposed finalists from organization departments, it is often easy for them to go through party or legislative congresses, where voting can be little more than an approving process. The popularity of particular candidates may be reflected in the percentage of votes they receive, but rarely are candidates outside the list elected (Song 2004). Second, though it is a procedural requirement, there are not always more nominees on the ballot than the seats to be filled, making it hard for potential write-ins to win sufficient votes.

Finally, enforcement may itself be manipulated, when supervision is lacking. Some local officials have come up with ways to ensure desired voting outcomes. They can persuade voting members to acquiesce to their desired candidates. Yang Xiuzhu of Wenzhou, Zhejiang, among the best-known cases of overseas flight, prevailed in the provincial people's congress to become a deputy head of the provincial construction bureau and a deputy mayor after a key city official lobbied the people's congress for four days. The voting procedure may be also manipulated to require that only those opposed to any nominees cast their votes. Those who touch their pencils, therefore, would clearly run the risk of offending the eventual winners. Instead of the secret ballot, people may also be asked to cast the ballot at the podium in front of all eyes, making it impossible not to vote for the proposed candidates.

Short of uniform enforcement and its adequate supervision, therefore, officials can be expected to calculate their own benefits and costs in dealing with new recruitment procedures. Where incentives for compliance are low, deviance is the inevitable preference.

"Political showcase projects"

Increased emphasis on performance records, especially during the "screening" phase, has given rise to another nefarious incentive: building up "political showcase projects." The quicker ascension of officials from more developed regions has further encouraged instrumental pursuit of developmental projects. These are usually lavish but dubiously useful projects launched by some officials to build up their political resume for the purposes of promotion, hence an abuse of formal recruitment procedures.

The key is the incentive behind those projects. Instead of local public interests, showcase projects are aimed at bolstering one's own political and career interests by generating quick growth rates within the current terms of the office holders. For some officials, such projects may also involve personal gains, e.g. kickbacks scrapped off from land allocation or construction projects.

The bad investments, moreover, can incur more harmful damages than individual corruption cases (Nian 2005; Hou 2005). Guided by short-term targets, investments may be ill-conceived, poorly executed, redundant and of little productive value. Some may be showy but shoddily constructed projects that meet short-term performance targets but deal long-term social and economic tolls. The two major disasters of 2008 have both shown the peril of such projects. Under the target of universal free education for nine years for all children, set by the Ministry of Education in the mid-1990s, many poor rural areas scrambled to expand school buildings. With limited funding, which was strained further by kickbacks, many school buildings were quickly assembled with substandard materials and shoddy construction. The result was the far more frequent, and far more devastating, destruction of new school buildings than older ones and non-school buildings in the Sichuan earthquake of 12 May 2008. During the unprecedented winter storms earlier in the year, likewise, electric poles erected in recent years collapsed while older ones stood intact. In one Guizhou county, as many as 90 percent of recently erected poles collapsed, while none of those built in the 1950s and 1960s did (*Yazhou zhoukan* 17 May 2008; *Beijing Youth* 15 February 2008).

Yet more damage is the huge financial losses incurred by showcase projects. Such projects are often funded by local government revenues and bank loans, made available through local officials' intervention. The low utility and lengthy time span of the projects, however, bring small returns economically while piling up huge debts for the local economy. Sometimes the original project promoters have left, thanks to promotions based on the "achievement" of those showcase projects, while their unfinished projects leave non-performing loans to their successors and to banks. Sometimes local officials raised funds by issuing bonds to the local public but could not pay returns to local citizens who purchased them. Sometimes they raised funds by withholding the wages of local state employees, including public school teachers (Nian 2005). Nationwide, redundant constructions alone may have cost the country 4 trillion yuan in losses in the two decades since the mid-1980s (Nian 2005).

Another form of damage of showcase projects has been the facilitating of career moves of corrupt officials, or the problem of "promotion alongside corruption." Because showcase projects are valued as "promoting development" or "attracting foreign investment," etc., they can help facilitate the promotion of many corrupt officials. As they climb up officialdom, these officials have yet greater opportunities to sponsor more showcase projects and exert further damage.

Buying and selling official posts

Buying and selling office has become the leading category of corruption in recent years. While its initial surge may be attributed to the effects of decentralization or weakened top-down supervision, why has the surge been sustained, despite more recent personnel reforms to increase bottom-up monitoring?

Above all, cadre incentives to cast their bet with key officials have continued under new recruitment measures. The mechanism of preselecting candidates for promotion encourages potential nominees to curry favors with those officials, and sometimes just the one top official at the party committee or the organization department. The enhanced autonomy of this top official, moreover, has made it easier for such favor-currying to have real outcomes. Instead of the quality of their work, aspiring candidates may be motivated to pay more attention to building connections, finding patrons and catering to the idiosyncrasies of key superiors. The latter can show a special preference for compliant and pleasing followers. The often de facto system of "a few people selecting cadres, and the selection of cadres among a few people" encourages the sale of office (*Dang Feng Lian Zheng* 2001; Chu 2001). An unruly chief can decide whom to nominate and for what position. He can advance or hinder a nominee, cover up a nominee's bad record, or push through totally unqualified candidates.

In poor regions, the relative shortage of economic opportunities can stimulate a special incentive to use office buying for career advancement. *Shi quan*, or substantive power, entails authority over tangible resources involving developmental assistance and anti-poverty funds. Career moves also bring improvements in salaries and material comforts, in terms of job location, rank category, and residential and transportation amenities. These perks are especially important for officials in poor regions. Most of all, buying office is an investment whose return buyers expect to reap once in office. Some individuals even take out loans to bribe for office, out of calculations that they will be able to generate far more returns. For the provider's side, the relative lack of bribes from a strong business sector leaves office selling as the main source of extra income for local officials in such regions. A cycle of "using money to get power, using power to get more money, then using money to get more power," has become a key path to personal and professional advancement for corrupt officials in poor regions (He 2003).

Table 4.1 is a list of office sellers with the largest amount of bribe taking as reported in the Chinese press in 2000–06. It provides some cursory evidence for a strong association between the level of development and office selling: all of the offenders held offices in less developed provinces, and most in rural or less metropolitan regions within those provinces.

Office for sale has done the most to undermine the CCP's recruitment system. The practice entails giving decision powers to unqualified or unscrupulous individuals. Those motivated to purchase office, in turn, may abuse it for personal gains. At the same time, office sellers usually have to protect the poor job performance of their clients. Nefarious appointments also help the patron to build a chain of cronies inclined to yield to one another's influence-peddling. When such officials are devoted to office buying and selling, rather than genuine job performance, in short, it is a clearest indictment of the failure of the recruitment system, and ultimately, of effective governance that personnel reforms aim to bring about.

Table 4.1 Worst office sellers, reported 2000–06

Name	Position	Province	Bribe take (million yuan)	Bribe givers
Chen Zhaoyuan	County PS*	Anhui	9+	—
Cao Yongbao	District deputy PS (1994–2004)	Sichuan	1.53	—
Han Guizhi	Deputy head, provincial PD** and Provincial PS (1996–2003)	Heilongjiang	7+	Ma De, etc.
Li Chenglong	County PS (1990s)	Guangxi	16 (several millions of which for office selling)	—
Li Tiecheng	County PS (1992–2000)	Jilin	1.44	162
Ma De	Small city PS (1993–2002)	Heilongjiang	5+	200+ (half of all officials above bureau level)
Sun Chuyan	Small city PS (1995–2001)	Hebei	0.4	20+
Shang Dian	County PS	Liaoning	6.21	30+
Wu Bao'an	County PS (Sept. 2003–June 2004)	Shanxi	1.18	
Yang Zexing	County PS	Anhui	0.7	70+
Zhang Gaiping	Borough PS (2000–05)	Shaanxi	1.07	27
Zhang Huaqi	County PS	Anhui	5.3	95

Dark side of personal life

Yet another blind spot in the new recruitment procedures, i.e. the difficulty of scrutinizing candidates beyond their professional life, has contributed to a failure to screen out or stem misdeeds in the so-called social and lifestyles of office seekers.

Personal lapses have become key manifestations of cadre corruption since the 1990s. According to statistics from the draft group for the revision of the Marriage Law (adopted in 2001), over 95 percent of disciplined officials had mistresses, and 60 percent of corruption cases involving officials had to do with "hoarding concubines."[2] The need to keep up with the expenses of maintaining mistresses and concubines is often the original driving force that launches officials down a path of graft. Keen on the material side of the exchange, the women involved usually need to be sheltered privately and expensively. Multiple mistresses require yet greater "maintenance fees." Along with rich entrepreneurs, corrupt officials are among the few groups associated with this practice. This has become serious enough that one main purpose of the revised Marriage Law was to protect all women involved. Despite the statistical correlation between mistress keeping and graft taking, the screening process does not cover lifestyle problems per se. Organization departments may be unaware or oblivious to hints of problems, thanks to benign neglect or a new sense of privacy. Given that the phenomenon was nonexistent in the pre-reform days, its rise since then cannot be attributed to human nature alone. The failure to deter personal lapses points to problems in the recruitment system itself.

Helping offspring in business pursuit or overseas education is another aspect of the personal side eluded by the screening process. Lending a hand to one's offspring often amounts to corruption because the kind of help has changed significantly over time. In the 1980s, the worst that officials did was to lend help to their relatives in speculating controlled goods. The notorious "prince-ling party" first made their fortunes from such activities. Since the 1990s, the stakes have become higher: from securing loans and land to developmental rights and construction contracts; and from preferential policies to tax relief.

Casino gambling is yet another activity of the personal arena eluded by the recruitment process. It constitutes corruption when officials and CEOs reach into their company or official accounts to finance their bets. Since the mid-1990s the gambling capitals of the East and the West—Macau and Las Vegas—have both targeted mainland officials as the leading source of growth. Losing hundreds of million in US dollars each year, Chinese gamblers have become the darlings of international gambling houses thanks to their generosity in playing money that is not their own and their inclination to keep quiet after huge losses (Chen 2001; Pomfret 2002). Because of its overseas locations and clandestine nature, gambling defies easy detection.

Promotion amid corruption

Together, the various problems in the recruitment system contribute to a phenomenon known as *bianfu biansheng*, i.e. "promotion alongside corruption." The popular phrase speaks to the failure of the recruitment system, at least partially, at preventive deterrence or timely detection. Weak deterrence in turn encourages incentives to disregard formal procedures.

An indication of failed deterrence is the smooth rise of individual officials while they simultaneously engage in corruption. Reports of exposed cases show that a majority of individuals involved have managed to do so. Worse still, the time lag between one's first violation and eventual exposure has increased significantly, despite more reforms. Among the cases processed between 1978 and 2002 involving officials above the deputy ministerial level, the average time lapse was only 1.43 years in the 1980s (1980–88). By contrast, the average increased to 6.31 years (1998–2002), with the longest lag being 16 years (see Table 4.2). This is particularly striking in the second period, marked by the beginning of recruitment reforms since 1996, when feedback from below was given more importance. The extended time lag means that individual offenders have managed to pass through the screening process. The reality encourages incentives to continue deviant behavior in private, to cite the best-known cases in the second period.

Another strong indication that the recruitment system does not instill sufficient disincentives against misdeeds is the rise of young offenders among official ranks. It has been an official policy to quicken the promotion of younger officials to reduce the so-called "59er" phenomenon, whereby

Table 4.2 Time span between initial violation and final exposure

Name	Highest position	Number of years
Hu Changqing	Deputy Governor, Jiangxi Province	5
Cheng Kejie	Governor of Guangxi (1992–98), Deputy Chair of NPC Standing Committee, 1998–99	6
Ma De	Party Secretary, Suihua city, Heilongjiang Province	7
Liu Fangren	Party Secretary, Guizhou Province (1997–99)	8
Yang Lifeng	Head of State Tax Bureau, Liuzhou City, Guangxi	10
Li Tiecheng	County Party Secretary, Liaoning Province	12
Qi Huogui	Party Secretary, Dongfang City, Hainan Province	13

Source: *Dang Feng Lian Zheng* (2004), 9: 15.

officials about to retire at the mandatory age of 60 years plunge into graft as a last opportunity to cash in their power. Key officials in the mid-50s are now retreated to less prominent positions as a preventive measure. Yet the official campaign to "youth-fy" the officialdom does not seem in itself able to reduce nefarious incentives. Data from prosecutorial agencies in recent years show that those under 35 comprise a leading age group of offenders (Wen 2004).

In another sign of decreasing disincentives, the educational level of younger offenders is getting higher. Of the 364 offenders in Guangzhou's case, cited above, 62.9 percent, or 229 had completed three years of college and above, and 17 had graduate degrees. These ratios were higher than was the case for other age groups. These developments show that the promotion of better-educated, younger people may not in itself reduce corruption, and that, further, younger offenders may have more confidence in the networks they have built and the informal rules of officialdom than in the formal recruitment procedures.

While increased local autonomy makes it easier for the unscrupulous to win nominations and offices, finally, it is difficult to remove top officials at a given level once they are appointed. This can serve as yet another disincentive for good behavior. Since their appointment and promotion have been approved by the party organization at the next higher level, the grassroots organization has no power to remove or demote those appointees. For example, neither a mayor nor the city council nor the local people's congress can recall an errant deputy mayor. Complaints have to be filed with the provincial party committee, which then meets to discuss the case. The control of the higher authority here is designed as a checking mechanism, but it can become a loophole for wayward officials to seek protectors both locally (so that complaints will not be filed to the higher level) and at the higher level (so that filed complaints will be ignored). This is yet another reason for the problem of "promotion while engaging in corruption."

Conclusion

The chapter has attempted to show that the relation of China's recruitment system to corruption is a complex one. The optimistic view, to the effect that China's personnel reforms have helped to clean the bureaucracy, improve government efficiency and reduce corruption, is an incomplete one. Distorted incentives and implementation gaps have resulted in shortfalls in reality. At the same time, progress is still more real than the pessimistic assessment of the center's total loss of accountability and control over local bureaucracy and personnel. This loss has not been universal but more serious where the center is weak. It is at those weakest links, generally, that more of the morally challenged officials manage to get selected and promoted to key positions, and go on to engage in yet greater abuse.

The core problems in the realities of the CCP's cadre recruitment are the manipulation, superficial compliance, non-compliance, and even fraud, by those who decide on personnel appointments and those who seek them. These problems in turn allow the recruitment system to corrode in some cases and fail in others. What is the fundamental cause? As shown in the chapter, the inherent limitations of the institutional procedures provide incentives for cadre deviance and corruption, while the realities of local variance enable these in practice.

Does this mean that cadre deviance and corruption are inevitable in a non-competitive recruitment system and a vast country of wide regional disparities? The answer is not necessarily definitive. After all, there was much less cadre deviance and corruption during the much more authoritarian Mao era. Would direct elections resolve China's recruitment problems? Much as the personnel reforms, village elections have worked better in more developed regions and poorly in remote and less developed ones. In the latter, vote buying or lineage-based voting have become commonplace, while post-election corruption remains rampant. By contrast, Singapore and Hong Kong have done well in managing a clean professional bureaucracy and efficient governance, without comprehensive direct elections.

In this context, the CCP's introduction of mechanisms aimed at intermediate accountability is still a good beginning and a realistic platform at present. The merits are twofold. The first is gradualism: intermediate procedures allow the gradual cultivation and expansion of democratic values and practices. The second is stability: the halfway measures allow trial-and-error experiments and a more smooth, and solid transition to deeper and wider democratic procedures. The key, however, is an earnest and serious enforcement of even those intermediate measures across the board.

Appendix

Major personnel reform decrees since 1995

(1) 9 February 1995: CCP Central Committee, "Temporary Regulations for the Selection and Appointment of Key Officials for Party and State Organs;" lays out six principles and four procedures for key cadre recruitment. The latter includes democratic nomination, scrutinizing, deliberation, and decision.
(2) 3 March 1999: CCP Central Committee Personnel Department, "Notification on Further Improving the Work of Open Selection of Key Officials;" lays out procedures for the open selection of party and state cadre.
(3) 22 June 2000: CCP Central Committee, "Program for Deepening the Reform of the Personnel System;" lays out ten-year targets for reforming the personnel system, with emphasis on mechanisms that allow cadres to "move up and down, move in and out."
(4) 14 December 2000: CCP Central Committee Personnel Department, "Opinions on Promoting the Public Announcement of Finalists for Key Party and State Offices before Formal Appointment;" suggests that finalists for key offices be publicly announced within a certain administrative scope

and time frame, so that the rank and file have an opportunity to make comments and objections.

(5) 9 July 2002: CCP Central Committee, "Working Guidelines for the Selection and Appointment of Key Officials for Party and State Organs;" lays out procedures for the open selection and competition for key party and government posts at sub-national levels, including the public announcement of open positions, candidate application and verification of credentials, administration of exams and opinion polls, discussion and recommendation of finalists by organizational departments, and discussion and decision by the party committee.

(6) February 2004: CCP Discipline Inspection Commission and CCP Central Committee Personnel Department, "Notification on the Exit of Party and State Cadre from Concurrently Held Posts in Commercial Firms."

(7) March 2004: CCP Politburo
   (a) "Temporary Regulations for the Open Selection of Key Party and State Cadre;"
   (b) "Temporary Regulations for the Appointment of Key Party and State Cadre through Open Competition;"
   (c) "Procedures for Voting on the Proposed Candidates and Recommended Candidates for the Chief Executive Positions of the Immediate Lower-level Party Committees and State Administrations, by the Plenary Session of Higher-level Party Committees;"
   (d) "Temporary Regulations for the Resignation of Party and State Officials;"
   (e) "Opinions on Participation in Commercial Activities by Key Party and State Cadre after Resignation."

Notes

1 The recruitment of cadre for such key positions is the prerogative of party committees and branches at different sub-national levels and within ministerial levels at the center. Recruitment below the *ke* rank locally is the prerogative of local party or government chiefs. Recruitment of officials at the levels of provincial party secretaries and central ministers is the prerogative of the central party's organization department. For the Chinese cadre's rank system, see Sun (2004: 46).
2 "Statistics from the 'Marriage Law' draft group show that 95 percent of corrupt officials kept concubines," *Dang Feng Lian Zheng* (2001), 8: 29.

References

Bo, Z.Y. (2004) "The institutionalization of elite management in China," in B.J. Naughton and D.L. Yang (eds) *Holding China Together: Diversity and National Integration in the Post-Deng Era*, London and New York: Cambridge University Press.

CCPDIC General Office and Research Office (ed.) (2005) *Strengthening Deterrence against Corruption, the Construction of Better Party Ethics and Governance, and the Struggle against Corruption*, Beijing: Foursquare Press.

Chen, F. (2001) "Casinos in Macau: graveyards for corrupt officials," *Dang Feng Lian Zheng*, 6: 39–40.

Chu, Z.K. (2001) "Reflections on major corruption cases," *Dang Feng Lian Zheng*, 10: 17–19.

Dang Feng Lian Zheng (2001) "The key to fighting corruption is to stop it at the source," *Dang Feng Lian Zheng*, 1: 13–15.

Gilley, B. and Nathan, A. (2003) *China's New Rulers: the Secret Files*, New York: New York Review of Books.

He, S.N. (2003) "Methods to end corruption in personnel matters," *Dang Feng Lian Zheng*, 3: 18–20.

Hou, Y.C. (2005) "Remedying mistaken approaches to political achievements," *Zhongguo Gongchandang*, 12: 98–100.

Hu, J. (ed.) (2005) *Strengthening the Building of the Party's Governing Capacity*, Beijing: Party History Publishing House.

Nian, X.G. (2005) "Political showcase projects and their remedies," *Zhongguo Gongchandang*, 10: 74–78.

Pei, M.X. (2006) *China's Trapped Transition: the Limits of Developmental Autocracy*, Cambridge, MA: Harvard University Press.

Pomfret, J. (2002) "China's high rollers find a seat at table—in Vegas—wealthy aren't afraid to blow millions, especially when the money isn't theirs," *Washington Post*, 26 March.

Sheng, Q.Y. (2001) "Promotion despite corruption: a problem not to be ignored," *Dang Feng Lian Zheng*, 1: 21–22.

Song, Y. (2004) "From the phenomenon of transportation department chiefs to the phenomenon of personnel department chiefs," *Feng Huang Zhou Kan*, 19.

Sun, Y. (2004) *Corruption and Market in Contemporary China*, Ithaca, NY: Cornell University Press

Tian, Y. (2004) "Incremental reform of the system for recruiting key party and state officials," in X.L. Xu (ed.) *The Party, Government and Society in China's Incremental Political Reform*, Beijing: CITIC Publishing House.

Wen, S.T. (2004) "New developments in corruption," excerpted from *2004: Analysis and Forecasts about China's Social Developments, Dang Feng Lian Zheng*, 9: 13–15.

Whiting, S.H. (2004) "The cadre evaluation system at the grass roots: the paradox of party rule," in B.J. Naughton and D.L. Yang (eds) *Holding China Together: Diversity and National Integration in the Post-Deng Era*, London and New York: Cambridge University Press.

Xu, H.B. and Guo, X.D. (2004) "The institutional sources of corruption in personnel matters and strategies to deal with it," *Dang Feng Lian Zheng*, 11: 23–26.

Yang, D.L. (2004) *Breaking the Leviathan: Market Transition and the Politics of Governance in China*, Palo Alto, CA: Stanford University Press.

Yang, L. (2005) "Latest violations in personnel matters," *Liao Wang* (Outlook Weekly), 22: 34–35.

5 The institutionalization of Party discipline inspection in China

Dynamics and dilemmas

Ting Gong

Questions about institutions are important for the social sciences. Social scientists have always been interested in explaining institutional arrangements and analyzing their effects with regard to the conduct of specific social functions. This is particularly evident in the new institutionalism, which suggests that human behavior takes place and can only be understood in the context of institutions. These include formal or informal organizations, rules of politics, ways of communication, the logic of strategic situations, and cognitive or interpretive frameworks. They influence the ways in which individuals pursue certain courses of action, behave as members of a collective, and select desirable goals and means. Even if institutions fail to shape individual behavior in the fashion that was desired, the answer can be obtained only from the institutions themselves (Immergut 1998; Hall and Taylor 1996; Steinmo et al. 1992; DiMaggio and Powell 1991). New institutionalists also argue that institutions, although by definition they connote stability, are subject to incremental and discontinuous changes themselves (Scott 2001: 48). Institutions are, therefore, "maintained and reproduced" in the change processes (Pierson 2004: 14).

This chapter analyzes the disciplinary inspection system of the Chinese Communist Party (CCP) and particularly its functional evolution and institutional peculiarities within this new institutionalist framework. Disciplinary inspection (*jilu jiancha*), a key feature of Leninist vanguard parties, has become an indispensable core of the Party apparatus in China. The institutions in charge of discipline inspection (that is, the Disciplinary Inspection Commissions; hereafter DICs) possess the power to make policy, carry out political supervision, and serve as key agents in the Party's current life-or-death struggle against corruption. Yet discipline inspection remains, arguably, the least understood element of Chinese politics. In Western scholarship, no systematic study has been devoted to the CCP's disciplinary inspection system in recent years, and little is known about its latest developments.[1]

This chapter identifies and analyzes the origins, dynamics, and outcomes of the discipline inspections carried out by DICs to see how institutions can shape, or fail to shape, the behavior of individual Party members. More specifically, it addresses the following questions: How has the system of Party disciplinary inspection evolved and what forces have prompted its changes? Why is discipline inspection essential for the political sustainability and organizational growth of the CCP? To what extent can discipline inspection or, broadly, formal-legal institutions as such, be expected to regulate the individual behavior of Party members? How can the CCP maintain a balance between the disciplinary restriction and moral construction of its members?

To answer these questions, this chapter begins with the formation of the CCP's disciplinary inspection system, which sought to provide organizational integrity and sustainability. It then discusses how the system evolved in new social and economic environments, and examines the functions and mechanisms of discipline inspection against the backdrop of such changes. The chapter presents, in its last section, a critical look at the system's design and capacity by detecting and analyzing its embedded dilemmas and deficiencies.

The origin of Party discipline inspection

The idea of discipline inspection originated with V.I. Lenin, the founding father of the Russian Communist Revolution. In his work *State and Revolution* (1917), Lenin wrote that to fight bureaucratism effectively, a Communist Party had to make institutional arrangements with regard to the election and dismissal of officials, salaries and rewards, and the routine supervision of its rank and file. The Soviet model of Party discipline inspection was designed and established to do just that. It was a highly centralized system characterized by a central supervision commission that had almost the same status as the Party's Central Committee and a vertical chain of disciplinary inspection commissions that linked the center to the very lowest level of the Party organization. These institutions performed the ordinary daily duties of maintaining the Party discipline, but they also participated actively in the internal power struggle and organizational purges of the Soviet Communist Party. Their role was controversial, to say the least (Cocks 1979: 178–85).

The system of discipline inspection was introduced to China during the CCP's founding years, which came as no surprise because the institutional structure of the CCP was modeled upon its Soviet counterpart. In practice, self-discipline served as an indispensable means for the CCP to maintain a leading role in the Chinese revolution. Iron discipline conformed with the basic requirement of a Leninist vanguard party that Party membership must be highly selective; only dedicated revolutionaries were to be recruited to represent the best elements of Chinese society. The disciplinary inspection system was thus not only ideologically important but also practically necessary. It emerged as a result of the Party's needs for legitimacy and institutional coherence. The evolution of the disciplinary inspection system thereafter proved to be a process of "self-reinforcing" or "path dependency" (North 1990; Arthur 1994; David 1994), based upon such needs.

Discipline inspection first appeared in the Party Constitution at the 2nd National Congress of the CCP in 1922. The very first Party Constitution devoted an entire chapter to the subject and especially to the importance of organizational discipline, but at that time there was no mention of corresponding institutional arrangements. Disciplinary supervision was understood in the early years more as a general attitude that should suffuse the Party membership than as an institution that would monitor their behavior. In the early years there were neither designated agencies nor standardized procedures for implementing Party discipline supervision. The responsibility for discipline inspection was undertaken mainly by local Party committees at the different levels and was carried out in various ways. The sheer notion of disciplinary control, however, served the Party well in terms of organizational mobilization and development, for it subordinated individual members to collective goals.

The CCP's disciplinary inspection began to get institutionalized in 1927 when the Party established disciplinary supervisory commissions at the central and provincial levels. The amended Party Constitution then added a special chapter on the institutional arrangements of the supervisory commissions of Party discipline and detailed the goals of these commissions. Practically, the Party urgently needed to impose disciplinary sanctions against members who were believed to have violated Party principles or discipline, as was indicated by the frequent rectification campaigns within the Party organization that took place in the ensuing years when the supervisory commissions handled numerous cases resulting from organizational purges. For instance in the late 1920s and early 1930s, the CCP launched a large-scale political campaign against embezzlement, waste, and bureaucratism in the areas it controlled. The central supervisory commission, then called the Worker–Peasant Inspection Committee, issued a series of directives concerning the scope, targets, and reform methods of the campaign. It actively investigated allegations against individual Party members, which led to the jailing and execution of many Party officials. It was also during this campaign that the CCP for the first time established auditing agencies at various levels of its government as an additional measure to maintain its institutional purity (Gong 1994).

Disciplinary inspection became even more important when the CCP bogged down in the internal power struggle in the following years. Discipline control agencies contributed a great deal to the Party's organizational purge of former leaders Zhang Guotao and Wang Ming in the 1930s and in the Party's largest rectification campaign in Yanan in the 1940s. During those years the disciplinary inspection agencies were reorganized several times, and their names were changed from review (*shencha*) committees (1928), to Party affairs (*dangwu*) committees (1933), to supervision (*jiancha*) committees (1945), for the purpose of institutional enhancement. The functions and jurisdictions of the discipline agencies were further clarified in the amended Party Constitution that was introduced at the CCP's 7th National Congress in 1945.

As Tolbert and Zucker point out, institutions stay alive not only as a property or state of an existing social order but also as a process, including the processes of further institutionalization and deinstitutionalization (Tolbert and Zucker 1996). The CCP disciplinary control organs were born to serve the ideological and organizational consolidation needs of a Leninist party. Their role was further reinforced in the Party's frequent campaigns against its real or perceived enemies both inside and outside the Party. The development of disciplinary inspection institutions continued after 1949, even though the CCP itself had transformed from a revolutionary party into the ruling institution. In the early years after the People's Republic of China was founded, strengthening the Party's organizational discipline stood out as an urgent task. The CCP, now the ruling party, faced the immense work of rebuilding a war-torn country and consolidating the newly established regime. At the same time, the Party leaders perceived a powerful self-indulgence among many revolutionary veterans, who became increasingly disconnected from the Party's cause and were now only interested in personal enjoyment. The Party could brook no further delay in institutionalizing and strengthening its discipline, for it had to "check the grave danger of the Party being corrupted by the bourgeoisie" (Mao 1977: 64).The CCP Politburo issued *The Decision to Establish the Disciplinary Inspection Commissions at the Central and Local Levels* in November 1949, immediately after the founding of the new government of the People's Republic.[2] It required that disciplinary inspection commissions be reinstalled as soon as possible at all levels of the Party organization. The number of full-time discipline inspection officials increased by a factor of five, from 1,500 to 7,200, during the period from 1951 to 1954 (Wu 2004; Yang and Jiang 2005). The DICs and their members worked vigorously to safeguard the Party's "iron discipline" to help the CCP maintain a legitimate leading position in new China. In 1953 alone, the DICs at various levels handled a total of 409,532 cases and took disciplinary measures against 74,671 Party members, including two senior officials who joined the Party in the 1920s.[3] These officials received harsh punishments, and their cases were widely publicized to show the Party's determination to keep its organizational purity and integrity. Disciplinary inspection was firmly reiterated in the first post-1949 constitution the CCP made at the 8th Party Congress in 1956. It is worth noting, however, that when confirming the institutional arrangements and functions of discipline inspection, the Party placed a special emphasis on the fact that local Party committees had political supervision over DICs and on the requirement for disciplinary inspection to serve the Party's general cause.

The effort to reinstitutionalize disciplinary inspection in the early years of the PRC was interrupted by the Cultural Revolution. Neither the 9th nor 10th National Congress of the PRC made any mention of Party discipline inspection. DICs ceased to exist for more than ten years until they were reinstalled in 1978 after the Third Plenum of the 11th CCP Central Committee.

Party discipline inspection in the reform era

Embarking on reform, the CCP shifted its policy orientation from an emphasis on class struggle to stressing economic modernization and gradually withdrew itself from the day-to-day administrative affairs of government. Given the new social and economic conditions, the Party's disciplinary inspection has become more important than ever before. To be sure, disciplinary inspection is still largely driven by the Party's anxiety to strengthen its political legitimacy and organizational sustainability. However, while the early efforts of the CCP were aimed at making the transition from a revolutionary party to a ruling one, today's challenge is how to make a Leninist institution conform to market changes. This goes far beyond—and may even directly contradict—its original institutional purpose.

Being a Leninist party does not necessarily mean the Party is opposed to change, although some may argue that Leninist institutions, by definition, are not able to survive market transformation.[4] The CCP was no doubt born as a revolutionary party, but institutional legitimacy and sustainability have always been its subconscious concerns and fundamental goals. The adaptation and reinforcing of the Party's disciplinary inspection after 1978 show the changing needs of the CCP in the reform context and its effort to cope with organizational problems in a new social and economic environment. Jepperson (1991) points out that institutions may develop contradictions with their environment, with other institutions, or with elementary social behavior. These contradictions, or other exogenous environmental shocks, may then serve as major driving forces behind institutional change. This does not mean, however, that institutions will fail. There are a number of ways in which institutions, once established, can change. They may further evolve, or become deinstitutionalized, or be reinstitutionalized.[5] This is exactly what we have seen in the CCP discipline inspection in recent decades—adaptation and change amid continuity in a reinstitutionalizing process.

Coming out of the ten-year Cultural Revolution, the Party discipline inspection system was completely deinstitutionalized. All the disciplinary agencies had ceased to function, and the staffs were disbanded. At the same time, the Party was confronted with mounting problems both inside and outside its organization, which required an "iron fist" of powerful disciplinary measures. Externally, for instance, the CCP had to restore its political legitimacy and institutional capacity for governance, both of which were considerably damaged by its disastrous political and economic policies in the earlier periods, especially during the ten years of the Cultural Revolution. The Party also had to cope with some thorny issues within its own organization, such as the ideological disorientation and moral decay of individual members, which had resulted not just from the disarray of the Cultural Revolution but also, paradoxically, from the new task the Party had set for itself: reform and modernization. Economic marketization undermined the appealing power of communist ideology for the Party's rank-and-file members and caused "organizational erosion from below" (Chen and Gong 1997). Unlike the collapse or shake-up of political authority during the Cultural Revolution, the marketization-induced institutional erosion was a process where the CCP felt it increasingly hard to maintain institutional control over the individual behavior of members. While there was no obvious sign of institutional breakdown, the conduct of Party members often departed from the formal rules and stated goals of the Party, as numerous corruption cases indicated. It was believed that an increasing number of Party members were becoming casualties of market reform as they failed to resist the enticement of money and fame (Myers 1989). The CCP consequently had to fight on both an economic and a moral front; that is, while encouraging people to enrich themselves with such slogans as "getting rich is glorious," the Party also had to restrain its members from engaging in excessive profit-seeking activities.[6]

The Party's disciplinary inspection system was thus strengthened in the context of an urgent need to prevent the moral degeneration and corruption of the Party's members. A new Discipline Inspection Commission of the CCP Central Committee was established in 1979, followed by the creation of many local branches in the next few years. This reorganization revealed the Party leadership's awareness of its urgent organizational problems and marked the beginning of the CCP's long and difficult reform-era battle against corruption.

The reinstitutionalized disciplinary inspection system has maintained its original structure as well as its mission. Institutionally, it is a hierarchical system composed of the DICs that parallel Party committees at every administrative level from the center down to counties. The DICs are charged with enforcing Party discipline and handling cases of disciplinary violation involving Party members. Despite the continuity in structure, however, some notable changes have taken place in the jurisdiction and functions of the DICs and in the overall role and status of discipline inspection in the Party apparatus. The CCP's disciplinary inspection system today presents a number of new features.

In terms of institutional design, the post-reform DICs are less under the control of the Party committees at the same level. While for a long time in theory the provincial and lower DICs were subject to the "dual leadership" of their immediate superiors within the inspection system (that is, the DIC at the next higher level) and the local Party committee of the same level, they were actually managed by the latter. The dual leadership was in fact an asymmetric institutional arrangement where Party committees were accorded a superior role over the DICs and exercised the real power in handling disciplinary matters. The DIC at the next higher level was merely expected to provide policy guidance or technical support for lower-level DICs. Since the beginning of reform in the 1980s, a more equal "partnership" has taken shape in order to enhance the role of the DICs in discipline inspection. Local Party committees and high-level DICs have acquired a relatively more significant role in supervising the work of local DICs. The new power balance between the two leading bodies was particularly emphasized at the Party's 12th National Congress in 1982 and has been practiced since then (Wu 2004).

Moreover, two institutional mechanisms have been added to further enhance the disciplinary authority of DICs over local Party cadres. The Central Disciplinary Inspection Commission (CDIC) dispatches ad hoc teams to various localities to conduct disciplinary inspection and to investigate alleged or suspected corruption cases among local officials. In August 2003, for example, the CDIC formed five inspection teams led by retired ministerial-level cadres (*Xuexi shibao*, 18 April 2007). Such teams report directly to the CDIC, and their work is exempt from the monitoring and intervention of local Party committees. They have the authority to call meetings, conduct interviews, and review documents relevant to the investigation. The opinion of an inspection team is crucial for determining the fate of local officials under investigation, as can be seen in the Shanghai pension fund scandal. In the summer of 2006, more than 100 investigators from the CDIC were sent to Shanghai to probe a corruption case in which more than US$ 400 million were siphoned off from the city's pension and housing funds. The investigation led to the sacking of the then Shanghai Party chief, who was also a member of the Politiburo of the CCP Central Committee, and the arrest of dozens of officials and business executives (*People's Daily*, 11 April 2008).

A second important mechanism aimed at enhancing the power of the DICs vis-à-vis local Party committees is related to the selection of the DIC members. The common practice for a long time was for the local Party committee at the same level to select DIC members, including the chief, who were then endorsed by the local People's Congress. Such an institutional arrangement made it difficult for the DIC to exercise supervision over local leading cadres, since those cadres controlled who became members of the DIC. In the late 1990s, the city of Zhangjiajie introduced a new method that moved the authority over the DIC leadership selection from the same-level Party committee to the DIC at the next higher level so as to reduce the possible interference of local officials with disciplinary affairs through personal connections. This experiment did not have much impact on other localities, and it faded away for lack of political attention and support. Nonetheless, the experiment triggered a scholarly debate concerning the DIC's organizational structure (Rong 2006; Mei 2004). A new model for DIC leadership selection and personnel management has recently come into view. After the Shanghai pension fund scandal, the Party Center decided in late 2006 to appoint the chief of DICs directly in the four centrally administered municipalities of Beijing, Shanghai, Tianjin, and Chongqing. For example, the CCP Central Committee appointed a deputy chief justice of the Supreme People's Court to be Secretary of the Shanghai DIC (*Ta Kung Pao*, 4 December 2006). The Center also suggested that non-native candidates should receive preferential consideration when appointing the head of provincial DICs (*Xuexi shibao*, 18 April 2007). The moves signaled the determination of the CCP central authority to reinstitutionalize its control over disciplinary matters because of its increasing dissatisfaction with the impotent disciplinary inspection at local levels.

The capacity of disciplinary inspection agencies

The capacity of DICs is another issue that the CCP has struggled with for a long time. When DICs were created, their main charge was simply to deal with disciplinary violations by individual Party members. As a result, their functions were confined to conducting investigations and then applying the disciplinary measures deemed appropriate to the cases before them. It was stipulated clearly in the 1945 Party Constitution that "the task and jurisdiction of the Party's central and local disciplinary organs is to impose or repeal penalties on party members and handle their appeals." Although the Party Constitution was amended several times after that, the provision concerning DIC responsibilities remained largely the same until the reform years. Under the mounting pressure to strengthen internal discipline so as to deal effectively with the increasingly rampant corruption among Party members, the CCP has significantly expanded the DIC mission charge. The capacity of DICs has been strengthened to include not only rule execution but also rule-making and adjudication.

The content of Party discipline inspection is based upon a combination of the various requirements for Party members stated in the CCP Constitution in general terms and specifically stipulated by the Party document *Some Criteria on the Inner-Party Political Life*, adopted in 1980. *Some Criteria* lists disciplinary requirements in eight areas: 1) political discipline—adhering to the Party's basic line, principles, policies, and decisions; 2) organizational discipline—upholding democratic centralism, that is, individual members are subordinate to the Party organization; 3) discipline in relation to publicity—faithfully disseminating the principles and policies of the Party; 4) discipline in relation to the masses—giving top priority to the interests of the general public and keeping close contact with them; 5) security discipline—adhering to the Party's confidentiality regulations; 6) economic discipline—preventing the abuse of power in economic activities; 7) personnel discipline—adhering to the merit principle in personnel matters; and 8) discipline concerning foreign affairs—protecting national dignity in the handling of foreign affairs. Since they are responsible for maintaining and strengthening discipline on such a wide scope, the DICs have a much broader and more active role to play nowadays than they did before. As a consequence, their capacity lies in four major areas: rule-making, disciplinary inspection and investigation, imposition of penalties, and the moral education of Party members. The DICs are responsible, for instance, for making, revising, interpreting, and implementing codes of conduct that all Party institutions and members must observe. In recent years the CDIC has become increasingly active in rule-making and has composed a significant number of regulations on behalf of the CCP Central Committee. Among the most recent ones are *The Regulations on Inner-Party Supervision* (2005), *Provisions on the CCP's Disciplinary Penalties* (2005), *Provisions about Establishing the Responsibility System for Party Construction and Clean Government* (2005), and *Interim Stipulations Leading Cadres' Integrity Report* (2006). It should be noted that the authority to interpret these regulations rests with the CDIC, as specified in these documents.

A significant development concerning the DICs' role and function took place in 2002 when the CCP's 16th Party Congress decided to empower the

CDIC as chief coordinator of all anticorruption efforts. The move came as a result of the CCP's renewed understanding of the corruption problem. And a more rigorous, systematic, and multifaceted anticorruption strategy was adopted because of the prevalence of corruption among Party officials. The Party realized that corruption was not just a matter of its public image but also a real threat to governance capability and regime survival. After the 16th Party Congress, several notable changes occurred in the official terminology about corruption. First, in anticorruption efforts the phrase "fighting and *preventing* corruption" replaced "fighting corruption." In the past, Party institutions, especially disciplinary inspection agencies, often busied themselves with individual corruption cases and spent less time on prevention of corruption in general. Adding the word "preventing" was meant to elicit more vigorous preventive measures that would nip corruption in the bud and change the post-mortem character of prior anticorruption drives. Second, the Party redefined anticorruption as "a critical task," not just "a serious battle." The CCP thereby broadened the scope of its anticorruption endeavor, making it clear that fighting corruption was a long-term mission, not a short-term battle. Finally, the Party began to emphasize the importance of building a legal basis for anticorruption policies. A significant number of rules and regulations were introduced in the next few years including, for example, *The Internal Supervision Regulations of the CCP* (2004), *Provisional Regulations on Open Selection of Party Officials* (2004), *Provisions on the CCP's Disciplinary Penalties* (2005), *Provisions about Establishing the Responsibility System for Party Construction and Clean Government* (2005), and *Interim Stipulations on Leading Cadres' Integrity Report* (2006).

By underlining the urgency for curbing corruption, these changes gave the DICs added prominence as China's leading anticorruption agencies. The DICs' responsibility for coordinating anticorruption efforts and policies was further confirmed by the *Interim Provisions on DICs' Role in Assisting the Party Committees with the Organization and Coordination of Anticorruption Work* in 2005 (*Zhongguo jijian jiancha bao*, 26 September 2005).

Another encouraging sign of the increasingly salient position of discipline inspection and the rise of DICs' political status within the Party apparatus is that the CDIC's annual plenary session usually has all members of the CCP's Central Standing Committee in attendance. In fact, in addition to the CCP Central Committee and the National People's Congress (which usually holds its annual plenum together with the National People's Political Consultative Conference), the CDIC is the only other national institution that holds its plenary session once a year. Held in the first month of the year, the CDIC annual plenum delivers its work report and projects future work.

The DICs' enhanced disciplinary capacity is manifested mainly in its authority to handle public accusations, conduct investigations, and impose a wide range of punitive measures.

First, the DICs are responsible for handling complaints and accusations against Party officials. For the public to report the wrongdoing of Party and government officials is by no means new in China. The People's Accusation Receiving Offices were established at various levels of government as early as in the 1950s. However, their function was not only limited, but it was also frequently interrupted by political campaigns. The practice of public reporting of wrongdoing was not fully institutionalized until the reform period, when various report centers (*jubao zhongxin*) for receiving public complaints were established as an important anticorruption measure. Citizens may lodge complaints or accusations at these centers in person or by phone, mail, or email, anonymously or not. The DIC processes these complaints according to the perceived importance of a case. Important cases—ones involving a large sum of money or a high-ranking Party official—will be followed up by the DIC, while those deemed less important are sent to the higher-level authorities of the concerned institutions for further action. Public reporting serves as a useful way to detect and deter official corruption. Statistics have revealed that about 80 percent of the cases handled by the procuratorial organs in China were originally stimulated by the actions of ordinary citizens (*Fazhi ribao*, 18 June 1994). However, because of their subordinate and dependent status in the Party's organizational structure, the DICs sometimes fail to act effectively and fairly in processing accusations; they also encounter difficulties when they try to protect whistleblowers.[7]

Second, DICs have the authority to conduct an investigation if they deem it necessary. In the investigation process, a DIC may take various actions such as contacting whistleblowers, questioning witnesses, and searching for physical evidence. A particularly forceful way of investigation developed in recent years is the informal but compulsory detention of officials alleged to have done wrong (referred to as *shuanggui* in China). It means that accused officials are required to stay for interrogation at a particular place for a period of time which may last for weeks or months. The method was first introduced in Article 28 of *The CCP's Regulation on Dealing with Cases of Party Discipline Violations*, which came into effect on 1 May 1994. It was reiterated by Article 20 of the *Administrative Supervision Law*, adopted on 9 May 1997, at the 25th session of the 8th National People's Congress Standing Committee. According to CCP policy, DICs at or above the county level can authorize such detention and determine when, how, and where the accused should be detained. The DICs' detention power is controversial because of its extralegal nature and lack of proper procedures. Scholars are concerned that this practice may open door for arbitrary detention and deprivation of personal freedom specified in Article 37 of China's Constitution (Zhang 2005).

Finally, following an investigation, the DIC may propose or implement disciplinary penalties against the accused, if the DIC believes that the charges have been substantiated. It may choose one of five disciplinary actions: warning, serious warning, removal from Party posts, probation within the Party, or expulsion from the Party. There is, however, one qualification. A DIC has the authority to give a warning or serious warning, but it may only propose the other three—dismissal, probation, or expulsion. The power to impose these more serious penalties lies in the hands of the Party committee at the corresponding level, and there is no guarantee that the Party committee necessarily concurs with the DIC's recommendations.

DICs may transfer a case to a procuratorate and court for prosecution and legal action. This step is taken only when the concerned case is believed to have violated not only Party discipline but also state law. However, in practice, this does not always occur smoothly because DICs may encounter the interference of local Party committees. As reported by a Chinese newspaper, for example, Tieli City of Heilongjiang Province passed a resolution entitled the "Notices of Coordinated Investigation and Enforcement between the Administration and Judiciary," which made it clear that local leading officials had to sign off on all important cases before they were sent to judicial institutions (*Fazhi ribao*, 3 April 1998). And even after a case has entered the legal process, the judicial work concerning the case may still be interrupted by the leaders of the local Party committee if they have questions about it. There is an institutional mechanism, called "disciplinary review," to prevent the excessive intervention by local Party committees. In this mechanism, a higher-level DIC accepts the appeals of a lower one and acts as an arbitrator to examine the facts and settle disagreements between a particular DIC and its corresponding Party committee. Such disciplinary review rarely takes place, however.

Embedded dilemmas

Discipline inspection has served the CCP as a means of ruling, a way of maintaining organizational control, and a source of regime legitimacy, even though various unstable political situations and Mao's radical policies caused oscillations in the importance and actual operation of the DICs in the early years. However, the Party's disciplinary inspection system leaves much to be desired in terms of its effectiveness in curbing corruption and other malpractices of Party members, because of certain problems embedded in its institutional design and policy capacity.

Dual leadership

The disciplinary inspection system has flaws in its institutional design. The structural features of an institution and the processes and mechanisms through which the institution influences individual actors are critically important, according to new institutionalism. The key question is whether the institutions are designed to be both adequate and appropriate for accomplishing the tasks or missions set for them. In China, disciplinary inspection agencies have acquired an increasingly salient role, and their current responsibilities far exceed those of their predecessors. However, the system has suffered from a fundamental defect since the beginning: the "dual leadership" problem.

As discussed above, local DICs have always operated under a dual leadership structure in which the local Party committee at the same level and the DIC at the next higher level of the Party's organizational chain both supervise them. This dual oversight is supposed to be equally weighted, and indeed, the vertical chain that links the DICs at different levels has been strengthened in recent years as a result of their improved status and expanded jurisdiction. In practice, however, a DIC is still more subordinate to the supervision of the local Party committee than it is to its superior in the DIC system. There are institutional reasons for this. For a long time, for instance, the position of a local DIC head was held concurrently by a deputy chief of the corresponding local Party committee. The person had to work in concert with the Party committee's "collective will" or sometimes simply comply with the Party chief.[8] In 2004 the CDIC introduced a measure to place all inspection teams it sent to central government agencies under its own direct control, thus removing them from the dual leadership structure. Where the experiment was carried out, the CDIC appointed the head of an inspecting team without involving the concerned local Party committee, and this person was therefore accountable to the CDIC only (Li and Wang 2006). However, this practice is confined to the central government only, and dual leadership still applies to local DICs.

Asymmetrical dual leadership renders the DICs vulnerable to political intervention at the local level in everything from staffing, to the definition of its work, to its day-to-day operation. It is ironic that these DICs, which are so far from working independently, are charged by the Party Constitution with "supervising" local Party committees and leading cadres. As subordinates in the political hierarchy and with their appointment, promotion, and personal welfare virtually all controlled by leading cadres of local Party committees, DIC members face tremendous difficulties in performing their supervisory duty independently. This is why, in recent years, the phenomenon of the "first in command's corruption" (*diyibashou fubai*) has drawn so much attention. The phrase refers to the situation where the chiefs of local Party committees (the top local leaders) assume great authority over resources and personnel as a result of the decentralization of power, but at the same time become increasingly free from effective institutional oversight and public surveillance, and they therefore become highly vulnerable to corruption (Gong 2006). This is well illustrated in the confession made by the former Party chief of Taian City of Shandong Province, who accepted more than 600,000 yuan worth of bribes and was sentenced to death. As he acknowledged, "an official like me has never been subject to any supervision" (An et al. 1996). Another fallen high-ranking official, the former deputy governor of Jiangxi, used an equally illustrative metaphor when he described disciplinary inspection as "placing a cat in a cattle pen—no use" (*Xinmin Weekly*, 6 September 2003).

It should be noted, however, that the dual leadership problem is more than just a matter of allocating responsibilities among different Party institutions. It points to a more deeply embedded deficiency in the Party's discipline inspection; that is, discipline inspection lacks substantial autonomy from the Party organization. Despite the fact that the DICs have assumed a much more prominent role in Party affairs in recent years, they remain just functional units, equal to others, within the Party apparatus. Because they lack independent discretionary power and strong political support, many local DICs are unable to break entrenched local *guanxi* (personal connections) networks. This explains why local DICs are so much less active and less effective than the CDIC in recent anticorruption activities (*Wen Wei Po*, 24 February 2007). For example, the CDIC largely performed a monodrama when it handled certain recent cases such as the Shanghai pension fund scandal and the vast bribery of the former vice mayor of Beijing who oversaw Olympic construction projects. In neither case did the CDIC fully engage the DICs in the respective cities. It is difficult in practice for local DICs to take any initiative in exposing big cases such as these since they are not in a strong position to confront powerful, well-connected local leading cadres; nor are they willing to risk their political careers to do so.

Morality by decree

In terms of policy capacity, one shortcoming of the DICs is that they rely on imposing morality by decree. This is rooted in the fact that discipline inspection long served the Party's political and organizational needs as an instrument. Institutionally a dependent component of the Party apparatus, the disciplinary inspection system has had to satisfy the Party's desire for organizational consolidation, adaptation, and legitimation. Recently the Party announced eight new rules against corruption, named by the media the "eight prohibitions." Under the new rules, Party and government officials are banned from a number of specifically defined economic activities such as purchasing property, automobiles, or other products for below-market prices, entrusting others to invest in securities and futures for them, or accepting gratuitous shares or "bonuses" from economic entities. The CDIC set a 30-day limit for corrupt officials to turn themselves in, requiring them to do so by 30 June 2007. If they did, they would receive leniency; if they did not, then they would face severe punishment when their wrongdoings were discovered (*Ta Kung Pao*, 4 July 2007). The Party expects such rules to guide its officials toward moral behavior. However, because of its required character, this "performance by design" approach has not been, and will not become, as effective as the Party desires in preventing the moral decay of Party members. In the tension between the incontestability of the individual's moral authorship and the imposed external forces that try to constrain or change it, as Harmon points out, there is no guarantee that the latter will always prevail (Harmon 1995: 134).

New institutionalism depicts three different ways in which social institutions and human behavior may interact. One is regulative, in which institutional constraints are imposed on the behavior of individuals within an institution to force them to act in certain desirable ways. The second is normative, in which institutions (defined as rules, norms, and other frameworks by new institutionalists) inform individuals of what they are "supposed" to do as their duty. While these first two modes emphasize the constraining functions of institutions, the third way draws attention to a cognitive influence that "enables" individuals to perform certain actions because the actions are conceived as routines or "the way we do these things" (Scott 2001: 57) What develops from the first two modes may be regarded as "objective responsibility," while the third translates into "subjective responsibility." The term "subjective responsibility," which appears in the writings of Cooper, Mosher, and Winter (Cooper 1998; Mosher 1968; Winter 1966), asserts the notion that people are moral agents and their behavior is often driven by their "inner sense" of responsibility or what they themselves perceive as the "right" way of performing their moral duty. In China, although a discipline inspection system has been gradually institutionalized within the CCP organization, there is a conspicuous deficit of subjective sources of discipline. For many Party members, following organizational disciplinary guidance is not a conscious choice they have made by themselves. The discipline inspection system has the disciplinary power to compel Party members to conform to the Party's political will out of fear of punishment. But it does not necessarily have morally persuasive authority over Party members that can engender an "inner sense of duty" to pursue high moral standards. To some extent, the discrepancy between the Party's disciplinary authority and its moral authority may be attributed to the fact that in China today the daily conduct of CCP members is largely guided by market forces and is therefore not always favorable to the Party's ideological and moral tenets. The traditional egalitarianism of communism has largely given way to a rich-is-glorious ideology. The politically prescribed roles of Party members may in fact conflict with socially constructed norms. Thus it remains a major challenge for the CCP leadership to determine how to cultivate subjective responsibility or moral decency among its members in a social climate that generally encourages individual advancement and materialistic aspirations. While codes of ethics and top-down inspection of the implementation of these codes are important for a vanguard party like the CCP, its leadership must learn how to understand and reform the *unwritten* "codes" that govern the daily conduct of its members. As these unwritten codes are beyond the reach of the Party, the CCP's effort at performance control through institutional imposition alone may not work. Instead, the CCP needs to do more to promote the self-discipline of Party officials and rank-and-file members.

Conclusion

The evolving trajectory of the CCP disciplinary inspection system shows that the Party is attempting to maintain its moral ascendancy and organizational decency amid rapid social change. As an important Leninist principle, discipline inspection has proven indispensable for the Party over time, even though its influence waxed and waned with leadership changes and policy shifts. Structurally and functionally, the disciplinary inspection of the CCP has never stayed static. Rather, it has gone through continuous reinstitutionalization, the process by which institutions adapt to new social conditions. The reconsolidation and further development of disciplinary inspection agencies in the post-reform period indicate clearly that the CCP understands the need for institutional renewal and policy adaptation to make disciplinary inspection more compatible with the changing environment and, in particular, with market conditions. This has led to a change in the dynamic of discipline inspection from being ideologically driven to being governance-based. However, for the Party, the essence of discipline inspection remains the same; it is intended to improve the moral conduct of Party members through top-down disciplinary measures. Such path-dependence is reflected in the dual leadership structure. All the disciplinary inspection agencies must abide by the Party's basic principle of "democratic centralism," which subjects lower-level officials and ordinary members to the authority of leading officials and justifies the control of higher-level institutions over lower ones. Thus when performing their supervisory functions, local DICs are ironically constrained by the very people who are supposed to be under their surveillance. Since DICs are just ordinary components of the Party apparatus, without institutional independence and autonomy, how they can be made to exercise effective supervision over other Party institutions and particularly over leading cadres remains a big challenge. If, on the other hand, they are granted independent status, then who will inspect the performance of the inspectors? Who guards the guardians is also going to be problematic under China's current political system. The dilemma will likely remain until more fundamental political changes take place, when, perhaps, public surveillance is fully developed to replace the conventional practice of the CCP's discipline inspection.

Notes

1 For two early studies on the CCP's disciplinary control agencies, see Sullivan (1984) and Yang (1984).
2 The Party's disciplinary agencies were not able to function normally during the war in the late 1940s; the CCP had to reorganize them in 1949.
3 Liu Qingshan and Zhang Zishan, who were accused and convicted of embezzling more than 1,550,000 yuan of public funds, received a death penalty.
4 See, for example, Shambaugh (2000).
5 For these views, see Powell and DiMaggio (1991), especially Jepperson (1991:143–63).
6 See, for example, the *Rules Concerning the Party's Political Life* (The Supreme People's Procuratorate 1989: 130), a very important Party document on regulating the Party organization by imposing institutional constraints.
7 For a detailed discussion, see Gong (2000).
8 The latest practice is that the local DIC chief serves as a standing member of the local Party committee.

References

An, J. Yi, D., and Chuan, J. (1996) *Taian fantan fengbao* (Anticorruption Storm in Tai'an), Beijing: Xinhua chubanshe.

Arthur, B.W. (1994) *Increasing Returns and Path Dependence in the Economy*, Ann Arbor: University of Michigan Press.

Chen, F. ard Gong, T. (1997) "Market vs Party in post-Mao China: the change of the Leninist institution from below," *Journal of Communist Studies and Transition Politics*, 13(3): 148–66.

Cocks, P. (1979) "The rationalization of Party control," in C. Johnson (ed.) *Change in Communist Systems*, Stanford: Stanford University Press.

Cooper, T.L. (1998) *The Responsible Administrator: An Approach to Ethics for the Administrative Role*, San Francisco, CA: Jossey-Bass.

David, P. (1994) "Why are institutions the 'carriers of history'? path dependence and the evolution of conventions, organizations and institutions," *Structural Change and Economic Dynamics*, 5(2): 205–20.

DiMaggio, P.J. and Powell, W.W. (eds) (1991) *The New Institutionalism in Organizational Analysis*, Chicago: University of Chicago Press.

Gong, T. (1994) *The Politics of Corruption in Contemporary China: An Analysis of Policy Outcomes*, Westport, CT: Praeger Publishers

—— (2000) "Whistleblowing: what does it mean in China?" *International Journal of Public Administration*, 23(11): 1899–1924.

—— (2006) "Corruption and local governance: the double identity of Chinese local governments in market reform," *The Pacific Review*, 19(1): 85–102.

Hall, P.A. and Taylor, R.C.R. (1996) "Political science and the three new institutionalisms," *Political Studies*, 44(5): 936–57

Harmon, M. (1995) *Responsibility as Paradox: A Critique of Rational Discourse on Government*, Thousand Oaks, CA: Sage.

Immergut, E.M. (1998) "The theoretical core of the new institutionalism," *Politics and Society*, 26(1): 5–34.

Jepperson, R. (1991) "Institutions, institutional effects, and institutionalism," in W. Powell and P. DiMaggio (eds) *The New Institutionalism in Organizational Analysis*, Chicago: University of Chicago Press.

Li, S. and Wang, H. (2006) "A historical review of the CCP's discipline inspection system," *Xinjiang shehui kexue*, 3:12–16.

Mao, Z.D. (1977) *Selected Works*, Vol. 5, Beijing: Foreign Languages Press.

Mei, L.H. (2004) "Jianguoyilai zhonggong jijian lingdaotizhi de biange yue fazhan" (The change and development of the CCP's disciplinary inspection leadership system since the PRC), *Lingnan xuekan*, 4: 58–62.

Mosher, M. (1968) *Democracy and the Public Service*, New York: Oxford University Press

Myers, J.T. (1989) "Modernization and 'unhealthy tendencies'," *Comparative Politics*, 21(1): 194–97.

North, D. (1990) *Institutions, Institutional Change and Economic Performance*, Cambridge: Cambridge University Press.

Pierson, P. (2004) *Politics in Time: History, Institutions, and Social Analysis*, Princeton: Princeton University Press.

Powell, W. and DiMaggio, P. (eds) (1991) *The New Institutionalism in Organizational Analysis*, Chicago: University of Chicago Press.

Rong, N. (2006) "Reflections on the development of the supervisory systems of the party and government in contemporary China," *Yunan xingzheng xueyuan xuebao*, 2: 29–32.

Scott, W.R. (2001) *Institutions and Organizations*, Thousand Oaks, CA: Sage.

Shambaugh, D. (2000) "The Chinese state in the post-Mao era," in D. Shambaugh (ed.) *The Modern Chinese State*, Cambridge: Cambridge University Press.

Steinmo, S., Thelen, K., and Longstreth, F. (eds) (1992) *Structuring Politics: Historical Institutionalism in Comparative Perspective*, Cambridge: Cambridge University Press.

Sullivan, L. (1984) "The role of the control organs in the Chinese Communist Party, 1977–83," *Asian Survey*, 24(6): 597–67.

Supreme People's Procuratorate (ed.) (1989) *The Selected Works on Keeping Government Honest and Fighting Corruption*, Beijing: Zhongguo zhengfa daxue chubanshe.

Tolbert, P.S. and Zucker, L.G. (1996) "The institutionalization of institutional theory," in S.R. Clegg, C. Hardy, and W.R. Nord (eds) *Handbook of Organization Studies*, London: Sage.

Winter, G. (1966) *Elements for a Social Ethic*, New York: Macmillan.

Wu, Z.J. (2004) "The evolution of the CCP's disciplinary inspection system," *Journal of Huainan Normal University*, 5: 34–36.

Yang, G. (1984) "Control and style: discipline inspection commissions since the 11th Congress," *The China Quarterly*, 97(1): 24–52.

Yang, X.G. and Jiang, G.H. (2005) "The history of the CCP's central disciplinary inspection institutions," *Journal of Hunan Institute of Humanities, Science and Technology*, 4: 17–20.

Zhang, B.W. (2005) "Shuanggui Shuangzhi: relative rationality and limited legitimacy," *Hebei faxue*, 1.

6 "Policing the police"

A perennial challenge for China's anticorruption agencies*

Stephen K. Ma

Introduction

In 1990, Gerald Caiden wrote that

> [p]ublic misconduct is uneven. Some areas of government are more prone to it than others simply because they exercise the greatest influence over public decisions. Key policymakers always are under heavy pressures to bend. Temptations also are great for any officials who handle large sums of money, have dealings with private businesses, or tackle illegal goods and services. Possibly, the prime target is law enforcement.
> (Caiden 1990: 58–60)

More than ten years have elapsed since then. Despite the efforts by the Chinese authorities to combat corruption in the public sector, the urgency to police the police became increasingly apparent as the rank of government officials in law enforcement being caught with corruption kept rising along the bureaucratic hierarchy. In October 2001, Li Jizhou, a Vice Minister of Public Security, was sentenced to death for bribery-taking, dereliction, and other crimes. Li was the highest-ranking administrator in law enforcement to be convicted since the founding of the People's Republic of China in 1949.

Though the hush money Li pocketed amounted to tens of millions of Chinese yuan, the case surprised few Chinese, if any, as corrupted bureaucratic behavior has been chronic and contagious since the nation embarked on the path of modernization and opened itself to the outside world. This chapter will probe into China's anticorruption agencies where the unethical bureaucratic behavior has been among the increasingly vexing pathologies the authorities have to cope with. The questions that merit exploration are: a) What happened to China's anticorruption agencies charged with the important task of cleaning the government bureaucracies? b) Is the corruption in anticorruption agencies a cause or a consequence of corruption in the public sector? and c) Why has "policing the police" become a perennial challenge for China's anticorruption agencies?

Anticorruption agencies in China

Concomitant with China's rapid and radical reforms there has been rampant corruption among its public officials. As an old Chinese saying proclaims that "not even a prairie fire can destroy the grass, it grows again when the spring breeze blows," corruption remains chronic and contagious and does not seem to be tapering off (Ma 1989: 40–52). To deal with the aggravating bureaucratic pathology, Chinese leaders have created new anticorruption agencies. As will be discussed below, from the early years of reform, a troika composed of agencies from the Chinese Communist Party's commissions for discipline inspection, the Ministry of Supervision, and the procuratorate was placed in charge of the task of fighting against corruption.

The CCP's Central Commission for Discipline Inspection was created by the Party's Constitution of 1977. Its original mission was to strengthen discipline among Party members and to restore internal democracy within the Party in the aftermath of the abusive practices by the radicals during the Cultural Revolution between 1966 and 1976. Soon after the post-Mao China inaugurated its new reformist policies, an increasing number of Party members were switching from "listening to the Party" to "listening to the purse." The commissions for discipline inspection at various levels found themselves more and more often involved in investigation of misconduct by the Party cadres. As a result, the crackdown on those who engaged in corrupt practices became an urgent task for these commissions.

As a component part of the State Council of the People's Republic of China, the People's Supervisory Commission was established in October 1949. It was renamed as the Ministry of Supervision in 1954 and discontinued in 1959. It was not until December 1986 that the Standing Committee of the 6th National People's Congress decided to restore the Ministry of Supervision in order to deal with administrative behavior within the government. Soon after, the Party's commissions for discipline inspection and the government's Ministry of Supervision or bureaus of supervision at the lower levels began to share not only offices but also much of their personnel, resulting in an intertwined relationship between the two. To uphold the Party's unified leadership, commissions for discipline inspection have always gained dominance. That explains why Ma Wen, currently Minister of Supervision, serves as Vice Secretary of the Party's Central Commission for Discipline Inspection.[1]

In order to institutionalize its own anticorruption efforts, the Supreme People's Procuratorate established the General Bureau of Anticorruption in 1989. Hence was born the troika of anticorruption in the early years of post-Mao China. Yet anticorruption efforts could barely keep pace with demand to contain corruption that was spreading rapidly across the nation.

As the need to curb corruption was becoming urgent and the importance of rule of law was being emphasized, the roles of bureaus of public security and courts became increasingly visible. Therefore, it is appropriate to state that anticorruption agencies in China today mainly include the Party's commissions for discipline inspection, the bureaus of supervision, the procuratorate or the bureaus of anticorruption under it, bureaus of public security, and courts.[2] Unfortunately, as observed by Melanie Manion, "in a setting of widespread corruption, corrupt enforcers and a shortage of enforcement resources, relative to the scope of the problem, pose significant obstacles" (Manion 2004: 201–3).

Indeed, very soon it was observed that none of them had the authority to lead and coordinate the efforts to combat corruption effectively. Subordinate to the Party committees at the same level and serving as their agencies of implementation (Sun 1995), the Party's commissions for discipline inspection were supposed to supervise the Party members. But unless backed up by their immediate superiors—the Party committees—the decisions meted out by these agencies were often difficult to implement. Bureaus of supervision within the administration, on the other hand, often found themselves in an awkward position when attempting to supervise leading cadres at the same level. Legal agencies under the procuratorates mainly dealt with criminals involved in embezzlement and bribery and therefore could not exercise the judicial supervision over bureaucratic misuse of power such as dereliction of duty.

As a result, the system of supervision over the bureaucracy had several loopholes through which corrupt officers could elude prosecution. Political interference often came to their rescue. Corrupt leading cadres seldom cared about the so-called "soft supervision" exercised by those from the bureaus of supervision within the administration at the same level. Because of a lack of sufficient authority, "soft supervision" could seldom hit them hard enough. There was also the so-called "blind area" where the cadres misused their power and did not have to worry about being caught because to correct such behavior was none of the above three agencies' business.

Did the Chinese authorities, used to monopoly of power, decide to follow the principle of checks and balances by letting three agencies share the responsibility of dealing with bureaucratic corruption? Of course not. A likely explanation could only be found in the top leadership's fear of an institution which is supposed to be established for the purpose of anticorruption but soon develops the potential of becoming a center capable of challenging the power of the ruling Party.

Therefore, although the establishment of anticorruption agencies can assist in the fight against corruption, other efforts will be required in order to make the anticorruption campaign more effective. Otherwise, as pointed out by Daniel Kaufmann, World Bank Institute Governance Director, it is just a myth that anticorruption commissions are the solution to curbing corruption (World Bank 2007: 171).

Corruption in China's anticorruption agencies

James Madison wrote in 1788 that

> If men were angels, no government would be necessary. If angels were to govern over men, neither external nor internal controls on government

would be necessary. In framing a government which is to be administered by men over men, the great difficulty lies in this: you must first enable the government to control the governed; and in the next place oblige it to control itself.

(Madison 1985 [1788]: 272)

Obviously, Madison's words apply to China's anticorruption agencies as well. These agencies must not only combat corruption in other government agencies but also, more importantly, keep themselves clean and clear from corruption. The latter mission is actually much more difficult than the former because, as stated earlier in this article, very often law enforcement is the prime target of corruption thanks to the temptations created by their work environment. It is an environment where they handle large sums of money made through illegitimate means, where they deal with suspects of corruption who may be their colleagues or friends, and where they work under unusually heavy pressure to bend the rules, to compromise the principles, or even to go along with them in their dirty deeds.

What happened in Shenzhen Intermediate People's Court in 2006 was illustrative of the gravity of the situation. Within a period of five months between June and October of that year, five judges were either arrested or detained for further investigation because of their involvement or possible involvement in corruption (Xinhua 2006a). In addition, more than twenty judges and eight lawyers were reportedly being questioned for their part in the case. Since so many in the Shenzhen Intermediate People's Court could have gotten into the scandal, the day-to-day work there had to be taken over by the Party's Municipal Commission for Discipline Inspection.

In fact, it was no longer a rare incident in recent China that a judge broke the law instead of safeguarding the law. As early as 2002, Tian Fengqi, Chief Justice at the Liaoning Provincial Higher People's Court, and Mai Chongkai, Chief Justice at the Guangdong Provincial Higher People's Court, both fell into disgrace for corruption. Tian's case was disclosed in September that year by the Party's Central Commission for Discipline Inspection and the Ministry of Supervision. He had the audacity to have accepted bribes worth several million yuan and to have aided in his son's business interests. Tian had to pay dearly for his misconduct. He was dismissed from his position, expelled from the Party (for which he had served as the Deputy Secretary of the Political and Legal Committee in Liaoning Province), and subjected to judicial investigation. He was sentenced to life in prison in May the following year. Similarly, Mai was expelled from the Party and removed from the vice-chairmanship of the People's Congress in Guangdong Province in October 2002. As provincial chief justice between 1989 and 1998, he had received 1.74 million yuan in bribes and was responsible for his son's receiving over 10 million yuan in bribes.

It is a well-learned lesson in Chinese history that if the upper beam is not straight, the lower ones will go aslant. In other words, when those above behave unworthily, those below will do the same. Altogether, 24,886 court employees were arraigned or prosecuted in 2002, or 2 percent of the country's judicial staff (Transparency International 2004: 178).

"To kill the chicken in order to frighten the monkey" is an old Chinese saying, suggesting that punishing someone can serve as a warning to others. That didn't seem to be working in recent China. While sentences including life in prison or death were being meted out, the warning more than often fell on deaf ears. Large numbers of state officials were advancing wave upon wave in their brazen pursuit of ill-gotten wealth. One wonders what has made corruption in the nation's anticorruption agencies a seemingly incurable cancer threatening to incapacitate the authorities' efforts to build up an honest government. "Policing the police," namely to make the anticorruption agencies less corruptible, has become a formidable problem for the Chinese leadership.

Causes of corruption in China's anticorruption agencies

Caiden offers a list of factors contributing to government officials' corrupt behavior. These include psychological, ideological, external, economic, political, sociocultural and technological explanations (Caiden 2001: 21–26). Psychologically, "the root cause of corruption is found in the defects of human character inherent in the human conditions; few are above temptation" (ibid.: 23) Anticorruption officers are not exceptions.

Ideologically, there are doctrines that endorse corruption (ibid.). "It is glorious to become rich" has been a slogan widely used by the post-Mao leadership to promote productivity. It was hoped that the goal of a prosperous life would prompt people to work harder and produce more. What was ignored was that there were many other ways and means, legal or illegal, that could lead to a prosperous life. One of them is through corruption.

"Corruption is contagious" (ibid.). Corruption spreads and infects rapidly, thanks to avarice in human nature: insatiable greed for material wealth. It was this excessive desire to acquire or possess more that made any measure to forbid the presenting of gifts and "red envelopes" a mission impossible. In dealings with bureaucrats, one could hardly move a single step without fat "red envelopes" or with only meager ones. In fact, as a former secretary of a provincial commission for discipline inspection disclosed in an interview, unlike years before, when a red envelope used to bribe a government official contained only several hundred yuan, it often held tens of thousands of yuan now (Xinhua 2006a).

"Scarcity is clearly a key source of corruption" (Caiden 2001: 24). Although China's is no longer an economy of shortage, scarcity still exists, only in a different kind. Instead of scarcity of food or clothes, it is now scarcity of expensive vehicles or luxurious mansions that drive the greedy crazy.

"[C]orruption seeks out key decision makers and the most powerful officials" (ibid.: 25). For quite some time, there were discussions exploring the causes for corruption of *Yibashou* or "first in command." They held primary administrative responsibility. They were the principal decision makers. They had most power in their hands. Of course, they were the number one target of corruption.

"Internal socialization and peer group pressure ensure that public officials go along with or at least keep quiet about deviance. Whistle-blowers who reveal internal wrongdoings are considered treacherous" (ibid.). The so-called "code of silence" has been existing within the Party and government hierarchies. Though witnessing misconduct within their own organizations, many party members often chose to maintain silence, which has become the "black breeding ground for corruption" (Xinhua 2006b).

Faulty technology and faulty administrative systems "permit those inclined to corruption to remain unseen and unknown, to evade detection, and to escape investigation"(Caiden 2001: 21–26). Post-Mao China launched its reformist policies in the late 1970s and early 1980s. "Reform corruption develops because reform is seldom followed by corresponding regulations" (Ma 1989: 48). More than two decades have elapsed since then, but the administrative systems remain faulty in segments of the bureaucratic machinery. Arbitrary demand for fees and fines was just one example. They produced a perfect channel for accosting innocent citizens for money and accepting bribery.

It should also be noticed that post-Mao China has witnessed a steady retreat of the state which has both "increased mechanisms *for* cadre misconduct and reduced disincentives *against* it," as pointed out by Yan Sun (Sun 2004). This was particularly true for anticorruption agencies because the nature of their work has created a unique environment where corruption fighters had to face unusual challenges. On the one hand, temptations were particularly high as they were dealing with illegal activities daily and handling a large amount of illegal wealth regularly. It requires a strong will and a great sense of public good over private interest to resist the tantalizing bait in order not to fall into the trap. On the other hand, restraints against corruption were often in short supply because it was too often that anticorruption agencies focused on their first mission of government—to control others—at the expense of the second mission—to control themselves. A former head of a provincial commission for discipline inspection admitted openly that there was no supervision over him when he was serving as a key leading official of supervision in the province (Xinhua 2006b).

Plenty of temptations coupled with a lack of supervision have made corruption a big issue in anticorruption agencies, including law enforcement, the legal system, and the judiciary. That explains why "bribes are most commonly paid around the world to the police, and are substantially more frequent than to other services" and why there were "enormous concerns regarding corruption in processes of law enforcement, particularly when viewed alongside the sector identified as the third most common recipient of bribes: the legal system and judiciary," as indicated in the "Global Corruption Barometer 2006" issued by Transparency International (2006: 6).

Moreover, the special inter-institutional relationship between the CCP and the anticorruption agencies has often jeopardized the effectiveness of the latter's operation and sabotaged morale among anticorruption officers. For example, the Party's dominance has resulted in the judiciary's inferior status. As Ting Gong observes, courts and procurators must report to the Political-Legal

Secretary of the local Party Committee (*zhengfa shuji*). As Party members, court presidents and vice presidents are always expected to demonstrate political loyalty to the Party. On the other hand, it is the Party that holds the personnel and purse power within the judiciary. Major judges and procurators are always selected by the Party Committee. The budget of each court is always determined by the local government where it sits. In addition, "legal decision-making and implementation are often subject to bargaining and manipulation of local governments" (Gong 2004).

Even the Party's commissions for discipline inspection could not fare better. Though themselves being part of the ruling party and enjoying the highest status among all the anticorruption agencies, they too seldom had an easy time in their dealings with the Party. Wei Jianxing, the former Secretary of the Central Commission for Discipline Commission, allegedly tendered his resignation on the eve of the opening of the fifteenth plenum of the CCP's Central Committee in the fall of 2000, protesting over the impotence of his institution in dealings with corrupted officers. It was indeed lamentable to realize that more than 100 senior government officials at or above the rank of lieutenant governor were removed from their positions and expelled from the Party in the two decades since the mid-1980s and that all these cases were unveiled by anonymous letters rather than through investigations by anticorruption agencies. Wu Guanzheng, Wei's successor submitted his resignation in August 2005 because he found himself in an even worse situation. Not only did the anticorruption campaign made little progress under his leadership. A total of 144 anticorruption officers at the provincial level were discharged from their posts and kicked out of the Party in 2004 (Guang 2005a: 19–20). Both numbers alone speak for themselves. Anticorruption agencies in China were born with their hands and feet bound due to the institutional design, a design that guarantees the Party's absolute rule at the expense of the other institutions' autonomy and capacity. As a consequence, not only did anticorruption agencies have to fight battles both front and rear in their anticorruption campaigns, the improper political interference also led to disappointment among anticorruption fighters and even their degeneration.

Neither Wei nor Wu resigned before their terms expired. Yet their gripes and grumbles were not without reason. Many of their reports about leading cadres' unlawful practice, including their extravagant expenditure, were withheld from distribution. They were frustrated by their inability to resist the political interference from the Party and to resolve the "abnormal relationship" between the Party's Central Secretariat and the Central Commission for Discipline Inspection (Guang 2005b: 17–18).

Corruption in anticorruption agencies: a cause or consequence of corruption in the public sector?

There is no doubt that many factors have contributed to corruption in the public sector, including the anticorruption agencies. The question we must also explore is whether corruption in the anticorruption agencies can contribute to administrative misbehavior in the public sector. It is obvious that *corruption in anticorruption agencies increases the probability of corruption in other parts of the government.* If a watchdog fails to perform properly, those being watched will face less or even no restraint over their conduct and tend to behave more irresponsibly.

In addition, *dishonest behavior by anticorruption officials disappoints the public's expectations of a clean government and dampens citizens' enthusiasm for participation as watchdogs, thereby damaging the mechanism of external supervision over state bureaucracy.* Han Jianlin, Director of the Bureau of Anticorruption in Jiangsu Provincial Procuratorate, could not resist the temptation and slipped into the trap set up by corrupted officials. He was removed form the position in June 2004, becoming the first chief anticorruption officer at the provincial level to fall in disgrace (Zheng 2004). The case not only disclosed the depth of "collective corruption" in government but offered one more example of how heroes turned into villains (Ling 2005), as remarked in a commentary on the website of the *People's Daily.* What was even more detrimental to the regime was the public's further declining confidence in authorities' ability to build up an honest government.

Moreover, *crooked anticorruption officers are in the best position to silence whistleblowers, effectively muffling criticisms of wrongdoings within the government.* Zeng Jinchun served as the Party's Municipal Secretary for Discipline Inspection of Chenzhou City in Hunan Province for more than ten years and was detained in September 2006. Only after he fell out of power did people reveal that materials by whistleblowers exposing his misconduct since he took the position in 1995 were collecting dust, piling up as high as two meters (Yi 2006). Zeng's iron-handed suppression of different voices certainly contributed greatly to the city's becoming a "disaster area" of corruption.

Finally, *anticorruption agencies, staffed with or led by corrupted officers, sustain corruption in the public sector by putting a misleading façade of a government fighting against corruption.* That explains why the public no longer reacted favorably to an official proposal in early 2007 to establish a new anticorruption agency called the Bureau of Corruption Prevention. Opinions voiced on line suggested that people wondered whether the new measure was just a speech more of ornament than of ideas. One comment on the website of China Radio International, for example, pointed out straightforwardly that it was simply unnecessary because more agencies of anticorruption do not necessarily mean less corruption (Li 2007). The National Bureau of Corruption Prevention (NBCP) was established in September anyway. It was noteworthy that the NBCP website crashed just hours after its launch on 18 December, as droves of people logged on to complain about corruption among officials. "The enthusiasm that greeted the launch of the website reflects the growing frustration felt by the public toward corruption at government level, which has been accentuated by several high-profile cases in recent years." Meanwhile, one of the comments was straightforward, saying that "[t]he corruption problem in China is a fatal illness. Establishing more institutions will not solve the problem."[3] It was lamentable to witness the apparent lack of confidence among the public in the usefulness of anti-corruption agencies as the authorities were trying to redouble their efforts to combat corruption.

Clearly, to a larger degree, corruption in the anticorruption agencies has contributed to administrative misbehavior in the public sector. Turning a blind eye to this fact could only render plans and programs of combating corruption fruitless and, more importantly, make the infected state apparatus incorrigible and the corroded government institutions crumble and collapse eventually.

Challenges in "policing the police" for China's anticorruption agencies

As discussed earlier in this article, the nature of work conducted by anti-corruption agencies has created a unique environment for anticorruption officers. They have to deal with the unusual challenges in "policing the police," namely the challenges in keeping themselves clean. The difficulty emanates from particularly high temptations and a lack of sufficient supervision over their behavior. While there is little that can be done in regard to the high temptations, the goal of exercising effective supervision over anticorruption agencies is not unattainable.

The debate between Carl Friedrich and Herman Finer on responsible government in the early 1940s can serve as a useful guideline for our discussion. The former emphasizes inner constraint over administrative behavior while the latter stresses the importance of external control (Friedrich 1940; Finer 1941). Neither is perfect, yet both contribute to healthy administrative behavior which is essential for building up a clean government.

Codes of ethics are an important component of inner constraint. During its 96th Annual Conference in Louisville, Kentucky, in 1989, the Executive Committee of the International Association of Chiefs of Police has adopted the Law Enforcement Code of Ethics, which covers areas such as Primary Responsibilities of a Police Officer, Performance of the Duties of a Police Officer, Discretion, Use of Force, Confidentiality, Integrity, Cooperation with Other Officers and Agencies, Personal/Professional Capabilities, Private Life (CSEP 1989). The post-Mao Chinese leadership did not resort to ethical codes until the early 1990s. The Ministry of Public Security issued the codes on "ten forbids" for police officers in September 1993, requiring that police officers refrain from:

1 bending the law for the benefit of relatives and friends;
2 confiscating and fining regardless of state policies;
3 collecting fees arbitrarily;
4 being involved directly or indirectly in business activities such as dancing halls, karaokes, restaurants, hairdressing salons, massage clinics, and Video/ DVD viewing centers;

5   interfering in business disputes on behalf of other individuals and enterprises;
6   conducting commercial business;
7   marketing products of social public security forcefully;
8   accepting gifts and securities while serving the public;
9   soliciting free food and goods;
10 being involved in, protecting, and covering up smuggling.[4]

A few months later, in January 1994, the Professional Ethical Codes for People's Police were made public and came into effect. They were concise, with only eight lines emphasizing the eight moral characters that police officers must possess:

1   be loyal to the Party, the Constitution, and the motherland;
2   serve the public wholeheartedly;
3   enforce the law impartially;
4   be honest;
5   be united in cooperation;
6   be devoted to the profession;
7   observe discipline;
8   be civilized in providing public service.[5]

Code of ethics can help "define acceptable conduct" by "providing guidance to public officials on doing good and avoiding evil" (Plant 2001: 309). The above "ten forbids" and "eight musts" were designed to achieve that goal in China's police force, an important unit in the nation's campaign against corruption. To reaffirm the official determination to combat corruption in police force, the Chinese authorities made public in September 2006 the "Declaration of Honest Government in China's Public Security" (Zhou 2006). The oath of conduct requires that all police officers, for the sake of the nation's prosperity and the people's peace and tranquility, fight against all criminal activities until their last drop of blood and that, for the sake of their sacred mission, they be content with scanty means and lead an honest life while serving the public.

However, codes of ethics are not a panacea for the bureaucratic pathology. As Terry L. Cooper has pointed out, they "usually lack the specific concrete sanctions of legislation and are much broader in the types of conduct covered. ... Many carry only the authority of professional peer esteem and have no formal means for enforcing their prescriptions" (Cooper 1998: 145). For example, An Huijun, Director of the Bureau of Public Security in Luo Hu District of Shenzhen City, allegedly solicited sex service from her male colleagues and was detained for investigation in October 2003 (Luo 2004). It was disclosed in November 2006 that He Qi, Deputy Director of the Bureau of Public Security in Shang Luo County of Shannxi Province, defying the police's mission of combating criminal activities, committed flagrant crimes of organizing prostitution, selling drugs, extortion and robbery for almost ten years (Yin et al. 2006). Xu Xiaogang, Deputy Director of the Bureau of Public Security in Jiangxi Province, extorted a total of 450,000 yuan from the master of an underground society in order to assist his mistress in opening her business.[6] Apparently, these corrupted officers let the codes of ethics in one ear and immediately out the other.

Inner constraints can also be achieved through education. Courts, where justice is administered and where corrupted officials are prosecuted, tried, and sentenced, have become an increasingly important battleground in combating corruption in recent China. However, as a scholar of law observed, some of the courts at different levels turned out to be "disaster areas" of corruption themselves. Lu Haijun at the Zhongnan University of Economic and Law believed that those courts were staffed with judges who were "three ignorants" (*san mang: wenwang, famang, liumang*) meaning they were ignorant literally, legally and behaviorally (Xinhua 2006b). To respond to exacerbating judicial corruption, the authorities were working hard to improve the quality of judges. In the past there were no required qualifications for members of the judiciary, who typically also held prominent political positions as the judiciary was not independent. In March 2002, China introduced for the first time a professional examination for lawyers, judges, and prosecutors. Meanwhile, training of the judiciary was also being strengthened. In July 2002, the Supreme People's Procuratorate, Tsinghua University, and the World Bank jointly opened a series of special anticorruption courses for procurators (Transparency International 2004: 179). Though coming in slowly, these efforts should yield positive results in the years to follow.

External controls were problematic as well. A retired provincial secretary for the Party's Commission for Discipline Inspection admitted that there was no supervision over him when he was serving as a key leading official of supervision in the province (Xinhua 2006a). Why was it so difficult to implement external control over anticorruption agencies? There were several factors at play. To begin with, talking about corruption within the anticorruption agencies was always taboo as it could tarnish the regime's image as a clean government, raising severe doubts about the authorities' determination to combat corruption and shaking considerably the public's confidence in the official capacity to curb and contain corruption. Therefore, the issue of corruption in anticorruption agencies was never placed on the agenda for deliberation.

In addition, effective supervision over anticorruption agencies would require a multiplicity of control over them, which could significantly challenge the party's monopoly of power, including the exclusive power to handle matters involving corrupted state officers. The Party's generalist committees "exercise leadership over discipline inspection committees in many specific ways. These include the *nomenklatura* system, party groups, and party member discipline" (Manion 2004: 203). This was true for other anticorruption agencies as well. A multiplicity of control over them could effectively terminate the CCP's grip over these very important institutions, which undermines "the overarching Leninist political design of mainland China" (Manion 2004: 202). It was therefore highly unlikely that the Party would forgo its privilege of administration as the sole ruling class.

Moreover, a multiplicity of control over anticorruption agencies would require the active participation by average citizens who watch their behavior from outside. To keep a close eye on the daily activities of the anticorruption officers, however, was never an easy task. It could carry the risk of being considered hostile to the cause of anticorruption. Anyone who had the courage to question the integrity of these agencies or those working there could be arbitrarily labeled as suspects of misconduct no matter how justified their inquiries were, if these agencies or individuals had something to hide. Even more threatening, the reprisals could be particularly harsh. Zeng Jinchun, the Party's former Municipal Secretary for Discipline Inspection of Chenzhou City in Hunan Province, for example, used exactly the power in his hands and avenged any criticism of his misbehavior. He made himself the most terrified figure in the city by punishing relentlessly almost everyone there who attempted to unveil his evil deeds (Yi 2006).

All these difficulties of fighting corruption in anticorruption agencies have posed serious challenges to the wisdom of anyone determined to curb and contain corruption. What should we bear in mind while trying to overcome these obstacles on our way toward a clean government? There are several issues that we must deal with carefully. All of them have something to do with *the dual nature* of anticorruption agencies. The first is *the issue of dual mission*. As pointed out by Madison, government has a dual mission of controlling the governed and itself. So do all the anticorruption agencies. They too must carry out a dual mission: to combat corruption in other parts of the state bureaucracy as well as in their own agencies. Indeed, the second mission is probably more demanding than the first one because anticorruption agencies' primary and principal goal is always to focus on corrupted behavior among state officers in other government institutions rather then within their own organizations. In addition, checking other people's conduct is often less difficult than checking one's own because the latter requires a higher level of emotional intelligence, including a higher level of self-awareness, self-discipline, and self-management, which "influence a person's ability to succeed in coping with environmental demands and pressures" (Robbins 2001: 109). It was the lack of self-discipline that caused a key anticorruption officer his Party membership. Du Xiangcheng, a former Deputy Secretary of the Party's Commission for Discipline Inspection in Hunan Province, was recently caught with a foreign prostitute in a hotel room during his official business trip to Beijing (Xia 2007). While details are scanty, the scandal has once again illustrated the utmost importance of upholding a high degree of self-discipline among officers within the anticorruption agencies.

Another item that we must bear in mind is *the issue of dual environment*. Agencies of anticorruption work in an environment that requires sufficient supervision but also adequate autonomy. Only in an environment where these agencies operate under effective supervision, supervision from different institutions, can they be held accountable. Only in an environment where these agencies enjoy proper autonomy can they focus on their operations without unnecessary interference. There were anticorruption officers unhappy with their agencies, either for lack of independence or for lack of supervision. Luo Ji, who served as the first Director of China's General Bureau of Anticorruption in the late 1990s, complained that the agency had a lower status and less autonomy than its counterpart in Hong Kong, the Independent Anticorruption Commission. As a result, its ability often fell short of its ambitions (Wang 2004). Recently, we heard the criticism that anticorruption agencies did not have enough supervision, as mentioned earlier in the article. Both opinions were reasonable, though they failed to realize that anticorruption agencies operate in a dual environment where there must be sufficient supervision as well as adequate autonomy. Neither of these two conditions can be dispensed with.

There is also *the issue of dual loyalty*. Anticorruption officers are all Party members whose allegiance lies first and foremost with the CCP. It is the CCP that assigns them to combat corruption. They demonstrate their loyalty to the Party by fulfilling the task thoroughly and completely. Being devoted to their duty means being faithful to the Party. There is no conflict between the two loyalties. Difficulties have arisen when they were to discipline and prosecute certain corrupted officials but the Party told them not to, especially when evidence pointed to important figures within the Party. Should anticorruption officers place their primary loyalty in the Party or in their profession when the interests of the two conflict with each other? It was their dual loyalty that made it uniquely difficult to find an answer to the question. Wei and Wu, both being the chief anticorruption officers and serving at the Standing Committee of the Party's Politburo, the most powerful decision-making body in the country, realized that they were still powerless when trying to resolve the quandary. As mentioned earlier, they had no choice but to resign. Although their requests were turned down, the dilemma facing the anticorruption fighters remained and continued to haunt them in their daily operation.

Conclusion

Anticorruption agencies in China have been charged with the important task of cleaning the government. Unfortunately, they have become a dirty "disaster area" of corruption. In addition to a series of factors contributing to corruption in the public sector in general, plenty of temptations coupled with a lack of supervision have made corruption a big issue in anticorruption agencies.

Recent development in China has indicated that to a larger degree, corruption in the anticorruption agencies has contributed to administrative misbehavior in the public sector. Although little can be done in regard to the high temptations, the goal of exercising effective supervision over anticorruption agencies is attainable. What we must bear in mind while trying to cope with corruption in anticorruption agencies is that these agencies are actually assigned a dual mission, that they have to operate in a dual environment, and that anticorruption officers have a dual loyalty. Only with a full understanding of these challenges they are faced with can we proceed on our way toward a clean government, fostering and fortifying the sense of duty, morality, and accountability among anticorruption officers. Still, this is just one of the first steps. Therefore, "we need to stand firm, protect our cherished values, and resist going with the flow, the latest fads and fancies of the moment, however smartly dressed up. We must stick to what has been proven to work and improve the lot of all humanity" (Caiden 2007: 273). Yet what exactly can we do to address these challenges in order to promote and preserve an adequate sense of personal integrity in anticorruption agencies? The question merits more of our exploration if we are determined in our pursuit of an honest public administration.

Notes

* This chapter is a revised version of an article entitled "The dual nature of anticorruption agencies in China," which has appeared in *Crime, Law and Social Change*, 49 (2, March 2008).
1 Ma Wen also serves as the head of the newly established National Corruption Prevention Bureau (NCPR), which aims to address the lack of preventive policies against corruption in private companies and non-governmental agencies, see Xinhua (2007a).
2 It should be pointed out that there are several other agencies that are also involved in anticorruption activities to a different degree. One example is the National Office of Audit, which was established in 1983 under the State Council. See He (2005).
3 The National Bureau of Corruption Prevention (NBCP) was set up on 17 September 2007. See *China Daily*, 20 December 2007. See also Xinhua (2007b).
4 See http://www.xs.gd.cn/fg/police/14803.html (25 August 2006). The "ten forbids" were reissued in February 2006. See also www.mps.gov.cn/gab/flfg/info_detail.jsp? infoId = 614 (accessed 22 November 2006).
5 See www.xs.gd.cn/fg/police/16235.html (accessed 22 November 2006).
6 See www.chinanews.com.cn/sh.news/2007/01–12/853054.shtml (accessed 1 November 2006).

References

Caiden, G. (1990) "Abuse of public trust: fact or way of life?" *USA Today Magazine*, July; reprinted in H.R. Balanoff (ed.) *Public Administration 1990–91: Annual Editions* (3rd edn, 1993) New York: William C. Brown.
—— (2001) "Corruption and governance," in G.E. Caiden, O.P. Dwivedi, and J. Jabbra (eds) *Where Corruption Lives*, Bloomfield, Connecticut: Kumarian Press.
—— (2007) "The civilizing mission of public administration," in Demetrios Argyriades, O.P. Dwivedi, and J.G. Jabbra (eds) *Public Administration in Transition: A Fifty-year Trajectory Worldwide,* Portland, Oregon: Vallentine Mitchell.
Cooper, T.L. (1998) *The Responsible Administrator: An Approach to Ethics for the Administrative Role* (4th edn), San Francisco: Jossey-Bass.

CSEP (Center for the Study of Ethics in the Professional) (1989) "Law Enforcement Code of Ethics," International Association of Chiefs of Police, online. Available at http://ethics.iit.edu/codes/coe/int.assoc.chiefs.police.law.enforcement.coe.1989.html (accessed 30 March 2007)

Finer, H. (1941) "Administrative responsibility in democratic government," *Public Administration Review*, 1: 335–50.

Friedrich, C.J. (1940) "Public policy and the nature of administrative responsibility," in C.J. Friedrich and E.S. Mason (eds) *Public Policy: A Yearbook of the Graduate School of Public Administration*, Cambridge, MA: Harvard University Press.

Gong, T. (2004) "Dependent judiciary and unaccountable judges: judicial corruption in contemporary China," *China Review*, 4(2): 33–54.

Guang, J. (2005a) "Wu Guanzheng, secretary of the central commission for discipline inspection, tenders his resignation," *Cheng Ming Monthly*, September.

—— (2005b) "The central commission for discipline inspection shakes the central secretariat," *Cheng Ming Monthly*, November.

He, L.D. (2005) "Neidi fantan guanyuan gangshi peixun" (China's anticorruption officials receive training in Hong Kong), 21 December, online. Available at www.hn.xinhuanet.com/2005–12/21/content_5868214.htm (accessed 20 February 2006).

Li, H.J. (2007) "National Bureau of Corruption Prevention is completely unnecessary," 13 March, online. Available at http://gb.cri.cn/9083/2007/03/13/1965@1495183.htm (accessed 13 March 2007).

Ling, C (2005) "Tracing the changing trend of corruption by analyzing the high-profile cases," 22 March, online. Available at www.people.com.cn/GB/14576/14528/3261594.html (accessed 9 November 2006).

Luo, C.P. (2004) "Luohu's public security chief was 'double detained' for receiving sex bribery," 7 December, online. Available at www.qzwb.com/gb/content/2004–12/07/content_1455513.htm (accessed 8 December 2004).

Ma, S.K. (1989) "Reform corruption: a discussion on China's current development," *Pacific Affairs*, 62(1, Spring): 40–52.

Madison, J. (1985 [1788]) "Federalist No. 51," reprinted in A.T. Mason and G.E. Baker (eds) *Free Government in the Making* (4th edn), New York: Oxford University Press.

Manion, M. (2004) *Corruption by Design: Building Clean Government in Mainland China and Hong Kong*, Cambridge, MA: Harvard University Press.

Plant, J.F. (2001) "Codes of ethics," in T.L. Cooper (ed.) *Handbook of Administrative Ethic* (2nd edn), New York: Marcel Dekker.

Robbins, S.P. (2001) *Organizational Behavior* (9th edn), Upper Saddle River, NJ: Prentice Hall.

Sun, F.H. (1995) "Dangqian fubai yu shehuizhuyi jiandu tizhi yanjiu" (A study on the current corruption and socialist system of supervision), *Beijing Shehui Kexue*, February: 127–34.

Sun, Yan (2004) *Corruption and Market in Contemporary China*, Ithaca: Cornell University Press.

Transparency International (2004) *Global Corruption Report 2004: Special Focus: Political Corruption*, London: Pluto Press.

—— (2006) "Report on the Transparency International Global Corruption Barometer 2006," online. Available at www.transparency.org/policy_research/surveys_indices/gcb/2006, (accessed 20 March 2007), p. 6.

Wang, C (2004) "The first anticorruption bureau chief unveils the story of how the anticorruption institutes come into being," 5 March, online. Available at http://news.163.com/2004w03/12482/2004w03_1078456738210.html (accessed 14 April 2004).

World Bank (2007) "Data regulation: measuring governance and corruption," in W. L. Richter and F. Burke (eds) *Combating Corruption, Encouraging Ethics: A Practical Guide to Management Ethics* (2nd edn), Lanham, MD: Rowman and Littlefield.

Xia, S.F. (2007) "Du Xiangcheng, Hunan's vice secretary of commission of discipline inspection, was ousted from the Party for involving in obscene activities," 12 April, online. Available at www.chinanews.com.cn/sh.news/2007/01–12/853054.shtml (accessed 1 November 2006).

Xinhua (2006a) "Former secretary of provincial commission for discipline inspection on ten years' fight against corruption," 2 November, online. Available at http://news.xinhuanet.com/lianzheng/2006–11/02/content_5280509.htm (accessed 3 November 2006).

—— (2006b) "Numerous Shenzhen judges were detained, senior officials come to Guangdong," 6 November, online. Available at http://news.xinhuanet.com/legal/2006–11/06/content_5295601.htm (accessed 8 November 2006).

—— (2007a) "China's new corruption prevention body eyes non-governmental agencies, companies," 17 September, online. Available at http://english.peopledaily.com.cn/90001/90776/6265690.html (accessed 20 May 2008).

—— (2007b) "Anticorruption website crashes on the first day," 20 December, online. Available at www.chinadaily.com.cn/cndy/2007–12/20/content_6334248.htm (accessed 20 May 2008).

Yao, W.S. (1995) "Lianzheng zhuanmen jizhi jianshe chutan" (A preliminary study on mechanisms promoting an honest government), *Zhongguo Faxue*, April: 19–24

Yi, S (2006) "How Chenzhou's secretary of commission for discipline inspection abuses his power," 8 October, online. Available at http://news.xinhuanet.com/lianzheng/2006–10/08/content_5176342.htm (accessed 9 October 2006).

Yin, B.M., Zhan, B.Y., and Li, S.F. (2006) "Vice bureau chief of Shanyang public security was prosecuted for organizing prostitution," 3 November, online. Available at http://news.xinhuanet.com/legal/2006–11/03/content_5284390.htm (accessed 4 November 2006).

Zheng, L.Z. (2004) "Jiangsu's anticorruption bureau chief Han Jianlin was 'double-detained'," 19 June, online. Available at http://finance.sina.com.cn/careerlife/20040619/0907823577.shtml (accessed 20 June 2004).

Zhou, R.H. (2006) "Declaration of honest government in China's public security," 30 September, online. Available at http://news.xinhuanet.com/legal/2006–9/30/content_5156550.htm (21 November 2006).

7 Preventing corruption through performance measurement

The case of China

Hon S. Chan and Jie Gao

During the past half century, Chinese authorities have relied on enforcing anticorruption measures in a campaign style to curb the power abuse of the cadres for private gain. The features, function, logic, and effects of conducting these anticorruption campaigns have been the focus of mainstream literature. However, studies indicate that campaign-style enforcement methods are by nature ad hoc measures designed to relieve public resentment or to cool down the overheating economy rather than a systematic strategy for controlling corruption (Manion 2004; Quade 2007). Though conducting routine anticorruption campaigns may temporarily deter cadres' corrupt behavior, eventually it leads to the intensification of high-stakes, high-level corruption in Chinese public sectors (Wedeman 2005).

Having recognized the weaknesses of campaign-style anticorruption strategies, Chinese authorities have begun moving towards institutional building and more forceful implementation of anticorruption policies since the 1990s. To this end they have initiated various measures and made some progress toward regulating the stock and real-estate markets, restructuring the state-owned enterprises, rationalizing the cadre personnel management system, and improving supervision by local people's congresses and anticorruption agencies (He 2000). In particular, the Chinese authorities have put much emphasis on developing a target-based responsibility system for building an upright "Party style"[1] and clean government in Party and government organizations, state-owned enterprises, and various social institutes. The rationale is to clarify the responsibilities of leading cadres at all levels for controlling corruption by using clearly defined performance targets and measures. Each year, local leadership cadres are required to sign performance contracts with the next-higher-level authorities for building an upright Party style and clean government. At each level, the task is translated into a number of concrete tasks or targets. Each leading cadre is held responsible for accomplishing one or several specific targets. In some localities, concrete, quantifiable indicators have been developed to measure the accomplishments of the leading cadres with regard to the assigned targets. Failure to attain the targets entails severe penalties for leading officials, such as an intra-Party warning, salary reduction, demotion, or even removal from their current positions. It is clear that the central authorities have intended to establish a long-term mechanism for preventing corruption by strengthening the performance accountability of local leading cadres.

However, the increasingly rampant corruption during the past twenty years reveals that implementing this target-based responsibility system for building an upright Party style and clean government has not achieved noticeable results. The work reports of the People's Supreme Procuratorate indicate that the number of corrupt local officials at and above the county level reached 13,929 in 2008, a 665 percent increase over the 1999 figure. The number of corruption cases involving amounts over 500,000 yuan was 1,773 in 1999, while those involving amounts over 1 million yuan reached 35,255 in 2008 (Supreme People's Procuratorate of the People's Republic of China 2008). Apparently the adoption of concrete and objective cadre evaluations has not done very much to curb the cadres' corrupt behaviors. So, what is going wrong? Is it possible for the target-based responsibility system to prevent local cadre wrongdoings? What are the strengths and weaknesses of this system? To date, mainstream literature has done little to address these issues.

This chapter selects one locale to examine closely the target-based responsibility system for building an upright Party style and clean government. Empirical data come from two months of fieldwork investigation conducted in a single Chinese inland county (Zhouzhi) in July 2006 and August 2007. Based on in-depth interviews with 23 local leading cadres and a careful examination of related official documents, reports, and other materials, this paper argues that the target-based responsibility system is sound in theory but weak in practice. The system is designed mainly to institute an *ex ante* mechanism to prevent corruption at its source by clarifying the tasks and responsibilities of each leading cadre in controlling corruption. But we have found that implementing the system has met with a number of difficulties. Some are related to how targets are measured and may not be too difficult to overcome. Because of local variance in socioeconomic and political conditions, officials in different localities have adopted different ways of prioritizing evaluation targets. While officials in some localities focus on anticorruption, those in other places do not make this the most important target. But the most fundamental problem in implementing the target-based system is that political patronage always compromises its effectiveness. Because of the way that authority is distributed among the Party committees, the discipline inspection commissions, and the procuratorate, the senior leadership can interfere with cases of corruption whenever they wish. A Party committee can deal with corruption on a case-by-case basis. Owing to these problems, adopting the target-based responsibility system for corruption control results in nothing more than pouring old wine into new bottles.

Background

In the late 1990s, after the Chinese Communist Party (CCP) had completed four intensive anticorruption campaigns, corruption in local governments was still rampant, which was increasingly tarnishing the regime's image and undermining the government's legitimacy. The CCP's top leaders determined to experiment with ways to enhance institution building and policy enforcement in order to deal with the problem. Efforts were made to develop and enforce concrete measures in order to systemize corruption-control mechanisms. In 1998, the CCP Central Committee promulgated a milestone document that proposed making the appraisal of the local leading cadres' accomplishments in corruption control a component of their annual performance evaluation. The responsibilities of leading cadres at all levels were to be clarified at the beginning of each year in the form of performance targets. At the end of the year, the next-higher-level Party committee's organization department would send an inspection team to evaluate the leading cadres' accomplishments in anticorruption work. The next-higher-level anticorruption agencies—the Party discipline inspection commission, the supervision bureau, the court, and the procuratorate—were to assist the same-level Party committee in monitoring the system's implementation. Based on the evaluation results, the Party committee and the anticorruption agencies would decide whether to reward or punish a cadre (Central Committee of the Chinese Communist Party 1998).

As a set of national guidelines, the central document did not specify in detail how anticorruption work should be translated into concrete targets in local organizations. Nor did it give specific suggestions as to how to evaluate local cadres' performance on anticorruption work. Instead, it allowed local officials considerable discretion in stipulating their own anticorruption targets and formulating specific indicators to evaluate the work accomplishment based on these targets. Because of this, local anticorruption agencies with different responsibilities had a certain leeway in developing "coping strategies" to meet the national requirements. If local leading cadres wanted to take anticorruption work seriously, they could develop concrete, quantifiable indicators for assessing accomplishment. If they did not want to take it seriously, they could adopt a responsibility system without any specific substance that would give it teeth.

Our investigated case illustrates how the target-based responsibility system operates at the local level. Zhouzhi County is under the administration of Xi'an, the capital city of Shaanxi Province. Shortly after the Central Party promulgated the milestone document in 1998, the Shaanxi Provincial Government required all its local governments to adopt the target-based responsibility system and evaluate its implementation annually. In 2000, the Shaanxi local governments began translating the anticorruption work into specific tasks and distributing concrete responsibilities with respect to their accomplishment to the leading cadres of Party and government organizations at various levels. The provincial discipline inspection commission, on behalf of the provincial Party committee, translated the broad directives into 37 specific tasks. Sixty-one organizations directly under the provincial government and eleven provincial Party committee members were held responsible, separately or jointly, for the accomplishment of these tasks (Shaanxi Provincial Government 2000). In a similar vein, city- and county-level discipline inspection commissions started to develop their own lists of responsible people and organizations, using the provincial list as a guide, and assigned specific tasks to subordinate offices and organizations. Since then, every year the discipline inspection commissions at various levels in Shaanxi Province have revised their tasks of building an upright Party style and clean government according to the new directives issued by the higher-level authorities, which they have distributed to all the same-level Party and government organizations, the people's courts and procuratorates, the people's congresses and political consultative conferences, social organizations, and state-owned enterprises.

Institutional design: preventing corruption at its source

In essence, the target-based responsibility system for building an upright Party style and clean government is a device to systemize corruption control by clarifying the objectives and responsibilities of each individual leading cadre. It builds a multiple-level accountability system that ties cadres at different levels together for accomplishing specific anticorruption tasks— leading cadres at the higher level are held responsible and punished for the wrongdoings of the next-lower-level cadres, and vice versa. To some extent, this institutional design may constrain the excessive use of the leading cadres' power. In the local governments of Shaanxi, the target-based responsibility system has created three levels of accountability—leading cadres at three different levels are held responsible for accomplishing the anticorruption work assigned by the Party discipline inspection commissions at the corresponding level.

For example, in 2007 the Zhouzhi County discipline inspection commission translated the higher authorities' general anticorruption directives into 75 targets (Table 7.1). Accomplishment of each target is under the supervision of one organization with primary responsibility and several organizations with secondary responsibility. These responsible organizations then translated each target into more concrete indicators corresponding to their job functions and distributed the newly made indicators further down to the leading cadres of subordinate offices and organizations.

Target 28 in Table 7.1 sheds light on how the three levels of accountability operate. At the county level, the deputy head of Zhouzhi County in charge of agricultural and environmental protection work is held responsible for accomplishing five targets. At a lower level, there is a further division of responsibility: the primary responsible organization, the County Farmers' Burden Alleviation Small Leading Group, coordinates and supervises the work of the secondary responsible organizations, which include the County Work Style Correction Office, the Supervision Bureau, the Agriculture Bureau, the Price Bureau, and the Finance Bureau. These secondary responsible organizations are required to develop their own specified indicators. The

Table 7.1 Division of responsibilities for building an upright Party style and clean government plus anticorruption work in Zhouzhi County (2007)

Task no.*	Tasks and requirements	Primary units	Main organizing units
2	(1) Strengthen supervision and inspection of the fulfillment and implementation of the Central Party's "Decisions on Several Important Problems for Constructing a Harmonious Socialist Society" and the Provincial Party Committee's "Implementing Opinions" so as to resolve the most pressing, direct, and practical problems and other issues and concerns of greatest interest to the people (2) Take concrete action to accomplish the various tasks and foster construction of a harmonious Zhouzhi County	County Discipline Inspection Commission; Party Committee General Office	County Government General Office; Planning and Development Commission; Finance Bureau; Agriculture Bureau; Environmental Protection Bureau; Supervision Bureau
18	(1) Strengthen the supervision and inspection of civil service wage reform and the standardization of subsidies and allowances (2) Firmly stop the unlawful distribution of money and other items of value and other activities that breach Party discipline and violate related rules and regulations	County Finance Bureau	County Government General Office; Discipline Inspection Commission; Supervision Bureau; Finance Bureau
28	(1) Take concrete actions to implement related rules, regulations, decisions, and policies that help to alleviate the farmers' burden and correct arbitrary fee collection, arbitrary fines, unlawful financing, and unlawful appropriation (2) Set strict rules on charging for agricultural water/electricity utilization (3) Investigate and deal with cases regarding the manufacturing or selling of false and inferior agricultural materials and the artificial marking-up of the prices of agricultural materials (4) Resolve serious problems that damage the farmers' rights and interests in land with regard to contracting, requisition, and expropriation of land (5) Resolve issues related to work in agricultural production, the life of the countryside, and farmer livelihoods	County Farmers' Financial Burden Alleviation Small Leading Group	County Work Style Correction Office; Supervision Bureau; Agriculture Bureau; Price Bureau; Finance Bureau

Continued on next page

Table 7.1 (continued)

Task no.*	Tasks and requirements	Primary units	Main organizing units
50	(1) Deepen reform of cadre personel management; implement the comprehensive evaluation methods for the leadership corps and leading cadres; take concrete actions to implement relevant systems and measures (2) Prevent the distortion of investigation results and the promotion or appointment of undesirable leaders	County Party Organization Department	County Discipline Inspection Commission; Supervision Bureau; Personnel and Labor Bureau
66	(1) Strengthen supervision and inspection of urban construction management and use of the allocated funds for the construction projects only	County Finance Bureau	County Supervision Bureau; Planning and Development Commission; Construction Bureau; Land Resources Bureau; Auditing Bureau
73	(1) Supervise and urge the leading cadres to promote good Party style (2) Have discipline inspection commissions at all levels carry out their duties and responsibilities to organize, coordinate, and supervise the work of building the work style of cadres under the leadership of the Party committee	Discipline Inspection Commission of the County	County Party Committee Organization Department; Working Committee of the Organization Directly under the Central Government and Supervision Bureau

Source: Zhouzhi County Discipline Inspection Commission (2007) "List of target-based responsibilities on building an upright Party style and anti-corruption work in Zhouzhi County," internal document.
Note:
* This table only lists tasks discussed in the text.

heads of both the primary and secondary responsible organizations are then held responsible for accomplishing the specified indicators.

Within the Finance Bureau, the target of alleviating the farmers' tax burden is assigned to the person in charge of collecting the agricultural tax. Hence, the head of the Agricultural Tax Section of the Finance Bureau takes primary responsibility for farmers' complaints about their heavy tax burden, together with two deputy heads of the Finance Bureau and the County Deputy Head. The career prospects of the leading cadres at three different levels (county, bureau, and section) are thus tied together as far as accomplishing the assigned targets is concerned.

The leading cadres' accomplishments in anticorruption work are to be taken as important evidence when making significant decisions regarding their compensations and careers. Failure to meet their assigned targets is supposed to result in severe punishment: leadership corps members with unsatisfactory achievement in anticorruption work are to receive criticism and salary reductions, and may be barred from participating in reorganizing the leadership corps.

The advantage of adopting such a multiple-level accountability mechanism is sound in theory. Since the corrupt behavior of the leading cadres is detrimental to both their own and their supervisors' careers, it is important that they assure the integrity of their subordinates. With multiple checks on the power of the leading cadres, the target-based responsibility system would thus appear capable of preventing corruption at its source.

As for the content of the performance targets on building an upright Party style and clean government, emphasis is given to using moral education to scour corruption from the cadres' thinking. As their own personal morality is vital in controlling corruption, cadres at all levels need to receive regular moral education on building Party style and preventing corruption. Each year general goals on moral education are issued by the province and distributed to cities and counties. The city- and county-level discipline inspection commissions then produce a list of responsibilities that include more concrete moral education targets (for example, setting up propaganda billboards and conducting regular meetings on building an upright Party style and clean government) and organizations responsible for accomplishing these targets.

For various reasons, such as deficient supervision, huge monetary temptations, and the desire for a luxurious lifestyle, many cadres choose to suppress their individual morality and break the law. But many other cadres have breached Party discipline only "slightly" and have not committed serious crimes. In logic, these individuals can still be re-educated and "rescued" from becoming corrupt (Dong 2003). Therefore, in recent years Shaanxi Province has focused particularly on strengthening the re-education of cadres who have a "tendency" towards corruption but whose wrongdoings are not serious enough to break criminal law. Local governments have developed three kinds of warning and admonishing targets for "problematic" leading cadres. First, cadres about whom the people have complained or who have violated moral rules should be warned. Second, cadres who have problems such as serious bureaucratism or being "too bold" in their work (i.e. being close to transgressing the established rules) should be admonished. Third, cadres having a "corrupt tendency" should be persuaded to correct their wrongdoings (Shaanxi Provincial Discipline Inspection Commission and Shaanxi Supervision Department 2003). Theoretically speaking, although it is difficult to differentiate among the three levels, the warning and criticism can help to prevent corrupt behaviors in advance. In some cases it has been possible to correct cadres' wrongdoings and in others to deter them from violating the law.

Implementation hurdles

In practice, however, implementation hurdles diminish the effectiveness of the target-based responsibility system for controlling corruption. Our investigation into the Shaanxi local governments and collected information from other parts of China indicate three major difficulties that make the smooth implementation of the target-based responsibility system uncertain.

Measuring targets

Obviously, high measurability for performance targets—targets that are concrete, precise, and easy to assess—is vital for tracking useful performance information on local cadres' accomplishments in anticorruption work and deciding on rewards and punishments. However, among the local governments of Shaanxi, the measurability of anticorruption targets varies across organizations. The leadership corps' support for the system is clearly highly important for developing targets that can be measured objectively and put into operation easily.

Performance targets adopted by some organizations, such as the Zhouzhi County Local Tax Bureau, are as abstract as, for example, "implementing full-scale open administration and improving management and supervision mechanisms." In addition, no organizations are held responsible for the accomplishment of each task. In fact, these targets are not formulated by the bureau itself. Most targets are formulated by the city as work requirements for all lower-level local tax organizations. The Zhouzhi Local Tax Bureau simply adopts the targets word-for-word as its own and subsequently distributes them to its sixteen subordinate organizations. Understandably, these targets bear little reference to the distinct job situation in Zhouzhi.[2] As far as the Zhouzhi Local Tax Bureau's particular situation is concerned, these targets are devoid of specific content.

Some leading cadres take the target-based responsibility system more seriously. For example, in 2004 the Weiyang District of Xi'an City used specific and quantified indicators to measure performance on building an upright Party style and clean government. The work was divided into six performance targets, including preventing corruption at its source, strengthening law enforcement and supervision, rectifying mistakes in work, and so on. Leading cadres' accomplishments on each performance target were measured by concrete and quantifiable indicators. An excellent goal accomplishment would receive more points in evaluation. For example, one indicator under the target of "preventing corruption at its source" was that "officials have realistically enforced the rules, separated revenues and expenditures, ensured that all revenue collection activities have been delinked from revenue management, and have gradually brought all administrative fees into annual budget planning." Four points were to be awarded for an excellent job on this, three for an average, and two for a poor (Weiyang District Government 2004). Clearly, with leadership support in developing specific, quantifiable indicators for measuring anticorruption work, the target-based responsibility system is likely to generate some positive results.

The same feature of using easily measurable targets and precise, quantifiable indicators for corruption control is also found in other regions of the country. For example, in 2005 Pingliang City of Gansu Province divided the major work on building an upright Party style and clean government into 38 specific tasks under six categories. In January 2006, the city conducted a quantified evaluation of the leadership corps' comprehensive performance of the allocated tasks. All these offices, organizations, and county governments were ranked by four grades—excellent, good, satisfactory, or bad. Seventy-seven organizations were ranked as "excellent," and not one organization received a "bad" rating. Individual leading cadres were also ranked by quantified assessment into four grades: excellent, competent, basically competent, and incompetent. Among the 473 county-level leading cadres, 148 (31.3 percent) received an "excellent" rating, 303 (64.1 percent) were "competent," nineteen (4 percent) were "basically competent," and three (0.6 percent) were rated "incompetent." Based on the evaluation results, the city investigated and finally disciplined 18 leading cadres. Twenty-six received warnings and admonishment in the year-end evaluation exercise (Pingliang City Party Committee and City Government 2006).

The measurability of the actual anticorruption targets shows that political will is important in trying to make government reform measures stick (Peters and Savoie 2000: 5–7; Chan and Li 2007). The examples mentioned above indicate that while officials at higher levels might put one set of priorities on the anticorruption targets, the local leadership corps carry out their own priorities, designing targets tailor-made to their own specific preferences and with their own evaluation criteria. Without leadership support, the target-based responsibility system is simply an exercise in paperwork.

Prioritizing goals

Under the current appraisal system, local leading cadres are held responsible for their accomplishments on a variety of targets. Besides anticorruption, local officials also need to accomplish many targets on social and economic development, such as enforcing birth control, ensuring safety production, improving the net annual income of peasants, attracting capital and investments, and so forth. To guarantee their own career advancement, local officials tend to give higher priority to accomplishing some targets (e.g. economic growth) than to pursuing the anticorruption work.

Most Xi'an local governments give four targets the weight to negate all others—family planning, production safety, handling of public complaints, and comprehensive social security.[3] If local officials fail to accomplish these targets, they lose the opportunity to attend the year-end evaluation, and hence the chance to obtain any bonuses, no matter how successfully they have met other targets. In addition, failure in the "targets that negate all others" may result in harsh penalties for leading cadres, such as salary decreases, demotions, or removal from current positions. Therefore, local leading cadres give these targets top priority for implementation as the results put substantial pressure on their future career prospects.

Also, it is common practice for local leading cadres to focus on accomplishing targets on economic development because these targets are formulated and assigned by governments at higher levels. The economic development targets are first established by the central government as broad policy objectives and then distributed to local governments at various levels in the form of more specific, concrete, and quantified indicators. To ensure local accomplishment of the national goals, targets are often set higher and higher at lower levels. For example, in 2005, the Central Government stipulated that the annual growth rate of the national GDP from 2005 to 2010 should be 7.5 percent (State Council of the People's Republic of China 2006). When this target was distributed to Shaanxi Province, the annual growth rate of the GDP was set at 11 percent by the end of 2010 (Shaanxi Provincial Reform and Development Commission 2006). Down a level, Xi'an Municipality was required to set its GDP growth to be set at 13 percent (Xi'an City Reform and Development Commission 2006), while the counties under the administration of Xi'an City were required to reach 12–13 percent (Zhouzhi County Government 2006). As China has adopted a one-level-down management system, the supervisors have full authority to make personnel decisions about subordinate officials. Hence, local officials tend to accomplish economic development targets rather than, say, the anticorruption targets because their own career prospects are tied to those of their supervisors.

Accomplishing economic development targets may in fact sometimes foster corruption in local governments. For example, He Minxu, the former Vice Head of Anhui Province, was removed from his position in June 2006 and prosecuted for "economic corruption, serious dereliction of duty, and deteriorated lifestyle." When He was Party Secretary of Chizhou City of Anhui Province in 2005, he provided businessmen with "preferential policies" aimed at attracting foreign investments for the special economic and technology zones in Chizhou. To obtain these policies, many businessmen bribed He with large sums of money and many sexual partners. In one case, He received 300,000 yuan as a bribe for transferring land use rights at an extremely cheap rate. The Central Discipline Inspection Commission (CDIC) found that He had taken over 8 million yuan during his term of office.[4] Indeed, cases of commercial bribery have become rampant ever since the CCP decided to further promote local economic development. Statistics show that during the first half of 2007, the procuratorates dealt with 24,879 cases of commercial bribery involving a total of 6.156 billion yuan.[5]

Patronage politics

As has been the case with all prior CCP anticorruption efforts, the target-based responsibility system for building an upright Party style and clean government operates under Party leadership. Party committees at all levels are still the chief units responsible for corruption control through their executive arm, the discipline inspection commissions at respective levels of government. The CDIC conducts its work under the leadership of the Politburo of the Central Party Committee, while the local discipline inspection commissions operate under the leadership of the Party committees at the corresponding levels. The next-higher-level discipline inspection commission has the power to overrule or alter decisions made by the discipline inspection commission on the level just below it. For example, Party committees at any level could decide to file charges against an ordinary Party committee member. The case-initiation decision, therefore, would occur before any decision to start an investigation, including a criminal one. That said, Party committees at various levels have broad, unregulated discretion to handle, on a case-by-case basis, cadres who have violated Party discipline. Party members, especially leading cadres, can be protected from the sanctioning of the discipline inspection commission because the power of case initiation is placed with the Party committee (Central Discipline Inspection Commission 1994).

In addition, Party members and cadres can be protected from more serious sanctioning by the criminal justice system. When a corruption case is reported to the anticorruption agencies, if the cadres are Party members the discipline inspection commission at the corresponding level always investigates the case first. After the commission confirms that the case has breached Party discipline and criminal laws, it transfers the related materials to the procuratorates at the corresponding level for further action (Central Discipline Inspection Commission and Supreme People's Procuratorate 1998). However, in practice political patronage between the Party committee and the cadre who has violated the law can easily delay, hinder, or even prevent the case from being transferred to the procuratorate.

Two recent cases illustrate how politics intrudes into the handling of corruption cases. After the CDIC looked into allegations of a diversion of Shanghai pension funds into real-estate and infrastructure projects in September 2006, Chen Liangyu, the former Party Secretary of Shanghai and a member of the Politburo, was arrested for aiding illegal business activity, shielding corrupt colleagues, and abusing his position to benefit relatives. Chen ultimately lost his positions in the Party and the government, including his membership in the Politburo. Some observers, including the *New York Times* (25 September 2006), insisted that this purge was actually a political fight between Hu Jintao, the new Party Secretary of China, and the heirs of the influential Shanghai-centered political machine built by Jiang Zemin, China's former leader. Hu's crackdown on the corruption of Shanghai senior officials was considered more of a political maneuver than a genuine effort to fight graft. However, the purge did not go easily. It was only after almost a whole year's investigation, in August 2007, that the Central Party decided to revoke Chen's Party membership and send his case for criminal prosecution. In March 2008, Chen was finally sentenced to eighteen years' imprisonment.

By comparison, Zheng Xiaoyu, former Director of China's State Food and Drug Administration, was prosecuted quickly after his case was investigated by the CDIC. The CDIC began investigating his case at the end of 2006, and by May 2007 he was being prosecuted for "corruption (taking bribes worth more than 6.49 million yuan) and dereliction of duty." Zheng was sentenced to death by a Beijing court and executed on 10 July. One important reason Zheng received a criminal penalty so quickly was that the consequences of his dereliction of duty proved extremely serious. Six medicines approved by the administration during his appointment turned out to be fakes that harmed people's lives (*China Daily*, 10 July 2007). His dereliction of duty discredited China's international reputation considerably and further weakened the CCP's already fragile political legitimacy.

The two cases show that since all related rules and regulations allow Party committees at the various levels to exercise their leadership over corruption control on a case-by-case basis, leading cadres can always interfere with the handling of corruption cases. Although the target-based responsibility system appears to have filled in a blank by establishing an accountability mechanism, it has not altered the CCP's fundamental rule in fighting corruption: the anticorruption agencies' decisions to punish a cadre are made more upon political considerations than on justice and fairness. The signal sent by such an institutional design—that corruption control is always placed under the purview and leadership of the Party committee—is that corruption may be tolerated and the perpetrator protected if he or she has a good relationship with superiors. Any anticorruption effort under political patronage can only be, as a Chinese idiom describes, a measure that "scratches the itch from outside one's boots."

Conclusion

Eleven years have passed since the target-based responsibility system on building an upright Party style and clean government was introduced in 1998. Although Chinese leaders have praised the system, which in a way has successfully instituted an *ex ante* mechanism, nonetheless collective corruption—

a group of corrupt people conspiring to pursue individual interests at the public expense—has now become the salient feature of corruption in contemporary China. Because the establishment and improvement of various corruption control mechanisms in recent years has increased the possibility of catching corrupt officials, a corrupt official will often seek to buy off his bosses at higher levels to get the all-important support and protection from above (Gong 2002). Many recent major corruption cases, including the Zhanjiang smuggling case and the Mu Suixin–Ma Xiangdong case in the late 1990s, have demonstrated the involvement of a wide spectrum of leading cadres across different systems and organizations, including the Party, government, judiciary, procuratorate, and public security organizations. As a mechanism for holding leading cadres accountable for their misconduct, the target-based responsibility system has simply not been effective in controlling collective corruption. This paper has shown that at least two contextual factors account for this.

First, the target-based responsibility system is still embedded within the Party cadre evaluation system. In practice this facilitates intrusion of the political will of higher-level authorities into how the system is implemented and evaluated. One of the most noticeable aspects of the evaluation system in local China is its emphasis on assuring that lower-level cadres will comply with the orders from their superiors. Policy goals that are crucial for national economic development (e.g. the GDP), regional economic growth (e.g. local government budget revenue), and maintenance of social stability (e.g. family planning and handling of mass complaints) are assigned and distributed level by level down the administrative hierarchy. The compliance of local officials with higher-level directives is taken as an important, if not the decisive, factor in their career advancement. The cadre evaluation system strives simply to promote an "inverse accountability," which means that accountability is geared toward the accomplishment of higher-level policy goals (Zhao 2007).

We see, therefore, that the importance, loci, magnitude, and intensity of the anticorruption work are largely decided by higher-level authorities. As we have shown, implementation of the target-based responsibility system varies across bureaus as well as localities. Different bureaus develop anticorruption targets with different ways of measuring them. Different localities give anticorruption a different priority in implementation.

The second contextual factor that undermines the entire target-based responsibility system is the cardinal principle of the Party control of cadres. In actual practice, this principle promotes a unified cadre personnel management system whereby Party committees at various levels monopolize authority over all significant personnel decisions. A corrupt cadre may still be promoted if same-level or next-higher-level Party committee members come together to protect the person. In other words, the political patronage system serves to insulate corrupt cadres. The same principle means that supervisory, disciplinary, procuratorate, and judicial organizations have no power to initiate cases of corruption unless the Party committee at the pertinent level gives its approval. If the pertinent Party committee decides to protect a corrupt cadre, it can simply decide against transferring the case to the supervisory organizations for judicial investigation. If the Party committee decides to give up protecting a corrupt cadre, it will first expel that individual from the Party and then send him or her to the supervisory organizations. Thus, the intrusion of political will into corruption control creates a scenario whereby equally corrupt cadres may end up with entirely different fates. Although tracking accountability is the most crucial step for making the target-based responsibility system effective, the real-world situation is that corrupt cadres are not always sanctioned even if they breach Party discipline and violate criminal laws.

We have seen the introduction of more transparent accounting, the separation of revenue and expenditure, the reform of the state treasury's collection and payment system, procurement system reforms, and more. What is missing is a system to deal with the excessive concentration of power. As Karklins (2005) points out, the logic of separating and sharing power is twofold: if there is no monopoly of decision making, the likelihood of corrupt decisions decreases because more people participate in the process and it is more difficult to hide illicit influences. Karklins further adds that demonopolizing power is in itself not enough; it needs to be combined with effective ways to oversee, check, and review decisions (Karklins 2005: 108). When these conditions are not met, it is difficult to expect an effective system of accountability for corruption control. Absent an intention and real efforts toward revamping the entire governance system, a system where power and authority are centralized by the Party committees at all levels, corruption appears embedded in the Chinese political system. Put in this light, it will not be easy for the CCP's new target-based responsibility system for corruption control to achieve the goals that have been set for it.

Notes

1 Party style refers to the cultivation of attitudes and behavior in implementing Party principles in politics, political thought, political organization, political life, and so on.
2 Interview with a deputy section-level cadre in the Local Tax Bureau of Zhouzhi County, Xi'an City, August 2007.
3 While some localities also make anticorruption work a target that negates all others, it was not a widespread phenomenon in Shaanxi local governments at the time of our investigation.
4 Online. Available at http://news.xinhuanet.com/politics/2008–01/04/content_73641 49.htm (accessed 24 June 2008).
5 Online. Available at http://english.people.com.cn/90001/90776/6243004.html (accessed 24 June 2008).

References

Central Committee of the Chinese Communist Party (1998) "Notification on building a target-based responsibility system on building an upright Party style and clean government," internal document.

Central Discipline Inspection Commission (1994) "Work regulations on examining cases by the discipline inspection organizations," online. Available at www.buaa. edu.cn/html/jijianjiancha/fagui/dj17.htm (accessed 23 June 2008).

Central Discipline Inspection Commission and the Supreme People's Procuratorate (1998) "Notice on establishing connection (or transfer) systems between the Party's discipline inspection commission and the supervisory organizations," online. Available at www.sxyc.gov.cn/town/tanshan/djw/djw/wsdxjljcjg17.htm (accessed 23 June 2008).

Chan, H.S. and Li, S.Z. (2007) "Civil service law in the PRC: a return to cadre personnel management," *Public Administration Review*, 67(3): 383–98.

China Daily (2007) "Former SFDA chief executed for corruption," 10 July, online. Available www.chinadaily.com.cn/china/2007–07/10/content_5424937.htm (accessed 24 June 2008).

Dong, L. (2003) "Building the warning and admonishing defense line, and improving the supervision prevention mechanism," *Discipline Inspection and Supervision in China*, 2.

Gong, T. (2002) "Dangerous collusion: corruption as a collective venture in contemporary China," *Communist and Post-Communist Studies*, 35: 85–103.

He, Z.K. (2000) "Corruption and anticorruption in reform China," *Communist and Post-Communist Studies*, 33(2): 243–70.

Karklins, R. (2005) *The System Made Me Do It: Corruption in Post-communist Societies*, New York: M.E. Sharpe.

Manion, M. (2004) *Corruption by Design: Building Clean Government in Mainland China and Hong Kong*, Cambridge, MA: Harvard University Press.

New York Times (2005) "Shanghai Party boss held for corruption," 25 September, online. Available at www.nytimes.com/2006/09/25/world/asia/25china.html?ex=1316 836800&en=13d906631f6a5225&ei=5088&partner=rssnyt&emc=rss (accessed 24 June 2008).

Peters, G. and Savoie, D. (eds) (2000) *Governance in the Twenty-First Century: Revitalizing the Public Service*, Montreal and Kingston: McGill-Queen's University Press.

Pingliang City Party Committee and City Government (2006) "Report on the fulfillment of the target-based responsibility system on building Party style and clean government in Pingliang City in 2005," online. Available at www.pingliang.gov.cn/ PingLiangWebSite/suborganization/document_information_detail.jsp?orgId=16&i_ DocId = 1558&styleCSS = 1&tag = WJZL (accessed 23 June 2008).

Quade, E.A. (2007) "The logic of anticorruption enforcement campaigns in contemporary China," *Journal of Contemporary China*, 16(50): 65–77.

Shaanxi Provincial Discipline Inspection Commission and Shaanxi Supervision Department (2003) "Strengthening the supervision mechanism, and actively exploring the building of warning and admonishing defense lines on fighting corruption," internal document.

Shaanxi Provincial Government (2000) "List of target-based responsibilities for building an upright Party style and anticorruption work in Shaanxi Province in 2000," internal document.

Shaanxi Provincial Reform and Development Commission (2006) "Outline of the eleventh five-year plan for national economic and social development of Shaanxi Province," online. Available at www.shaanxi.gov.cn (accessed 21 June 2008).

State Council of the People's Republic of China (2006) "Outline of the eleventh five-year plan for national economic and social development of the People's Republic of China," online. Available at www.xinhuanet.com (accessed 21 June 2008).

Supreme People's Procuratorate of the People's Republic of China (2008) "Work report of the Supreme People's Procuratorate in 1999 and 2008," online. Available at www.spp.gov.cn (accessed 23 June 2008).

Wedeman, A. (2005) "Anticorruption campaigns and the intensification of corruption in China," *Journal of Contemporary China*, 14(42): 93–116.

Weiyang District Government (2004) "Notification about the implementation method of the objective responsibility system for offices and organizations under Weiyang District," internal document.

Xi'an City Government (2006) "Outline of the eleventh five-year plan for economic and social development of Xi'an Municipality," online. Available at www.xa.gov.cn (accessed 24 June 2008).

Xi'an City Reform and Development Commission (2006) "Outline of the eleventh five-year plan for national economic and social development of Xi'an Municipality," online. Available at www.xa.gov.cn (accessed 21 June 2008).

Zhao, S.K. (2007) "The accountability system of township government," *Chinese Sociology and Anthropology*, 39(2): 64–73.

Zhouzhi County Discipline Inspection Commission (2007) "List of target-based responsibilities on building Party style and anticorruption work in Zhouzhi County," internal document.

Zhouzhi County Finance Bureau (2007) "List of division of responsibilities of Zhouzhi County Finance Bureau for the task for building Party style and clean government and anticorruption work," internal document.

Zhouzhi County Government (2006) "Outline of the eleventh five-year plan for national economic and social development of Zhouzhi County," online. Available www.zhouzhi.gov.cn/Html/zzgk/fzgh/115gh/index.htm (accessed 22 June 2008).

Zhouzhi County Local Tax Bureau (2007) "Performance contract on building Party style and clean government in 2007," internal document.

Part II

Corruption and institutional design

Learning across regions

8 Japan, Korea, the Philippines, China

Four syndromes of corruption

Michael Johnston

Introduction

Is there such a thing as "Asian corruption," in the sense of a particular pattern of corruption that extends across Asia, is clearly shaped by distinctive regional influences, and is not found elsewhere? If not, how do corruption problems vary among Asian societies, what are the key contrasts, what are their sources, and what are their implications for development and reform?

Numerous observers have invoked distinctively Asian varieties of corruption to account for the ways extensive abuses have coexisted with—and in some cases, have seemed to aid—rapid economic growth in several countries. The underlying notion is that there is something about Asia, its corruption, and/or its growth that checks the worst effects of abusive connections between wealth and power. On the other hand, if important variations among Asian societies are found alongside similarities to corruption elsewhere, what are the most important influences, and what deeper dynamics do they reflect?

Those questions are significant not just at a theoretical level but also in terms of reform. What might be called the "consensus playbook" of reforms—transparency, enhanced public management, building up civil society, political liberalization, privatization, independent judiciaries and news media—varies surprisingly little from one society to the next. Appropriate reforms require an understanding of the deeper, long-term forces shaping and sustaining corruption, their links to observable local influences, and careful thought as to how corruption controls might function in a given context. That sort of analysis is essential if we are to sort out important factors from the superficial, and if we are to avoid explanations that consist mostly of putting the label "Asian" on whatever we see in the region.

This chapter offers a discussion of Japan, South Korea, the Philippines, and China as examples of four "syndromes of corruption" (the analysis draws upon Johnston 2005). Those syndromes reflect deeper trends and contrasts in *participation* and *institutions*—in the ways people pursue, use, and exchange wealth and power, and in the state, political, and social institutions that both restrain and sustain those processes. Four syndromes cannot explain all contrasts in corruption—and the discussion will be incomplete in the sense that differences *within* countries, and a systematic approach to cultural factors, are left for future analysis. Nonetheless, the goal is to demonstrate that behind the façade of "Asian corruption" lie important variations as broad as any found globally, reflecting the development of specific societies. Further, while our focus on participation in economies and politics links the analysis to the liberalizing changes that have dominated policy agendas over the past generation, we put equal emphasis upon state, political, and social institutions, and upon the policy capacities of societies as a whole. Without strength in those latter areas it is unlikely that reforms of any sort will prove credible or effective.

Corruption in real societies: influences and contrasts

Why would we expect Asian corruption to be distinctive? Leaving aside the question of what is meant by "Asia," there are many possible answers, yet none has guided scholarly analysis in productive ways. History and culture are two obvious candidates, though both are too general to account for corruption patterns at any but the broadest levels of generalization. Causal arguments based on culture also have a way of becoming circular: people do things because of their culture, and we infer the content of their culture from the things they do. Moreover, historical and cultural factors differ significantly across the region, and thus would seem better able to account for differences than for overriding regional patterns. Technological and economic changes offer promising lines of inquiry, particularly to the extent that they reflect the timing of Asia's transformation and the global climate within which it has taken place. But here again there are important variations among and within societies— and corruption as a general problem predated economic and technological takeoffs in most cases. Regime types and political styles ought to influence corruption as well, but again there is too much variation, both among societies and over time in several societies, to make them the basis for some common corruption style.

Further, what is it that is so distinctive? As for amounts and trends, country-level corruption indices are still too problematical to tell us much; in any event, Asian societies are found at all levels on measures such as the Transparency International Corruption Perception Index (TI CPI), on which high scores are meant to suggest low levels of corruption (see Table 8.1).

At the level of specific deals and practices, bribery, extortion, electoral fraud and the like function in much the same way in Asia as elsewhere, even if the amounts of money involved in some cases are strikingly high. Political consequences of corruption resemble those in many other places: Chang and Chu (2006), for example, find that corruption erodes institutional trust in Asian countries in much the same ways it does elsewhere.

The most frequent reason for positing distinctively Asian corruption has been its apparent consequences: extensive corruption has coexisted with rapid economic growth in the region, and it has been tempting to argue that therefore *something* different must be going on. One problem with that approach, of course, is that if we look at Asian corruption with a presumption of difference, differences are what we are likely to find, whether they are linked to outcomes or not. At the very least we need a theory of what influences corruption problems in a given setting. But another difficulty with the economic-growth argument is that there is less to it than meets the eye. For the 20 countries listed in Table 8.1, the simple correlation between GDP per capita for 2006 (the latest year available for all) and TI scores for 2007 is 0.946 (p = 0.000). For GDP per capita and each country's *average* TI score, based on all data available over the 1997–2007 period, the correlation is 0.931 (p = 0.000).[1]

Such results should be viewed with considerable caution, but there seems no basis whatever for arguing that corruption encourages growth or affluence. (A more plausible argument is that institutional and other sorts of developments in several societies have aided *both* economic growth and corruption control and that growth, by creating new economic opportunities, reduces official leverage over citizens and citizens' incentives to pay up in many circumstances—ideas to be discussed below). Contrasts among societies also pose problems, again: an argument that distinctively Asian factors make corruption benign or helpful for growth would have to account for differences in scale and timing among corruption and growth trends in, say, Japan versus Korea, Taiwan, Malaysia, and Bangladesh. Similarly, it would have to make room for the economic meltdown of 1997–98 and for the variations in its severity from one country to the next. Finally, it would have to distinguish Asian cases from others in which moderate-to-significant corruption has also coexisted with sustained growth, such as Botswana since the 1960s, Spain and Russia in recent years, Italy during the 1980s and 1990s, or the United States in the late nineteenth and early twentieth centuries.

Table 8.1 TI CPI scores for representative Asian states, 2007

Country	TI CPI 2007	Country	TI CPI 2007
Singapore	9.3	Mongolia	3.0
Hong Kong	8.3	Vietnam	2.6
Japan	7.5	Nepal	2.5
Taiwan	5.7	Philippines	2.5
Malaysia	5.1	Pakistan	2.4
South Korea	5.1	Indonesia	2.3
China	3.5	Bangladesh	2.0
India	3.5	Cambodia	2.0
Thailand	3.3	Laos	1.9
Sri Lanka	3.2	Myanmar	1.4

Source: Transparency International Corruption Perception Indices, 1995–2007, online. Available at www.transparency.org/policy_research/surveys_indices/cpi.

Four syndromes of corruption

Understanding variations in corruption requires careful study of opportunities to acquire and use wealth and power, and of the institutions that sustain and restrain such activities. I have suggested (Johnston 2005) that rather than simply ranking countries on a single dimension of more or less corruption, we can observe four qualitatively different corruption syndromes. I have termed those syndromes "Influence Markets," "Elite Cartels," "Oligarchs and Clans," and "Official Moguls," and investigated ways in which they reflect particular combinations of political and economic participation, on one hand, and institutions—state, social, political, and cultural—on the other. Statistical analysis sorted 98 countries into groupings consistent with the four syndromes, and case studies suggested that the expected differences in corruption were frequently apparent.

To search for syndromes of corruption is, in effect, to ask *what are the underlying developmental processes, and problems, of which a society's corruption is symptomatic?* Huntington (1968), for example, suggested years ago that where economic opportunities are more plentiful than political ones, ambitious people use wealth to seek power. Where political opportunities abound and economic ones are scarce, by contrast, power pursues wealth. Similarly, a relatively weak state may be vulnerable to illicit private pressures, while a weak civil society might suffer from official predation. Groups of countries and corruption syndromes will scarcely exhaust all possible variations; they are merely ideal types intended to highlight patterns and connections for closer study.

Participation and institutions come in many forms, but the main issue is how wealth and power are sought, used, and exchanged, and whether state, political, cultural and social institutions effectively sustain and restrain such activities. Societies differ in terms of the range and balance of political and economic opportunities they offer; wide variations are also apparent in the strength of institutions protecting economic and political rights, and guaranteeing fair play. Weak official institutions may well coexist with a coercive state and strong social institutions: China's weakened Communist Party and its enduring traditions of *guanxi* are a case in point. Yet strong public institutions do not guarantee all is well: while the United States scores well on institutional indicators, it apparently has a civil society in decline (Putnam 2000).

Variations in participation and institutions tend to fall into identifiable patterns, as my statistical analysis showed (Johnston 2005: Ch. 3). Established democracies often have mature market economies, for example. But there are also consolidating or reforming democratic/market societies in which political and economic competition is still emerging; institutions in such societies are generally weaker than those in the first group. Countries in a third group are undergoing major, simultaneous political and economic change: opportunities of both sorts are rapidly expanding and institutions are very weak, making insecurity and, at times, violence facts of daily life. Finally, most undemocratic regimes, while offering few political opportunities by definition, have been liberalizing economically to varying degrees if only because of global pressures. Their political institutions tend to be weak and personalized; leaders may even be widely feared, but that is not institutional strength as such. Not surprisingly, their economic opportunities are exploited by a powerful few, and countervailing forces may be nonexistent.

These intentionally general groupings, I argue, correspond to four major syndromes of corruption: Influence Markets, Elite Cartels, Oligarchs and Clans, and Official Moguls, as summarized in Table 8.2.

Influence Market corruption

Influence Markets deal in access to decision makers and policy implementers within strong state institutions; often politicians serve as middlemen, trading connections for funds both legal and otherwise. Mature market democracies offer extensive political and economic opportunities, and generally have strong, legitimate institutions. They resemble each other in important ways, which may help explain why they are often held up as reform ideals. But many of these countries have not "solved" corruption problems; rather, they have been accommodating to wealth interests as well as persuading people to follow the law. In part for those reasons, corruption in influence-market societies may be the exception, not the rule, and is unlikely to cripple economic development. But these societies still have corruption problems: their banks are often the repositories of corrupt gains from elsewhere, and their multinational businesses have made illicit deals around the world. Competitive politics in these societies can check some kinds of corruption while encouraging others: citizens can oust a corrupt government, but the costs of running for office encourage politicians to put their connections out for rent.

Elite Cartel corruption

In other societies politics and markets are becoming more competitive, but institutions are weaker. There, networks of elites collude, using corrupt exchanges to shore up their positions. Official institutions that are only moderately strong both facilitate and (from the elites' standpoint) necessitate such linkages. Power and its links to wealth are in flux, creating new opportunities and risks for elites; much elite corruption may be defensive in nature. Those involved may have power bases in business, the military, the bureaucracy, a political party, or an ethnic or regional community, and corrupt linkages may integrate elites in both the public and private sectors. These systems will not be wholly undemocratic or uncompetitive, and in some respects Elite Cartel corruption will be a stabilizing force facilitating growth.

Table 8.2 Projected syndromes of corruption

Syndrome	Participation		Institutions		
	Political opportunities	Economic opportunities	State/society capacity	Economic institutions
Influence Markets	Mature democracies Liberalized, steady competition and participation	Mature markets Liberalized, open; steady competition; affluent	Extensive	Strong
Elite Cartels	Consolidating/reforming democracies Liberalized; growing competition and participation	Reforming markets Largely liberalized and open; growing competition; moderately affluent	Moderate	Medium
Oligarchs and Clans	Transitional regimes Recent major liberalization; significant but poorly structured competition	New markets Recent major liberalization; extensive inequality and poverty	Weak	Weak
Official Moguls	Undemocratic Little liberalization or openness	New markets Recent major liberalization; extensive inequality and poverty	Weak	Weak

Oligarch-and-Clan corruption

Some societies are experiencing simultaneous but poorly institutionalized economic and political transitions, putting a wide variety of opportunities in play. This syndrome corruption is defined by a disorderly, sometimes violent scramble among contending oligarchs seeking to parlay *personal* resources (e.g. a powerful family, a business, a bureaucratic beachhead, judicial or organized crime connections) into wealth and power. Unlike Elite Cartels, whose relatively established elites collude, Oligarchs are contending free agents in a climate of pervasive insecurity. Inability to enforce contracts or defend property through courts and law enforcement creates incentives for violence, making police and organized crime protection all the more marketable. It may be difficult to say just what is public and what is private, who is a politician and who is an entrepreneur, or even who is clearly corrupt and who is an innovator. There is considerable political competition in this type of case, but it is likely unpredictable with shallow social roots. Factions can be unstable and poorly disciplined; oligarchs, both seeking rapid enrichment and needing to buy support again and again, will exploit any fragments of government authority available. Reforms will often be smokescreens for continued abuse or revenge; privatization can become a legalized carve-up of state resources or outright theft.

Official Mogul corruption

In a final group of countries institutions are very weak, politics remains undemocratic or is opening up only slowly. Civil society is weak or nonexistent. Opportunities for enrichment abound, but power is personal and often exercised with impunity. Here, top political figures or their clients dominate the economy, and face few constraints from state institutions or competitors. Of our four corruption syndromes this one is the least focused-upon influence within the state: institutions and offices may be merely useful tools in the search for wealth. Neither rulers nor counter-elites (if any) enjoy much sustained popular support or credibility beyond that created through patronage or intimidation; as a result, some Official Mogul cases can be fragmented or unstable. Military leaders are thus useful corruption partners, but may well use past corruption as a pretext for taking power. Development of civil society is inhibited by both corruption and the political hegemony underlying it, and people will thus have little recourse in cases of official abuse.

These four corruption syndromes are ideal types, as noted. No country will have just one kind of corruption, and no syndrome will fit any one case perfectly. As we move from Influence Markets toward Official Moguls we shift from corruption focusing on official roles and processes to that which is scarcely institutionalized at all. The former uses wealth to buy bureaucratic influence or electoral success, while the latter is the open exploitation of power, and of the weak by the strong, in the pursuit of riches. Influence Markets and Elite Cartel corruption involve repeated transactions, and connections usable over a long term; indeed, Elite Cartel corruption may work primarily to forestall change. In Oligarch-and-Clan and Official Mogul cases corruption is far less predictable, often involving targets of opportunity or the whims of leaders acting with impunity. Finally, in the latter sorts of cases corruption may be not the exception but the norm.

Four groups of cases

Do these four scenarios have anything to do with reality? In the book-length analysis (Johnston 2005: Ch. 3) K-Means cluster analysis using indicators of participation and institutional strength produced four statistically significant clusters consistent with the categories discussed earlier. Influence Market (N = 18) countries included Austria, Canada, Germany, the Netherlands, Norway, Sweden, the United Kingdom, and the United States. The Elite Cartels group (N = 21) included Argentina, Belgium, Chile, Italy, South Korea, Poland, Spain, and Zambia among others. Oligarchs and Clans (N = 30) were exemplified, *inter alia*, by Albania, Colombia, Ecuador, Malaysia, Mexico, the Philippines, Russia, and Venezuela. Finally, Official Moguls cases (N = 29) included Algeria, Chad, China, Indonesia, Jordan, Nigeria, Syria, Tanzania, and Zimbabwe. The suggestion is emphatically not that countries in each group are alike, nor is it that they are common "system types"; rather, it is that they experience similar corruption problems reflecting common underlying patterns of participation and institutions. Case studies (Johnston 2005: Chs 4–7) generally bore out the expected contrasts of corruption.

Asian societies: four groupings

Classification data were available for thirteen societies in South, Southeast, or East Asia. They fell into all four categories, but were most numerous in Oligarchs and Clans (see Table 8.3).

There is a "regional flavor" to this distribution yet no single Asian type appears. Equally, there is no concentration of large or rapidly growing economies in any one category. I will suggest later on, however, that Influence Market and Elite Cartel corruption may be most compatible with broad-based growth (though they are in no sense "functional"), and that in India, China and elsewhere the question might be what sorts of *social* institutions not reflected in data on institutional quality are helping societies withstand the effects of corruption.

Four Asian cases

Influence Markets in Japan: leaders, factions, and tribes

Japan's Influence Markets connect wealth interests to decision makers within a well-institutionalized state (extended versions of these discussions appear in

Table 8.3 Asian cases classified by cluster analysis

Group 1: Influence Markets
Japan

Group 2: Elite Cartels
South Korea

Group 3: Oligarchs and Clans

Bangladesh	Pakistan
India	Philippines
Malaysia	Sri Lanka
Nepal	Thailand

Group 4: Official Moguls
China
Indonesia
Myanmar

Source: Johnston (2005: Ch. 3).

Johnston 2005: Chs 4–7). Politicians and contributions, some of the latter legal and others not, are integral to that process. A strong, centralized, and remote bureaucracy raises the value of mediation by politicians who have cultivated bureaucratic and parliamentary networks. The money involved can be astonishing: when former Liberal Democratic Party (LDP) Deputy Secretary General Kanemaru Shin was arrested for tax evasion in 1993, the valuables seized from his home were worth an estimated ¥3.6 billion, then roughly US$ 30 million. Boisseau (1997: 133–35) estimates that by the early 1990s the LDP spent about US$ 8 billion *annually* to keep its machine running. Kickbacks to LDP politicians from the winners of public works contracts ran a flat 3 percent of the value of the contract (Johnson 1995: 208). When we consider that in the mid-1980s domestic construction outlays in Japan totaled ¥53.6 trillion yearly (Woodall 1996: 1)—around $225 billion at then-current exchange rates—or that in the early 1990s around 15 percent of the LDP's *reported* contributions came from real estate and construction interests (Woodall 1996: 11)—we can sense the scale of the process.

Blechinger (1999: 57) has described Japan's party–business links as a kind of mutual services agreement, with the LDP dealing in access and business funding party operations. Trading in influence at high levels required a *zoku*—a network or political tribe. A *zoku* linked Diet members with a particular policy or economic sector to businesses and bureaucrats; some *zoku* members became virtual industry spokespersons (Johnson 1995; Blechinger 2000). Modified one-party politics created just enough political competition to make it worthwhile to put up cash to keep the LDP in power, *and* a near-monopoly over access that gave factional leaders leverage over donors. Corruption did not prevent a four-decade economic miracle; indeed, it fed upon prosperity. But Influence Markets have had significant *political* costs, aggravating the factional splits that brought the LDP down, temporarily, in 1993 and perhaps contributing to Japan's ineffective economic adaptations following the burst of the late-1980s bubble.

Korea: "money politics" and Elite Cartel dominance

Korea's corruption outwardly resembles the "money politics" seen in Japan. Large payments by businesses to political elites—both as "contributions" to parties or foundations and as outright bribes—for years bought favorable access to credit and major policy favors. But Korea's corruption was more centralized within top levels of the state, and was less a quid pro quo system than a continuous incentive flow supporting an elite network (Moran 1999; Steinberg 2000: 203–38). Those networks included presidents, their families, and their entourages; heads of the *chaebols* (huge family-controlled conglomerates); bureaucrats, and military and business leaders. Weakness in civil society and state institutions, and traditional attitudes toward authority, facilitated this style; but so did its ability, from the mid-1970s onwards, to deliver rising living standards on a breathtaking scale.

"Money politics" was simple in important respects: *chaebols* made payments to political leaders, their parties, or their pet charities. During the 1980s and early 1990s, such contributions ran as large as 22 percent of net profits (Woo 1991: 9). This immense cash flow underwrote party and legislative organizations and rewarded key bureaucrats and military figures for loyalty. A significant portion also funded gift-giving and vote-buying (Kang 2002a: 99). As democratization proceeded funds were slipped to opposition leaders in order to keep them compliant (Pye 1997: 220). In return *chaebols* got access to capital and foreign exchange on preferential terms, light regulation, and labor peace guaranteed by state power. Elite Cartels produced both wealth and control: stability attracted investment, and presidents could reward development "winners," making productivity and export growth, as well as loyalty, keys to admission to the cartel.

Democratization changed the dynamics of corruption in some ways but by no means eradicated it. Kim Young-Sam, winner of the first competitive civilian presidential election, took office in 1993 as a reformer. He mandated investigations of "money politics" under predecessor Roh Tae Woo, inquiries that eventually included the leaders of the top 30 *chaebols*. Nine businessmen were indicted, and five convicted; Roh himself was convicted and sentenced to jail. Kim Dae-Jung, later the first opposition candidate to become president, accepted $2.6 million from Roh, and suspicions extended to, but were denied by, Kim Young-Sam as well. Chun Doo Whan, president from 1981 to 1987, was brought to trial in 1996, convicted, and condemned to death (a sentence later commuted) for both corruption and his role in political violence in 1979 and 1980 (Moran 1998: 573–74; Blechinger 2000: 3–4; Steinberg 2000: 207; Kang, 2002b: 196–97).

Corruption both enriched the national elite and shored up their sometimes shaky hegemony. In economic development terms the result was both early benefits and deferred costs. *Chaebol*-driven growth enabled Korea to exploit niches in international trade, but as the maturing economy took on more global competitors politicized lending led to overcapacity; corporate governance was opaque. The practice of underwriting each others' loans turned corporate debt into a house of cards. These accumulating risks, and the lack of incentive for political leaders to demand accountability, deepened the 1997–98 financial crisis.

The Philippines: oligarchs, clans, and a weak state

Ferdinand and Imelda Marcos dominate popular images of Philippine corruption, but reality is more complex. Entrenched oligarchs, their families, and their personal clients have inhibited the growth of democratic forces while enriching themselves in both the public and private sectors. The nation is dominated by about 80 families (Sidel 1997, 2000; Moran 1999); some are provincial dynasties, while others have risen to prominence through banking or industry (Montinola 1999; Hutchcroft 2003). Some oligarchs have turned segments of the state into fiefdoms; others have used corrupt influence to keep the state out of their business dealings. Still others have simply stolen from the nation. The Marcos era—especially the long period of martial law (1972–86)—complicated the picture: favored families thrived while others saw property and privileges vanish. Corruption helped mobilize the "People Power" revolution of 1986, since which time reforms have proliferated but have been uneven in their effects.

Oligarchs and Clans derive much of their power and wealth from *outside* the state—to the extent that that distinction makes much difference—and exploit the state much more effectively than the state exploits them (Hutchcroft 1991: 424). Guaranteeing corrupt deals and in a setting of weak institutions is a chronic problem, however, and thus presidents are handy friends to have. Violence is part of the story too (Moran 1999: 582), particularly in remote areas; over the long run oligarchic privilege makes for a fragmented and unpredictable economy. During martial law Marcos cracked down on some oligarchs while channeling wealth to others. For example, he imposed a special tax on coconuts and copra to be collected by an agency run by Eduardo Conjuangco. With the proceeds Conjuangco acquired a bank, using a subsidiary to buy coconut processing facilities. Marcos then ordered that subsidies for the whole industry be restricted to that subsidiary, creating a virtual monopoly (Wedeman 1997a: 471). Imelda Marcos built a business empire of her own, diverting aid, bribe income, and organized crime money into a series of bank and asset accounts.

Once Marcos was toppled in 1986, there was little to restrain powerful families from regaining or extending their influence. McCoy describes the rise, fall, and restoration of the Lopez family, who began with large landholdings in the western Visayas sugar region and, with presidential connections over the years, became powerful in the media, transportation, and energy sectors as well as politics. During martial law Marcos moved against the Lopez empire and crushed its principal figures, one of whom had been his own vice-president. After 1986, however, the Lopezes were back—aided at first by President Aquino, who restored many of their industrial holdings, and later by building a new satellite-based media empire. McCoy portrays the Lopezes' return as part of a restoration of elite family power in a weak state (McCoy 1993: 513–17).

China: riding the tiger—for now

China is a fragmented case of Official Mogul corruption: in a climate of rapidly growing economic opportunities, tightly controlled (official) political opportunities, and weak state institutions, officials engage in corrupt activities with little to stop them. Corruption is pervasive and diverse; weakening party discipline and the absence of effective rule of law enabled cadres, already enjoying considerable privilege (Gong 1994: xviii), to amass and exploit fragments of power, which in turn became a path to wealth. In the years before Mao's death in 1976 and the launch of market reforms in 1978, corruption was a problem: favoritism was common, and production, in the centrally planned economy, was often falsely reported (Kwong 1997: 111). But it was generally controlled in scope and the stakes involved. Officially it reflected surviving feudal traditions and bourgeois values, or just individual deviance (Hao and Johnston 2002: 583–604).

Economic liberalization, while legitimating many market *mechanisms*, did not create well-institutionalized, national markets as such. Official profiteering (*guandao*) became a major problem, taking on various forms such as moonlighting, speculation, taking gifts, and bribery. Officials have been able to create lucrative monopolies in a gray sector neither clearly public nor private. Judicial institutions were reconstructed, but became politicized and unaccountable (Gong 2004), as did lending and credit. State bureaucratic capacity lags far behind the spread of markets, and the party has experienced organizational decay (Gong 1997: 285; Wedeman 1997b; Lü 2001; Cheng 2004). The result has been Official Mogul corruption on a fragmented basis, as officials and their cronies have been able to use fragments of state power or party influence to enrich themselves, at times with impunity.

For the first fifteen years of reform a two-track price system created incentives to buy commodities at artificially low planned prices and re-sell them on the market at much higher prices. Many managers overstated or simply skipped production under the plan and moved directly to the market, dealings concealed by cutting bureaucrats in on the profits. Teachers compelled students to buy books and supplies from them, railway workers traded in scarce freight and passenger space, and military officers sold fuel, supplies, and special license plates exempting holders from inspections, tolls, and fees (Hao and Johnston 2002: 583–604). Managers could tap into the cash and commodity flows of their enterprises with little risk of punishment (Cheng 2004).

City officials might wink at local manufacturers' tax obligations while levying special fees upon goods from elsewhere (Wedeman 1997a: 807). More recently tax fraud and embezzlement have been major moneymakers (Sun 2004: Ch. 3). Increasingly, Chinese corruption involves collusion among local officials and their business favorites (Gong 2002: 86).

Syndromes, Asian corruption, and reform

Much more could be said about all four cases, and about the extent to which the syndromes do and do not illuminate the corruption problems they experience. But if the above discussion has any validity, notions of "Asian corruption" need reassessment. There does not seem to be a distinctive form of corruption found across Asia and only in the region. Japan's corruption seems to have much in common with that of other advanced market democracies, and Korea's with places as different as Italy and Botswana. Oligarch-and-Clan corruption in the Philippines, while not as disruptive or violent as that found in Russia, the Caucasus, and many other places, still reflects influences and incentives common to societies where private networks fill a power vacuum. And China's Official Moguls use fragments of party–state authority to enrich themselves and their clients with few constraints.

What can be said about corruption and development? Japan's corruption reflects the power of business in an already developed political and legal system; it and the LDP's long run of modified one-party rule probably made needed economic adaptations more difficult. But as in the United States, the real costs of Influence Market corruption in Japan have come, not in the form of a devastated economy, but rather in political terms as the scope and credibility of political competition suffered.

Korea, ironically, may have been aided in its stunning growth and its surprising transition to democracy by its particular style of corruption. Elite Cartels hung together for all the wrong reasons, but they provided the sort of political security that official institutions could not, encouraging investment and allowing top figures to accommodate democratizing pressures gradually rather than lapsing into complete repression. Institutions that might elsewhere have been the backbone of democratic rule—constitutions, party systems, civil society—were weak during much of Korea's early democratic phase, and could benefit from considerable strengthening even today. The point is not that the Elite Cartel syndrome is "good corruption," but rather than in certain circumstances it may be preferable to many real (as opposed to ideal) alternative styles of politics and business.

What, then, are we to make of rapid growth in India and China—two economically liberalizing countries experiencing the most disruptive sorts of corruption yet emerging as economic superpowers? Few of the other Asian countries listed in the Oligarchs and Clans or the Official Moguls groupings are experiencing anything like India's and China's successes. Are there informal social institutions that mitigate the economic costs of extensive corruption—

factors such as the traditional role of "middlemen" in India, and *guanxi* in China—by reducing transaction costs and unpredictability, and by imposing a set of norms, expectations, and social sanctions that the formal institutional apparatus fails to provide?

The fact is we will never know. Judging the effects of corruption requires that we know what would have happened without it—something we cannot determine. Still, while there may not be distinctively Asian corruption there may be important Asian ways of dealing with it. Our syndromes analysis cannot yet tell us much about those factors, but such a level of analysis seems a promising place to look for relatively specific implications of cultural and historical variables as influences upon economic and political change.

Reform: beyond the "consensus playbook"

A final point has to do with institutions. All of the societies we have considered in this discussion have market economies; most have liberalized decisively in recent years, along with their neighbors in the region. For a number of years in the 1990s it was frequently argued that marketization and privatization—taking the state out of the economy, and thereby depriving its officials of any authority or discretion worth paying for—would by itself significantly reduce corruption. The resulting boost to markets would in turn encourage an upward spiral of both growth and good governance. Politics, too, was seen as a kind of dead weight upon such expansion, encouraging rent-seeking, facilitating corrupt access to essential state functionaries, and diverting resources into costly services and welfare benefits, thereby reducing profits and investments.

The comparisons of syndromes, as well as recent experience, however, suggest that the liberalization argument was incomplete. Quite apart from its ideological underpinnings and implicit assumptions that trends in GDP per capita equate to human well-being, that consensus style of reform devalued institutions in the state, political, and social domains. Oversight institutions upholding fair play in the market place, political parties and interest groups, and strong civil societies (among other kinds of social institutions) are essential to broad-based development with justice—and, consistent with that notion, to corruption control as well. Such institutions are essential for accountability in both politics and the economy—for restraining rapacious exploitation, collusion, and outright theft. Further, they help create a pluralized society in which multiple centers of power can check each other, using diverse resources and mobilizing broad coalitions of groups and interests. Neither economic markets themselves, nor visions of liberalized politics treating democracy as just another kind of market, can build or sustain those sorts of institutions. Yet without them a society cannot develop in balanced ways, and cannot check corruption. Such a vision may seem to re-establish Western market democracies as global ideas, but the Influence Market syndrome of corruption serves as a valuable reminder that they, too, have serious problems of corruption and accountability.

What the successful Asian societies in all four of our categories share is some sort of durable institutional framework. Both anticorruption reformers and advocates of justice have come to appreciate the value of such institutions; a detailed analysis of contrasting corruption problems in diverse societies can tell us much about how to build and sustain them, and about the consequences for societies where they are missing.

Notes

1 Data sources: Transparency International Corruption Perception Indices 1995–2007, online. Available at www.transparency.org/policy_research/surveys_indices/cpi (accessed 26 September 2007); GDP data are 2006 IMF estimates based on most recent data available, online. Available at http://imf.org/external/data.htm#data (accessed 14 March 2008). For Bangladesh, TI CPI average is for 2001–07; for Myanmar, 2003–07; for Mongolia and Nepal, 2004–07; for Laos and Cambodia, 2005–07.

References

Blechinger, V. (1999) "Changes in the handling of corruption scandals in Japan since 1994," *Asian-Pacific Review*, 6: 42–64.
—— (2000) "Corruption through political contributions in Japan: report on recent bribery scandals, 1996–2000," paper presented at a conference on Bribery and Party Finance, sponsored by Transparency International, Villa La Pietra, Florence, Italy, October.
Boisseau, J.M. (1997) "Gifts, networks and clienteles: corruption in Japan as a redistributive system," in D. della Porta and Y. Meny (eds) *Democracy and Corruption in Europe*, London: Pinter.
Chang, E.C.C. and Chu, Y.H. (2006) "Corruption and trust: exceptionalism in Asian democracies?" *Journal of Politics*, 68(2): 259–71.
Cheng, W.H. (2004) "An empirical study of corruption within China's state-owned enterprises," *The China Review*, 4: 55–80.
Gong, T. (1994) *The Politics of Corruption in Contemporary China: An Analysis of Policy Outcomes*, Westport, CT: Praeger.
—— (1997) "Forms and characteristics of China's corruption in the 1990s: change with continuity," *Communist and Post-Communist Studies*, 30: 277–88.
—— (2002) "Dangerous collusion: corruption as a collective venture in contemporary China," *Communist and Post-Communist Studies*, 35: 85–103.
—— (2004) "Dependent judiciary and unaccountable judges: judicial corruption in contemporary China," *China Review*, 4(2): 33–54.
Hao, F. and Johnston, M. (2002) "Corruption and the future of economic reform in China," in A.J. Heidenheimer and M. Johnston (eds) *Political Corruption: Concepts and Contexts* (3rd edn), New Brunswick, NJ: Transaction Publishers.
Huntington, S.P. (1968) *Political Order in Changing Societies*, New Haven: Yale University Press.
Hutchcroft, P.D. (1991) "Oligarchs and cronies in the Philippine State: the politics of patrimonial plunder," *World Politics*, 43: 414–50.
—— (2003) "Reflections on a reverse image: South Korea under Park Chung Hee and the Philippines under Ferdinand Marcos," paper presented at the East Asia

Institute, Korea University, and the Asia Center, Harvard University, 2000; revised 2003.

Johnson, C.A. (1995) *Japan: Who Governs? The Rise of the Developmental State*, New York: Norton.

Johnston, M. (2005) *Syndromes of Corruption: Wealth, Power and Democracy*, Cambridge and New York: Cambridge University Press.

Kang, D.C. (2002a) *Crony Capitalism: Corruption and Development in South Korea and the Philippines*, Cambridge and New York: Cambridge University Press.

—— (2002b) "Bad loans to good friends: money politics and the developmental state in Korea," *International Organization*, 56: 1.

Kwong, J. (1997) *The Political Economy of Corruption in China*, Armonk, NY: M.E. Sharpe.

Lü, X.B. (2001) *Cadres and Corruption: The Organizational Involution of the Chinese Communist Party*, Stanford: Stanford University Press; Cambridge: Cambridge University Press.

McCoy, A.W. (1993) "Rent-seeking families and the Philippine state: a history of the Lopez family," in A.W. McCoy (ed.) *An Anarchy of Families: State and Family in the Philippines*, Madison, WI: University of Wisconsin, Center for Southeast Asian Studies, in cooperation with Ateneo de Manila University Press.

Montinola, G. (1999) "Politicians, parties, and the persistence of weak states: lessons from the Philippines," *Development and Change*, 30: 739–74.

Moran, J. (1998) "Corruption and NIC development: a case study of South Korea," *Crime, Law and Social Change*, 29: 161–77.

—— (1999) "Patterns of corruption and development in east Asia," *Third World Quarterly*, 20(3): 569.

Putnam, R.D. (2000) *Bowling Alone: The Collapse and Revival of American Community*, New York: Simon and Schuster.

Pye, L.W. (1997) "Money politics and transitions to democracy in east Asia," *Asian Survey*, 37: 213–28.

Sidel, J.T. (1997) "Philippine politics in town, district, and province: bossism in Cavite and Cebu," *Journal of Asian Studies*, 56: 947–66.

—— (2000) *Capital, Coercion, and Crime: Bossism in the Philippines*, Stanford, CA: Stanford University Press.

Steinberg, D.I. (2000) "Continuing democratic reform: the unfinished symphony," in L. Diamond and B.K. Kim (eds) *Consolidating Democracy in South Korea*, Boulder, CO: Lynne Rienner.

Sun, Y. (2004) *Corruption and Market in Contemporary China*, Ithaca, NY: Cornell University Press.

Wedeman, A. (1997a) "Looters, rent-scrapers, and dividend-collectors: corruption and growth in Zaire, South Korea and the Philippines," *Journal of Developing Areas*, 31: 457–78.

—— (1997b) "Stealing from the farmers: institutional corruption and the 1992 IOU crisis," *China Quarterly*, 152: 805–31.

Woo, J.E. (1991) *Race to the Swift: State and Finance in Korean Industrialization*, New York: Columbia University Press.

Woodall, B. (1996) *Japan under Construction: Corruption, Politics, and Public Works*, Berkeley: University of California Press.

9 Curbing corruption in a one-party dominant system

Learning from Singapore's experience

Jon S.T. Quah

Introduction

Singapore is an unusual city-state in many respects. In June 1959, it attained self-government from Britain and the People's Action Party (PAP) government assumed office after winning the May 1959 general election. The newly elected PAP government inherited many problems: a population of 1.58 million that was growing at the rate of 4 percent; an economy based on entrepot trade and an unemployment rate of 5 percent; a serious housing shortage with half of the population living as squatters; labor unrest; rampant corruption; and a high crime rate. With a per capita gross domestic product (GDP) of S$ 1,330 (US$ 443) in 1960, Singapore was a typical poor Third World country struggling for its survival (Quah 1998: 105). Not surprisingly, Albert Winsemius, the Dutch economist leading the United Nations study mission to Singapore in 1960, was pessimistic about Singapore's future as he observed that "Singapore is going down the drain, it is a poor little market in a dark corner of Asia" (Tamboer 1996: 29).

However, after 49 years of PAP rule, Singapore has been transformed from a Third World to a First World country as its GDP per capita has increased by 40 times to S$ 52,994 (US$ 35,163) in June 2007. Singapore's official foreign reserves have also grown by 204 times from S$ 1,151.4 million (US$ 383.8 million) in 1963 to S$ 234,545.6 million (US$ 155,627.1 million) in 2007. The housing shortage has been solved by the Housing and Development Board's effective public housing program which has increased the proportion of the population living in public housing from 9 percent in 1959 to 82 percent in 2006 (Department of Statistics 2008).

By introducing legislation to curb labor unrest, crime, and corruption, and demonstrating the political will to enforce these laws impartially, the PAP government has succeeded in disciplining the labor force, reducing the high crime rate, and minimizing the problem of corruption. According to Transparency International's 2008 Corruption Perceptions Index (CPI), Singapore is perceived to be the fourth least corrupt country among the 180 countries surveyed and the least corrupt Asian country, with a CPI score of 9.2 (www. transparency.org). In contrast, corruption has "historically enhanced" Mexico's

Institutional Revolutionary Party's (PRI's) "ability to 'buy' and maintain the support of key sectoral leaders" through its administration of "a secure and permanent spoils system for those willing to abide by the political rules of the game" (Morris 1991: 39, 137). Why has the PAP in Singapore not succumbed to corruption like Mexico's PRI?[1] This chapter focuses on how the PAP government has minimized the problem of corruption and how it has been able to remain clean after being in power for 49 years.

The PAP's victory in the May 1959 general election led to its assumption of power and the beginning of its long and durable rule. Singapore's party system was transformed from a competitive system (May 1959–September 1966) to a de facto one-party dominant system in October 1966, when the thirteen opposition Barisan Sosialis members of parliament (MPs) boycotted parliament. It was transformed to a *de jure* one-party dominant system after the April 1968 general election, when the PAP won all the 58 parliamentary seats. The PAP repeated its feat of winning all the parliamentary seats in the 1972, 1976, and 1980 general elections. However, its monopoly of parliament was eroded in October 1981, when J.B. Jeyaratnam of the Workers' Party defeated the PAP candidate, Pang Kim Hin, in the Anson by-election. Nevertheless, the PAP government has remained in power as it was re-elected in the subsequent December 1984, September 1988, August 1991, January 1997, and May 2006 general elections.

Corruption in colonial Singapore

Corruption was a way of life in Singapore during the colonial period because of the low salaries of civil servants, the ample opportunities available for corruption, and the ineffective anticorruption measures employed by the British colonial government, which resulted in a lower probability of detecting corrupt offences and punishing these offenders if they were caught. In other words, corruption thrived during the colonial period because it was perceived by the public to be a low-risk, high-reward activity, as corrupt offenders were unlikely to be caught and punished.

Corruption was made illegal with the enactment of the Penal Code of the Straits Settlements of Malacca, Penang and Singapore in 1871. The 1879 Commission of Inquiry found that corruption was prevalent in the Straits Settlements Police Force among the European inspectors and the Malay and Indian junior officers. Similarly, the 1886 Commission of Inquiry confirmed the rampant police corruption in Penang and Singapore (Quah 1979: 24–27). However, the British authorities ignored the findings of these two commissions and did not introduce any anticorruption measure for the next 51 years until December 1937, when the first anticorruption law, the Prevention of Corruption Ordinance (POCO), was enacted.

Police corruption thrived during the colonial period as the local junior officers were poorly paid and made ends meet by moonlighting and/or accepting bribes from illegal gambling-house owners (Quah 1979: 28–31).

However, corruption was not confined to the police as other government agencies, including the customs, immigration, and internal revenue departments, provided more opportunities for corruption than those public agencies that had limited contact with the public, did not issue licenses or permits, and collected fees or taxes.

During the Japanese Occupation (February 1942 to August 1945), corruption was rampant because inflation made it difficult for the poorly paid civil servants to survive. Consequently, trading in the black market was a "way of life" as "everyone was surviving on some sort of black marketing" (Lee 2005: 142). Nepotism and corruption were "perfectly acceptable" and "bribery, blackmail, and extortion grew out of the violence and fear" that the Japanese authorities employed to rule Singapore (Lee 2005: 142, 205). Conditions deteriorated during the postwar period as corruption spread among civil servants because of their low salaries, and inflation and inadequate supervision by their superior officers provided them with ample opportunities for corruption with a low probability of being detected (Quah 1982: 161–62). As corruption had become a way of life for many Singaporeans, it is not surprising that the British Military Administration, which took over after the Japanese surrender in August 1945, was described pejoratively as the "Black Market Administration." Five years later, the Commissioner of Police, J.P. Pennefather-Evans, reported that graft was rife in government departments in Singapore (Quah 1978: 14).

The POCO was ineffective because its offenses were not seizable and limited the powers of arrest, search and investigation of police officers as warrants were required before arrests could be made. Second, its penalty of two years' imprisonment and/or a S$10,000 fine was not an effective deterrent. The POCO was enforced by the Anticorruption Branch (ACB) which was established within the Criminal Investigation Department (CID) of the Singapore Police Force (SPF) in December 1937.

The ACB was ineffective in curbing corruption for three reasons. First, it was inadequately staffed, with four senior officers and thirteen junior personnel, and had to compete with other branches of the CID for limited manpower and other resources. Second, the CID had many priorities and the function of combating corruption was only one of the sixteen duties of its Assistant Commissioner in May 1952. Indeed, apart from corruption control, some of his other duties included dealing with secret societies, gambling promoters, commercial crime, anti-vice, narcotics, criminal records, and missing persons (Quah 1978: 14–15).

However, the most important reason for the ACB's ineffectiveness was the prevalence of police corruption in Singapore during the colonial period. In view of the rampant police corruption, which was documented by the 1879 and 1886 commissions, it is difficult to understand why the British authorities decided in 1937 to make the ACB, which was part of the SPF, responsible for corruption control. The folly of this decision was made apparent nearly fourteen years later when three police detectives were implicated in the

October 1951 robbery of 1,800 lb of opium worth S$ 400,000 (US$ 133,330). This opium hijacking scandal exposed the ACB's weaknesses and its inability to curb corruption, especially within the SPF.

More importantly, the British colonial government realized its mistake of relying on the ACB to fight corruption when there was extensive police corruption. Consequently, the ACB was replaced by the Corrupt Practices Investigation Bureau (CPIB), which was formed as an independent agency in October 1952. However, as the British colonial government was not committed to the goal of eradicating corruption, it made the second mistake of not providing the CPIB with sufficient legal powers, staffing and funding. Thus, it was not surprising that the CPIB began with five staff members and by 1959 its personnel had only marginally increased to eight members (Quah 1978: 17).

The PAP government's anticorruption strategy

The PAP leaders launched their campaign for the May 1959 general election on 15 February at a pre-election rally at Hong Lim Green when the PAP chairman, Toh Chin Chye, revealed that "the Americans had given [S]$ 500,000 [US $ 166,667] to the SPA [Singapore People's Alliance]" (Lee 1998: 293). Three days later, Lee Kuan Yew identified Chew Swee Kee, the Minister for Education, as the person who had received S$ 800,000 [US$ 266,667] in 1957–58 from the Americans. Chew resigned from his position and the Legislative Assembly on 4 March, and the government appointed a commission of inquiry to investigate Lee's allegations. The commission confirmed that Chew

> had received from the United States political funds totaling $519,083.96 (Malayan currency) on 20 October 1957 and a further $182,509.51 on 24 April 1958 ... Without comment, the Commissioner listed the names of the beneficiaries of the total sum of $701,539.47 paid into Chew's personal bank account. Chew was himself the major beneficiary, drawing cheques in favour of himself amounting to $690,153.51.
>
> (Drysdale 1984: 210)

The commission's findings "confirmed what voters already knew—that Lim Yew Hock's government was corrupt, and worse, that it was now in the pay of the Americans." Indeed, the Chew Swee Kee scandal and "the unfavourable fallout from the commission of inquiry had put voters off" (Lee 1998: 295). The publication of the commission's report in the press on 27 May, three days before the general election, exposed the SPA's lack of integrity and seriously undermined its prospects for an electoral victory. The PAP's commitment to clean government and its exposure of the Chew Swee Kee scandal enabled it to win 43 of the 51 seats with 53.4 percent of the votes cast by 90 percent of the electorate in the 30 May general election. In contrast, the SPA won only four seats. At the press conference after the election results, Lee Kuan Yew declared: "The people's verdict is clear and decisive. It is a victory of right over wrong, clean over dirty; righteousness over evil" (Lee 1998: 305).

Corruption was a serious problem in Singapore in June 1959, when the PAP government assumed office. In his memoirs, Lee Kuan Yew explained why he and his colleagues were determined to keep Singapore free from corruption:

> When the PAP government took office in 1959, we set out to have a clean administration. We were sickened by the greed, corruption and decadence of many Asian leaders ... We had a deep sense of mission to establish a clean and effective government. When we took the oath of office ... in June 1959, we all wore white shirts and white slacks to symbolize purity and honesty in our personal behaviour and our public life. The people expected this of us, and we were determined to live up to their expectations ... We made sure from the day we took office in June 1959 that every dollar in revenue would be properly accounted for and would reach the beneficiaries at the grass roots as one dollar, without being siphoned off along the way. So from the very beginning we gave special attention to the areas where discretionary powers had been exploited for personal gain and sharpened the instruments that could prevent, detect or deter such practices.
>
> (Lee 2000: 182–84)

As corruption was a way of life and perceived by the public to be a low-risk, high-reward activity, the PAP government's mission was to minimize corruption and to change the public perception of corruption to a high-risk, low-reward activity. Accordingly, the PAP leaders introduced a comprehensive anti-corruption strategy in 1960 by enacting the Prevention of Corruption Act (POCA) and strengthening the CPIB.

As Singapore was a poor country in 1959, the PAP government could not afford to raise the salaries of the civil servants. On the contrary, it reduced the wages of senior civil servants by withdrawing their cost of living allowances to avoid a budgetary deficit of S$ 14 million (Quah 2003: 147–48). Thus, the PAP government's anticorruption strategy focused on strengthening the anticorruption laws to reduce the opportunities for corruption and to enhance the penalty for corrupt behavior (Quah 1995a: 395).

Prevention of Corruption Act

The PAP government's resolve to curb corruption was unequivocally stated by the Minister for Home Affairs, Ong Pang Boon, when he moved for the second reading of the Prevention of Corruption Bill in the Legislative Assembly on 13 February 1960:

> The Prevention of Corruption Bill is in keeping with the new Government's determination to stamp out bribery and corruption in the country, especially in the public services ... Therefore, this Government is

determined to take all possible steps to see that all necessary legislative and administrative measures are taken *to reduce the opportunities of corruption*, to make its detection easier and to deter and punish severely those who are susceptible to it and who engage in it shamelessly.

(Quoted in Quah 1978: 10, emphasis added)

The POCA was enacted on 17 June 1960, and had five important features which removed the POCO's weaknesses and strengthened the CPIB. First, the POCA's scope was broader with 32 sections in comparison with the POCO's twelve sections. Second, Section 2 defined corruption explicitly in terms of the various forms of "gratification." Third, the penalty for corruption was increased to imprisonment for five years and/or a fine of S$ 10,000 (Section 5) to increase the POCA's deterrent effect. Fourth, according to Section 13, a person found guilty of accepting an illegal gratification had to pay the amount he or she had taken as a bribe in addition to any other punishment imposed by a court. Finally, the POCA's most important feature was that it gave the CPIB more powers and a new lease of life. Section 15 gave CPIB officers powers of arrest and search of arrested persons. Section 17 empowered the public prosecutor to authorize the CPIB's director and his senior officers to investigate "any bank account, share account or purchase account" of any person suspected of having committed an offense against the POCA. Section 18 enabled the CPIB officers to inspect a civil servant's banker's book and those of his wife, child or agent, if necessary (Quah 1995a: 395).

To ensure that the POCA remains effective, the PAP government has introduced whenever necessary, amendments (in 1963, 1966 and 1981) or new legislation (in 1989) to deal with unanticipated problems or to plug legal loopholes. For example, in 1966, the POCA was amended so that a person could be found guilty of corruption without actually receiving the bribe as long as he had shown the intention of doing so. The POCA was also amended in 1966 so that Singaporeans working for their government in embassies and other government agencies abroad as Singapore citizens would be prosecuted for corrupt offences committed outside Singapore and would be dealt with as if such offences had occurred within Singapore (Quah 1978: 13).

The Minister for National Development, Teh Cheang Wan, committed suicide on 14 December 1986, twelve days after he was interrogated by two senior CPIB officers regarding the accusation by two developers that he had accepted bribes of S$ 1 million in 1981–82. Teh's suicide led to a commission of inquiry and the enactment of the Corruption (Confiscation of Benefits) Act 1989 on 3 March 1989.[2] Among other things, this new legislation enabled the court to issue a confiscation order against a deceased defendant (Quah 2007a: 20–21).

The Corrupt Practices Investigation Bureau

Learning from the British colonial government's lack of political will in curbing corruption as reflected in the CPIB's lack of legal powers, manpower and funding during its first eight years, the PAP government realized from the outset the critical importance of enhancing the CPIB's powers and providing it with the required manpower and budget for performing its functions effectively.

The CPIB is the anticorruption agency responsible for enforcing the POCA in Singapore. It performs these three functions:

1 to receive and investigate complaints alleging corrupt practices;
2 to investigate malpractices and misconduct by public officers with an undertone of corruption; and
3 to prevent corruption by examining the practices and procedures in the public service to minimize opportunities for corrupt practices (CPIB 2004: 3).

In addition to these functions, the CPIB also screens those candidates selected for positions in the Singapore Civil Service and statutory boards to ensure that only those candidates without a previous record of corruption or misconduct are actually recruited (Republic of Singapore 1994: 638).

The current CPIB director, Soh Kee Hean, has described the CPIB's "total approach to enforcement" which deals with both "big and small cases" of corruption in both the public and private sectors, "both giver and receiver of bribes" and "other crimes uncovered in the course of [the] corruption investigation" (Soh 2008a: 1–2). The CPIB has succeeded in its enforcement efforts because of its reliance on skilful interview techniques, careful planning and execution of field operations, and computer forensics (Soh 2008a: 2–3). More importantly, the CPIB's effective enforcement capacity can be attributed to its threefold emphasis on the capability building of its enforcement officers, building networks and partnerships with other public agencies in Singapore, and organizational excellence.

To improve their capabilities, the CPIB's enforcement personnel are exposed to both in-house and external training programs in Singapore and abroad on relevant management and professional topics. The CPIB has also organized Anticorruption Expertise regional workshops in Singapore on investigation techniques and computer forensics in anticorruption work in 2006 and 2007. For building networks and partnerships, it has conducted joint operations in Singapore with the Commercial Affairs Department and the Immigration and Checkpoint Authority (Soh 2008a: 3–4).

The CPIB's focus on organizational excellence is important and perhaps unique among the anticorruption agencies in Asia. Its commitment to organizational excellence is reflected in the many awards it has won, beginning with its certification as an ISO 9000:2001, since 1997. The significance of this award is that the key processes of the CPIB are documented and followed by its officers, and there is also a "regular surveillance audit by the ISO inspectors and regular reviews" of these processes "to keep them up to date" (Soh 2008a: 4). In 1998, the CPIB was awarded the Singapore Quality Class, which certifies the excellence of both public and private organizations in Singapore. In 2003, the CPIB became the first government agency in Singapore to receive the People Excellence Award.[3] Finally, the CPIB was given the Distinguished Public Service Award for Organizational Excellence in 2005 (CPIB 2008).

In line with its emphasis on capability building, the CPIB formed a Computer Forensic Unit in July 2004 to improve its investigative and evidence-gathering capabilities. It has also developed a Technology Masterplan to provide support for its operations and management systems. In 2006, the CPIB improved its system of recruiting investigation officers by introducing a three-stage process involving the use of psychometric tests to evaluate the candidates' aptitudes and competence, case analysis exercises to assess their thinking and people skills, and a structured interview (CPIB 2008).

In addition to its emphasis on investigation and enforcement, the CPIB adopts a proactive approach to its activities on corruption prevention and education. To prevent corruption, the CPIB reviews the procedures and practices in those government agencies where corruption has occurred and makes recommendations to remove the "loopholes and vulnerabilities." The CPIB relies on this review process "to identify potential problem areas and loopholes" in order to reduce the opportunities for corruption (Soh 2008b: 8).

The CPIB has an extensive outreach program to Singaporeans and visitors from other countries. It has a Public Education Group which conducts prevention and education talks for pre-university students, principals and teachers, newly appointed civil servants, law enforcement agencies like the police and immigration, and the management and staff of major organizations in key industries. The CPIB's effectiveness has attracted worldwide attention and it has received many visitors from other countries, including the staff of anticorruption agencies and those foreign officials visiting Singapore under the Singapore Cooperation Program. The CPIB also assists the anticorruption agencies in other countries by arranging attachments for their staff from 21 countries during the past two years (Soh 2008b: 5). Finally, the CPIB conducts anticorruption training courses for civil servants at various levels in Singapore with the Civil Service College. Table 9.1 shows that the number of persons attending the CPIB's corruption prevention and education activities has increased from 3,670 in 2005 to 9,750 in 2007.

The CPIB has grown by eighteen times from a small staff of five members in 1952 to its current strength of 89 personnel in July 2008 (CPIB 2008). Even though the CPIB has increased its manpower during the last 56 years, it is still a small agency as its staff constitutes only 0.14 percent of the 64,539 civil servants in Singapore in 2006 (Department of Statistics 2007: 44). Table 9.2 shows that the CPIB is the smallest of the eight anticorruption agencies compared. However, it is also apparent from Table 9.2 that the CPIB has the third best staff–population ratio of 1:53,086 and per capita expenditure of US$ 1.79 after Macao's Commission Against Corruption and Hong Kong's Independent Commission Against Corruption. In other words, the PAP government has demonstrated its political will in curbing corruption by providing the CPIB with adequate staff and funding. Indeed, the CPIB's budget

Table 9.1 Number of persons attending CPIB's corruption prevention and education activities, 2005–2007

Activity	2005	2006	2007
Prevention and education talks	2,500	4,500	7,000
Visits by foreign delegates	1,000	1,500	2,000
Visits by local organizations	20	200	350
Student visits	150	200	400
Total	3,670	6,400	9,750

Source: CPIB (2008).

has increased from S$ 1,024,370 (US$ 474,245) in 1978 to S$ 12,726,405 (US$ 7,666,509) in 2005 (Quah 2007a: 24). On the other hand, the unfavorable staff–population ratios and low per capita expenditures of the anticorruption agencies in South Korea, Thailand, India, the Philippines, and Indonesia reflect their governments' lack of political will in combating corruption.

The CPIB's location within the PMO since 1969 has raised concern about its independence among policy-makers in those Asian countries who are interested in the transferability of Singapore's anticorruption strategy and the possibility that the political leaders can use the CPIB-style agency against their political foes (Quah 2007a: 23–24). However, even though the CPIB comes under the PMO's purview, it has not failed to investigate all allegations of corruption against political leaders and senior civil servants in Singapore as the PAP government is committed to curbing corruption. The four PAP leaders investigated for corruption by the CPIB included: the Minister for National Development, Tan Kia Gan, in 1966; a Minister of State, Wee Toon Boon, in 1975; Phey Yew Kok, an MP and trade union leader, in 1979; and Teh Cheang Wan, Minister for National Development, in 1986. The senior civil servants who were found guilty of corruption and imprisoned were the Director of the Commercial Affairs Department, the Chief Executive Officer of the Trade Development Board, and the Deputy Chief Executive of the Public Utilities Board (Quah 2007a: 25–26).

To ensure the CPIB's independence, the Constitution of Singapore was amended in 1991 to establish the elected president. Article 22G empowers the CPIB's director to investigate ministers and senior bureaucrats without the prime minister's consent if he obtains the consent of the elected president. This means that the CPIB can investigate the prime minister if it obtains the elected president's permission to do so (CPIB 2003b: 2.16). Thio Li-Ann has argued that the elected presidency in Singapore was "an institutional response to curb the untrammeled power of the parliamentary executive" as the "existence of a *de facto* single-party dominant state" has "thrown the checks and balances dynamic into disequilibrium" (Thio 1997: 101). In short,

Table 9.2 Comparative data on eight anticorruption agencies in 2005

Anticorruption agency	Personnel	Budget (US$)	Population	Staff–population ratio	Per capita expenditure (US$)
Macao CAC	112	10.6 million	488,100	1:4,358	21.72
Hong Kong ICAC	1,194	85 million	7 million	1:5,863	12.14
Singapore CPIB	82	7.7 million	4.3 million	1:53,086	1.79
South Korea KICAC	205	17.8 million	47.8 million	1:233,171	0.37
Thailand NCCC	924	22.8 million	64.2 million	1:69,481	0.36
India CBI	4,711	30.3 million	1,081.2 million	1:229,505	0.28
Philippines Ombudsman	957	12 million	81.4 million	1:85,057	0.15
Indonesia CEC	305	18 million	222.6 million	1:729,836	0.08

Sources: CAC (2006): 119, 123; ICAC (2006): 28; Republic of Singapore (2007): 371-372; CBI (2006): 38, 44; KICAC (2006): 6; Office of the Ombudsman (2006): 73, 91; ONCCC (2006): 85, 117; and Davidsen, Juwono and Timberman (2006): 52.

the elected presidency is designed to check the power of the prime minister in Singapore's one-party dominant parliament as, "without certain safeguards, it would be quite easy for a corrupt prime minister to squander the country's hard-earned official foreign reserves" (Quah 2008: 29).

Evaluating Singapore's anticorruption strategy

The CPIB has enforced the POCA impartially without fear or favor because of the support it has received from the PAP government. Indeed, the effectiveness of Singapore's anticorruption strategy is reflected in Table 9.3, which shows Singapore's consistently favorable rankings and scores on Transparency International's Corruption Perceptions Index (CPI) (1995–2008), Hong Kong's Political and Economic Risk Consultancy (PERC) annual surveys (1995–2008), and the World Bank's governance indicator on the control of corruption (1996–2007).

Singapore's effectiveness in curbing corruption can be attributed to a large extent to the CPIB's effectiveness in impartially enforcing the POCA as reflected in these performance indicators: (1) the CPIB exceeded its target of completing 62 percent of its investigations within 30 days by an average of 31.3 percent during 1999–2002; (2) it exceeded its target of completing 90 percent of cases in a year from 1999–2002; (3) it increased its prosecution rate from 47 percent in 2000 to 60 percent in 2002; (4) it investigated an average of 60 percent of the reports during 1998–2002 (CPIB 2003a: 3.24, 3.25, 5.36, 14.96); and (5) it has

Table 9.3 Singapore's ranking and scores on CPI, PERC, and control of corruption, 1995–2008

Year	CPI rank and score	PERC rank and score	Control of corruption percentile rank
1995	3rd (9.26)	1st (1.20)	NA
1996	7th (8.80)	1st (1.09)	97.6
1997	9th (8.66)	1st (1.05)	NA
1998	7th (9.1)	1st (1.43)	100.0
1999	7th (9.1)	1st (1.55)	NA
2000	6th (9.1)	1st (0.71)	99.5
2001	4th (9.2)	1st (0.83)	NA
2002	5th (9.3)	1st (0.90)	99.5
2003	5th (9.4)	1st (0.38)	99.0
2004	5th (9.3)	1st (0.50)	99.5
2005	5th (9.4)	1st (0.65)	99.0
2006	5th (9.3)	1st (1.30)	98.1
2007	4th (9.3)	1st (1.20)	96.1
2008	4th (9.2)	1st (1.13)	NA

Note: The CPI score ranges from 0 (most corrupt) to 10 (least corrupt); and the PERC score ranges from 0 (least corrupt) to 10 (most corrupt).
Sources: Compiled from www.transparency.org, info.worldbank.org/governance/wgi/sc_chart.asp, www.cpib.gov.sg, "Singapore Rankings" (2008), and Channelnewsasia.com (Hoe 2008).

consistently achieved a conviction rate of between 95 percent and 99 percent (CPIB 2008).

The CPIB's effectiveness has also been confirmed by its favorable public perception in the October 2002 survey of 1,000 Singaporeans. First, 13 percent of these respondents rated corruption control in Singapore as excellent, 42 percent as very good, 39 percent as good, and only 7 percent as fair. Similarly, 71 percent of the respondents agreed or strongly agreed that the CPIB had done well in solving corruption offenses; 61 percent of them trusted the CPIB to keep Singapore corruption-free; and 56 percent of them agreed or strongly agreed that the CPIB was world-class in curbing corruption. Finally, nearly 70 percent of the respondents said that the CPIB was impartial in its investigations, and 65 percent of them believed that the CPIB had not abused its investigation powers (CPIB 2003a: 5.40, 14.97).

However, it would be inaccurate to attribute Singapore's success in minimizing corruption solely to the CPIB's efforts. Apart from the political will of the PAP government, Singapore's ability to curb corruption has also been assisted by its reliance on meritocracy, the policy of paying competitive salaries for political leaders and senior civil servants, the elimination of red tape, and the reliance on e-government to reduce the opportunities for corruption.

Singapore inherited the tradition of meritocracy from the British colonial government, which established the Public Service Commission (PSC) in January 1951 to keep politics out of the civil service and to accelerate the pace of localization. The PAP government has maintained the tradition of meritocracy by retaining the PSC to ensure that civil servants are recruited and promoted on the basis of merit. The PSC has succeeded in attracting the "best and brightest" citizens to join the civil service by awarding the best students in their cohort with scholarships and retaining them after their graduation (Quah 2004: 93–96). In November 1992, Prime Minister Goh Chok Tong asserted that meritocracy was the key to Singapore's success as "it is this practice of meritocracy in the civil service, in politics, in business and in schools, which has allowed Singaporeans to achieve excellence and to compete against others" (Goh 1992: 15)

One year later, Senior Minister Lee Kuan Yew stressed the importance of meritocracy to seventeen leaders from ten African countries attending a conference in Singapore on "The Relevance of Singapore's Experience for Africa": "A strong political leadership needs a neutral, efficient, honest Civil Service. Officers must be recruited and promoted completely on merit ... They must be adequately paid so that temptations will not be difficult to resist" (Lee 1994: 5).

Having attracted the "best and brightest" Singaporeans into the civil service and government, the challenge was to retain them, especially in the wake of competition for talent in the private sector since the 1970s. During its first twelve years (1959–71), the PAP government could not afford to raise the salaries of civil servants even though a 1968 report on public sector salaries had recommended wage increases of more than 25 percent for most civil servants (Quah 2003: 148). However, Singapore's rapid economic growth during the 1970s and 1980s resulted in higher salaries and substantial bonuses in the private sector and led to a brain drain of talented civil servants. The PAP government sought to stem the brain drain by increasing the salaries of civil servants and political leaders periodically from 1972 to January 1994. In October 1994, a White Paper on *Competitive Salaries for Competent and Honest Government* was presented to parliament to justify the pegging of the salaries of ministers and senior civil servants to the average salaries of the top four earners in six private sector professions. This policy of paying competitive salaries has succeeded in preventing political leaders and permanent secretaries from leaving for private-sector jobs. However, this policy has been "ineffective in preventing Division I officers below the head of department level" from leaving the civil service (Quah 2003: 158).

As unnecessary regulations provide opportunities for corruption, the PAP government has initiated various measures to reduce these opportunities by cutting red tape. The Service Improvement Unit was formed in April 1991 to improve the quality of service in the civil service and statutory boards by obtaining public feedback on the removal of unnecessary regulations (Quah 1995b: 339–40). In May 1995, Public Service for the 21st Century (PS21) was introduced to improve the quality of service and prepare the civil service to welcome and accept change. As part of PS21, the Cut Waste Panel was formed in September 2003 "to receive suggestions from the public on where the government can cut waste, remove frills and make savings in the delivery of public services" (Quah 2007b: 167–68).

The PAP government also relies on e-government to enhance transparency and reduce opportunities for corruption by simplifying the procedures for obtaining business licenses. In 2004, the On-line Applications System for Integrated Services (OASIS) was launched to enable the public to "apply, renew or terminate 85 different types of licenses" online. Similarly, to reduce the opportunities for corruption and improve efficiency and transparency in procurement, the online procurement portal known as *GeBiz* was introduced to enable government procurement to be done through the internet (Soh 2008b: 7).

Singapore's success in cutting red tape is manifested in its first ranking among 178 countries in the World Bank's "Doing Business" survey in 2008 (World Bank 2007: 4–6). By implementing the above measures, the PAP government has reduced the opportunities for corruption through the elimination of red tape and the reliance on e-government.

Conclusion: keeping the government honest and effective

The critical challenge facing the PAP government in institutionalizing good governance in Singapore is the need to maintain and preserve the tradition of honest and effective government. As there is no guarantee that future political leaders will remain honest and incorrupt, the current anticorruption strategy should be continued and periodically reviewed and fine-tuned to ensure its continued effectiveness.

In July 2005, Prime Minister Lee Hsien Loong revised the code of conduct to prevent ministers and their families from accepting gifts or services which place them in a position which conflicts with their public duty. Members of Parliament (MPs) are required to be careful in accepting directorships and to report their interests in companies to avoid conflicts of interest (Lim 2005: 1). Prime Minister Lee explained that these measures were necessary because:

> The integrity and reputation of the PAP MPs and Government is our most precious asset, which has been built up over half a century. If we lose this, we will lose the respect of voters and the confidence of investors, and Singapore will go down.
>
> (Quoted in Koh and Lee 2005: H3)

Similarly, 23 years ago, Prime Minister Lee Kuan Yew asked this question in parliament: "How is Singapore to preserve its most precious assets?" His answer was:

> An administration that is absolutely corruption-free. A political leadership that can be subject to the closest scrutiny because it sets the highest standards. It is not easy, because if we lose this, then our reason for our existence, our *raison d'être* ... will disappear.
>
> (*Straits Times*, 23 March 1985: 14)

Singapore's success in combating corruption and its ability to maintain the tradition of clean government for the past 49 years under the PAP government are important assets which should be safeguarded for the country's long-term survival. Hence, to institutionalize good governance in Singapore, the PAP government or any future government must be able to persuade talented citizens to join the government and civil service and to motivate them to behave ethically and rationally for the national interest. In the final analysis, whether the PAP government will succeed in attaining this objective will depend also on the presence of these five preconditions: (1) continued political stability to prevent the exodus of foreign investment and talented citizens to other countries; (2) maintaining the tradition of clean government by continuing the effective anticorruption strategy; (3) implementing sound macroeconomic policies to ensure sustained economic growth; (4) maintaining racial harmony to ensure political stability and prevent discrimination towards minority groups; and (5) sharing the benefits of economic growth among all citizens to minimize income inequality and enhance the government's legitimacy.

Acknowledgement

I am grateful to Mr Soh Kee Hean, director of the CPIB, and his two senior colleagues who kindly granted me an interview on 27 June 2008 and shared their extensive knowledge and relevant information on the CPIB with me. However, they are not responsible for the views expressed in this chapter.

Notes

1 Mexico is ranked 72nd with a score of 3.5 on the 2007 CPI.
2 This Act was expanded and renamed as the Corruption, Drug Trafficking and Other Serious Crimes (Confiscation of Benefits) Act, Chapter 65A, in 1999.
3 The process of "transforming business through People" in the CPIB is documented in CPIB (2003b).

References

CAC (Commission Against Corruption) (2006) *2005 Annual Report of the Commission Against Corruption of Macao*, Macao: CAC.

Central Bureau of Investigation (2006) *Annual Report 2005*, New Delhi: CBI.

CPIB (Corrupt Practices Investigation Bureau) (2003a) *Swift and Sure Action: Four Decades of Anticorruption Work*, Singapore: CPIB.

—— (2003b) *Transforming Business through People Excellence: Corrupt Practices Investigation Bureau 2003 People Excellence Award Winner*, Singapore: CPIB.

—— (2004) *Corrupt Practices Investigation Bureau*, Singapore: CPIB.

—— (2008) Interview with the CPIB's director and two senior officers on 27 June 2008 and subsequent information provided in emails of 3 and 11 July 2008.

Davidsen, S., Juwono, V., and Timberman, D.G. (2006) *Curbing Corruption in Indonesia 2004–2006: A Survey of National Policies and Approaches*, Jakarta and Washington, DC: Center for Strategic and International Studies and United States–Indonesia Society.

Department of Statistics (2007) *Yearbook of Statistics 2007*, Singapore: Department of Statistics.

—— (2008) "Key annual indicators," online. Available at www.singstat.gov.sg/stats/keyind.html (accessed 8 August 2008).

Drysdale, J. (1984) *Singapore: Struggle for Success*, Singapore: Times Books International.

Goh, C.T. (1992) "My urgent mission," *Petir*, 11–12 (November/December).

Hoe, Y.N. (2008) "Singapore voted cleanest Asian economy in PERC survey," Channelnewsasia.com. Online. Available at www.channelnewsasia.com/stories/singaporelocalnews/view/334265/1/.html (accessed 8 August 2008).

ICAC (Independent Commission Against Corruption) (2006) *2005 Annual Report, Hong* Kong: ICAC.

KICAC (Korea Independent Commission against Corruption (2006) *Annual Report 2005*, Seoul: KICAC.

Koh, L. and Lee, L. (2005) "Board seats: code updated for MPs," *Straits Times*, 6 July.

Lee, G.B. (2005) *The Syonan Years: Singapore under Japanese Rule 1942–1945*, Singapore: National Archives of Singapore and Epigram Private.

Lee, K.Y. (1994) "Can Singapore's experience be relevant to Africa?" in *Can Singapore's Experience be Relevant to Africa?* Singapore: Singapore International Foundation.

—— (1998) *The Singapore Story: Memoirs of Lee Kuan Yew*, Singapore: Times Edition.

—— (2000) *From Third World to First, The Singapore Story: 1965–2000*, Singapore: Times Media Private.

Lim, L. (2005) "Rules for ministers updated," *Straits Times*, 6 July.

Morris, S.D. (1991) *Corruption and Politics in Contemporary Mexico*, Tuscaloosa: University of Alabama Press.

Office of the Ombudsman (2006) *2005 Annual Report*, Quezon City: Office of the Ombudsman.

ONCCC (Office of the National Counter Corruption Commission (2006) *The National Counter Corruption Commission*, Bangkok: ONCCC.

Quah, J.S.T. (1978) *Administrative and Legal Measures for Combating Bureaucratic Corruption in Singapore*, Occasional Paper No. 34, Singapore: Department of Political Science, University of Singapore.

—— (1979) "Police corruption in Singapore: an analysis of its forms, extent and causes," *Singapore Police Journal*, 10(1): 7–43.

—— (1982) "Bureaucratic corruption in the ASEAN countries: a comparative analysis of their anti-corruption strategies," *Journal of Southeast Asian Studies*, 13(1): 153–77.

—— (1995a) "Controlling corruption in city-states: a comparative study of Hong Kong and Singapore," *Crime, Law and Social Change*, 22: 391–414.

—— (1995b) "Sustaining quality in the Singapore civil service," *Public Administration and Development*, 15(3): 335–43.

—— (1998) "Singapore's model of development: is it transferable?" in H.S. Rowen (ed) *Behind East Asian Growth: The Political and Social Foundations of Prosperity*, London: Routledge, 105–25 (Ch. 5).

—— (2003) "Paying for the 'best and brightest': rewards for high public office in Singapore," in C. Hood, B.G. Peters, and G.O.M. Lee (eds) *Reward for High Public Office: Asian and Pacific Rim States*, London: Routledge.

—— (2004) "The public service commission in Singapore: an evaluation of its first 50 years," in A. Nakamura (ed.) *Public Reform, Policy Change, and New Public Management*, Tokyo: EROPA Local Government Center.

—— (2007a) *Combating Corruption Singapore-Style: Lessons for Other Asian Countries*, Maryland Series in Contemporary Asian Studies No. 2, Baltimore: School of Law, University of Maryland.

—— (2007b) "Administrative reform in Singapore: an evaluation of Public Service 21 (1995–2004)," in D. Argyriades, O.P. Dwivedi, and J.G. Jabbra (eds) *Public Administration in Transition: Essays in Honor of Gerald E. Caiden*, London: Vallentine Mitchell.

—— (2008) "Good governance, accountability and administrative reform in Singapore," *American Journal of Chinese Studies*, 15(1): 17–34.

Republic of Singapore (1994) *The Budget for the Financial Year 1994/95*, Singapore: Budget Division, Ministry of Finance.

—— (2007) *The Budget for the Financial Year 2007/2008*, Singapore: Budget Division, Ministry of Finance.

"Singapore Rankings" (2008) Online. Available at www.sedb.com/edb/sg/en_uk/index/why_singapore/singapore_rankings.html?showM (accessed 9 August 2008).

Soh, K.H. (2008a) "Corruption enforcement," paper presented at the Second Seminar of the International Association of Anticorruption Associations in Chongqing, China, 17–18 May 2008.

—— (2008b) "Role of awareness and education in the fight against corruption," paper presented at the Asia Anticorruption Conference in Qatar, 9–11 June 2008.

Tamboer, K. (1996) "Albert Winsemius: 'founding father' of Singapore." *IIAS Newsletter*, 9 (summer): 29.

Thio, L.A. (1997) "The elected president and the legal control of government: *quis custodiet ipsos custodes*," in K.Y.L. Tan and P.E. Lam (eds) *Managing Political Change in Singapore: The Elected Presidency*, London: Routledge.

World Bank (2007) "*Doing business in 2008*," Washington, DC, online. Available at www.doingbusiness.org/documents/FullReport/2008/DB08_Full_Report.pdf (accessed 8 August 2008).

10 Combating corruption in India

Challenges and approaches

O.P. Dwivedi, D.S. Mishra,
and Meera Mishra

Introduction

A survey conducted on tracking corruption in eleven public services extra-polates that 145.4 million households paid bribes worth Rs 210.68 billion during the year 2005 (CMS 2005: 13–14). This means an average of nearly Rs 1,500 was paid as extra money by households in receiving one or more of these services through the year. The study focused on corruption experienced by the general public in securing services from government to which they are entitled; if it were to cover the extent of corruption at other levels such as businesspersons paying bribes to tax officials, and mega corruption in pro-curements of public works, equipments and consultancy services, the fluidity of corruption money would be astounding. In another study concerning drought management in Bolangir district of Orissa province, 63 percent of the respondents stated that the government's welfare schemes were riddled with corruption (Srinivas and Nayar 2007: 20–21). Not surprisingly the Chief Economic Advisor to the Finance Ministry said that one had to chase every rupee[1] of public expenditure to see whether it was producing results or not and whether it was actually building the roads or educating the child it was meant to (Lahiri 2007: 26).

Transparency International (TI) placed India 72nd among 180 countries with a Corruption Perception Index (CPI) of 3.5 in its Annual Report pub-lished on 26 September 2007 (TI 2007). CPI ranges between 10 (most clean) and 0 (most corrupt). The low score raises alarm and throws a challenge to those who are responsible for Indian governance systems to take measures which will rescue the country from the ill-effects of corruption. A study conducted on non-resident Indians (NRIs) by the US-based Association for India's Development (AID), a non-profit organization, revealed that 81 per-cent of respondents had to pay bribes at some stage or other for receiving services for themselves or for their parents (Das 2007: 9).

Studies suggest a strong correlation between corruption and poverty. Cor-ruption not only prevents a country from deriving optimum benefits from its resources in nation-building but also endangers national well-being and security, thus hitting the most vulnerable and deprived disproportionately

(Dwivedi and Mishra 2007: 717–20). While corruption has spread at all levels in the governance system like a disease, this essay briefly outlines its status and examines its causes, including the perplexing question as to why there is soaring corruption in a society which is deeply religious and abides by strong public and private morals. The essay cites instances from government studies regarding corruption and suggests specific measures to tackle this major impediment to growth and equitable distribution of and access to public services. The paper proposes certain out-of-the-box approaches as alternatives to traditional methods of controlling corruption which have not yielded adequate results over the years.

The state of corruption in India

The resounding success of *Munnabhai MBBS*, a Bollywood film about fighting corruption in public life through Gandhian principles (*Gandhigiri*) shows how the public at large associates itself with day-to-day experiences of corruption. CMS (2005: 1–4) mentions that 62 percent of respondents said that they had personal experience of paying bribes or "using contacts" to get jobs done in public offices. The same survey revealed that three-fourths of citizens believe that the level of corruption in public services is increasing. According to this survey, the police stands out highest on the corruption index followed by the judiciary (lower courts) and land administration. The level of corruption varies in different parts of the country and over different government sectors including essential services like health, education, water supply and other civic amenities. The existence of such a high level of corruption impelled Justice Markandeya Katju of the Supreme Court of India to remark that corrupt persons should be hanged from the nearest lamp post (Panchu 2007: 11). Former Chief Vigilance Commissioner, N. Vittal (1999: 1) mentions that owing to the corruption and inefficiency in four specific departments— Customs, Central Excise, Income Tax and the Enforcement Directorate—and the resultant failure to curb illegal activities and evasion of taxes, the Indian economy is experiencing a high quantum of black money estimated to be around Rs 400–401,000 billion. He further states that a substantial portion of the film, urban construction and various other small industries are thriving on this illegally generated wealth. Moreover, the use of such money in elections promotes nexus between criminals and politicians. This state of affairs has existed for more than four decades, as the Santhanam Committee lamented: "We wish we could confidently and without reservation assert that at the political level, Ministers, Legislators, party officials were free from this malady" (Santhanam Committee 1964: 12). The situation has subsequently become more acute.

Although, in the last two decades, newspaper headlines have reported various scams involving highly placed politicians, bureaucrats and businesspersons, there have not been any significant convictions. The Central Vigilance Commission (CVC) points out that public procurement is one of the major sources of corruption (CVC 2004: 9). Khare (2007: 8) states the paradox of the media, which is expected to be a watchdog for probity in public life, having lost its strength because those involved in it are corruptible for positions of power and personal financial gains. Vittal (1999: 2) mentions that initially in the post-independence era individuals attempted to corrupt institutions, but later corruption became institutionalized and an inevitable culture in public life. In a study of the metropolitan water supply and sanitation of India, Davis (2004: 55–61) mentions five major areas of corruption: (1) speed money for seeking new electric connections/getting repairs; (2) collusive action for illegal connection or falsifying bills; (3) commissions in award of contracts for works and services; (4) kickbacks in execution of works/procurement of machinery and equipments; and (5) transfers to "plum" positions.[2] In some instances, government agencies are known to use front organizations for the perpetuation of corruption (CVC 2004: 10). In a study by CVC (2001: 9) concerning India's elite Indian Administrative Service (IAS), it was found that 66 percent of cases of alleged misconduct concerned undue favor and/or causing undue loss to the organization, 11 percent the possession of assets disproportionate to known sources of income, and 6 percent the demand/acceptance of bribes. If this is the status of the elite service, the extent of corruption in other services can be guessed.

It is against this background that the Supreme Court of India made the observation on 3 February 2000 that corruption in a civilized society is like cancer which, if not detected in time, is sure to render malignant the polity of the country, leading to disastrous consequences for the socioeconomic–political system. The Court added that corruption is not only anti-people; it is aimed at and targeted against them (referred by Srivastava 2001: 84). Like his predecessors, Dr Manmohan Singh, prime minister of India, pointed out that corruption is eating away the vitals of institutions of governance and the society and is a threat to the national well-being. Reiterating national resolve for providing a corruption-free, transparent, accountable, responsive and responsible governance system, the prime minister urged zero tolerance to corruption and a multi-pronged approach to stem the rot (CBI Bulletin 2006a: 11).

Why so much corruption in a religious country like India?

Corruption literature outlines various economic, socio-cultural, political, legal, ethico-religious, administrative and psychological explanations for the existence of corruption in different societies. It elucidates how rent-seeking behavior is reinforced in public life. But what is paradoxical about the Indian society is the coexistence of a very high level of public and private religiosity on the one hand and the prevalence of corrupt practices on the other. It may be thought that with such religious upbringing and moral beliefs, people would automatically be more ethical (compared to societies where religion has less prominence) and not indulge in or condone corruption. But the relationship between corruption and religious practices and rituals (in the Indian context) is complex. Even though religion plays a prominent role in people's everyday life, they do not appear to subscribe to moral behavior associated with religion. This paradox is discussed further in the following paragraphs.

Rituals are intricately woven into the fabric of religion in the country but they may be innocently or deliberately misinterpreted to suit personal convenience. Popular beliefs abound that, by making specific offerings to a deity, donating funds and building temples, bathing in holy rivers, one can seek absolution of one's sinful deeds, including corruption. It is, therefore, not surprising to find people visiting temples, beseeching special favors, including "quick fix" solutions, not only to cover up their corrupt deeds or unethical behavior but also to pacify their consciences. The authors suggest that in those nations where religiosity abounds, corruption is tolerated more than in other nations. A review of the past ten years of Transparency International CPI indicates that scores were poor in those nations where religiosity is prominent, suggesting that people possibly interpreted their religious beliefs conveniently to rationalize their conduct.

Besides religiosity, another factor in tolerating corruption is the influence of ascriptive considerations. Indian society is highly associated/connected on the basis of family, kinship, caste, neighborhood, ethnic origin and religious affiliations that call for individual loyalties. Dwivedi (1967: 247–49) points out that when it comes to choice between loyalty and merit, even civil servants are influenced by the former. Close social networks and emphasis on loyalty make nepotism a culturally acceptable phenomenon. In brief, ascriptive considerations lead to unethical and corrupt practices.

To some extent the growing ethical deficit in the society could be linked to the disintegration of the extended or joint family system; the collective conscience of large family settings introduced internal checks and balances among individuals and induced a sense of duty and responsibility towards the larger family and society. But with growing industrialization, urbanization, the rise of materialism and resultant nuclearization of families, those values have been overtaken by greed and self-righteousness, and one's obligation to the extended family, society and the nation is forgotten.

Traditionally Indian culture does not endorse materialism and monetary goals as a noble pursuit in life. Instead, those who shun materialism are idolized. However, during the past two to three decades, with the rise of the neo-rich groups, the lure of materialism has taken over the traditional emphasis on renunciation as an act deterring the aggressive pursuit of financial gains. Corruption provides a quick short-cut for fulfilling such desires, which are ever growing in a materialistic world. The growing nexus between politics and crime and the liberal use of deviously earned money to boost political careers sends out the signal that the ends (power, supremacy) justify the means (corruption).

Basu (2007: 28) discusses this phenomenon by explaining why countries like India develop such a tolerance which eventually makes combating corruption and related unethical activities an uphill task for reformers. For example, among several government school teachers, there is large-scale absenteeism, and suboptimal use of paid time. Amazingly, the public, despite inconveniences, neither agitates nor demands accountability. Is this skewed sense of tolerance a deeply ingrained fatalism in the society?

Access to basic services and a life of dignity is an arduous task for the common person. From getting a child admitted into school to obtaining an uninterrupted supply of cooking gas, every aspect of the common person's life is riddled with competition in the midst of scarcity, leaving little room for considerations for societal common goods. In fact, an ingrained apathy results from this everyday struggle and a moral quandary does not bother people if they have to pay bribes to get services or jump the queue.

Institutional grounds for combating corruption

Dwivedi (1967: 246–47) argued that the colonial legacy of having two sets of rules, one for the ruling class and another for the ruled, had been imitated by indigenous politicians and bureaucrats who bent rules to suit their needs after independence. When politicians and bureaucrats jump queues or violate administrative procedures and norms, their behavior is in turn copied by junior employees. Another aspect is that the British introduced several layers of checks and balances to control administrative decision-making, based on their inherent distrust of the locals; such layers exist even today and act as gates which have to open through the offering of bribes. Sixty years after independence it is unrealistic to blame "the colonial legacy" alone for the existence of corruption.

Vittal (1999: 6) points to the presence of large number of outmoded rules and administrative regulations, some of which ought to be scrapped, and others redrafted so as to make them relevant to the current situation. Maheshwari (2002: 312–15) mentions that Indian society has become highly legislated, where every problem seeks legal redress. With laws being passed each year without much attention to the resources required to implement them, procedures drafted under such laws remain complicated and require contacts at different levels for accessing government services; and every interface is prone to abuse.

Even though the Prevention of Corruption Act has existed since 1947 and has been replaced by its stricter version, the Prevention of Corruption Act, 1988, it has remained largely ineffective in controlling corruption. The conviction rates are abysmally low. A key provision of the Act deals with having wealth disproportionate to one's known sources of income. However, hardly anyone is convicted, owing to hyper-technical objections devised by lawyers to buy time in the courts. Panchu (2007: 11) mentions that the real issue in terms of the commission of corrupt acts does not even get discussed before the court(s) and peripheral issues take all the time. Vittal (1999: 2) mentions that the conviction rate in Indian courts is only 6 percent and nearly 30 million cases are pending. He adds that on average it takes more than ten years to dispose of a case, diluting the very intent of its filing.

The Discipline and Appeal Rules for public servants in India prescribe cumbersome procedures for framing charges, examining explanations, enquiries, producing witnesses and evidence, opportunities for cross-examination, and so on, before any punishment can be inflicted (Raj 1984: 127). Even those held for fraud or corruption have several escape routes, like administrative appeals, mercy petitions, administrative tribunals and the courts. In most cases the accused is reinstated after long-drawn-out procedures and can easily slip back in his or her position anonymously, as contemporaries in the meanwhile get transferred and moved on. They mingle in the system and continue the misdeeds for which they were punished.

In Indian administration, officers are moved from one post to another frequently, while the tenure of administrative/support staff and clerks is much longer. This helps the clerks gain a sound understanding of the relevant rules, regulations, procedures and precedents and helps them provide informed advice to the decision-makers based on their knowledge. However, this also means that they are able to influence the decision-making process as officers comply with whatever is noted in the files by them. This opens up scope for corruption, as those who are decision-takers may not have full exposure to the parameters for taking the decisions and are, therefore, helpless in the hands of those who are producing notes on the files. This kind of information gap has major potential for corruption in the system (Raj 1984: 118–21).

Under the parliamentary system, ministers are responsible for policy-making and for the functioning of their departments. This leaves the administrative officers without direct responsibility for their actions. Instead of using this immunity to be fair and fearless contributors to governance, public servants misuse this privilege by passing the buck when it comes to accountability for non-delivery or wrongdoings. Such long chains have been created for different administrative actions that it is very difficult to pin anyone down for action/ inaction. The existing checks and balances in the system only make accountability yet more cumbersome, offering loopholes for the corrupt officials to escape charges.

CVC (2004: 7) mentions that complaints continue to be the main means for the public to deal with corruption and harassment at the hands of public servants. The Commission has taken various measures to deal with public complaints effectively; however, this reactive approach leads to taking action after the corruption has already taken place. Now the Commission is emphasizing a pro-active preventive approach wherein systems are recast to close opportunities for corruption.

Varma (2004: 75–79) writes that in India, right from admission to prestigious schools to appointments through the Public Service Commission to government departments, or the transfer of government officials to "lucrative" posts where "extra" money can be made, to securing government contracts, or the willingness of street vendors to pay bribes to the police and/or municipal officers to be able to keep selling from their unlicensed stalls, corruption is rampant and systematic. Is this because of the prevalence of systemic corruption, embedded in the cultural software of the country where corruption exists as a form of pure rationality of the end justifying the means? Or perhaps it is a matter of simple expediency in an otherwise bureaucratized system. Could it be that the prevailing ethical decay is a function of weak moral leadership combined with a breakdown of basic values resulting from an upsurge of moral relativism? Furthermore, ethical deficit and double standards are pervasive in the public place, in business and even in primary groups. Who are the effective agents for closing the ethical deficit? Obviously, it is those who occupy public offices, have the mandate and the responsibility— political, legal, moral and fiscal—for good governance, who are accountable for their actions taken in the public domain, and thus answerable to the public for a large-scale decline in moral values.

From childhood through school years, Indians are raised in the tradition of compliance to authority. Students are discouraged from questioning their teachers, and children who question their elders are often reprimanded. There is an emphasis on social ties and reverence of powerful and senior people. Most Indians are trained to turn a blind eye even if they catch a familiar person cheating or stealing. Years of such training blunt the courage and interest in questioning authority. The Right to Information Act, 2005, makes the procedure more practicable as it removes the awkwardness of face-to-face questioning. However, as this is still new, it remains to be seen how it will change the landscape of governance in the country.

The Central Vigilance Commission plays a crucial role in combating corruption in India. It was established in 1964 as an apex body for exercising general superintendence and control over vigilance administration of central government organizations and agencies as per recommendations of the Santhanam Committee Report on the Prevention of Corruption. The Commission deals with cases involving lack of probity and integrity in the functioning of the government or its subordinate bodies. In compliance with the Supreme Court's pronouncements in a writ petition filed by Vineet Narain and others, the government of India has made it a statutory body through the CVC Act, 2003. The Commission has also been empowered to oversee investigations pertaining to the Prevention of Corruption Act, 1988, conducted by the Central Bureau of Investigation (CBI), the premier investigating agency of the country.

In its Annual Report of 2004, the Commission quoted specific instances to express the following concerns in matters related to integrity and disciplinary cases (CVC 2004: 39–62): (1) inordinate delay in disposal of cases, leading to charged officer(s) retiring or cases becoming time-barred; (2) manipulation through relevant papers being lost, dilution of charges or accepting resignations before punishment; (3) taking a soft approach by giving the accused the benefit of the doubt, resorting to token action, showing leniency in deciding the quantum of punishment, dilution of the penalty by appellate authority; and (4) a tardy approach to vigilance matters when a large number of cases are pending at different stages of investigation, leading to the dilution of disciplinary action.

Considering procurements as major area for corruption, the Chief Technical Examiners' Unit (CTE) of the Commission conducts inspection of various works, services and equipment and comes out with specific instances which may cause or have led to corruption in the respective matters. Accordingly, the concerned are expected to explain the deviations, improve systems, and initiate actions against the delinquents. CVC (2004: 63–77) lists various types of lapses and actions taken thereon. These are related to pre-tender, tender and execution of contract stages. As regards the investigation of criminal cases pertaining to misconduct by showing undue favor, obtaining bribes, amassing assets disproportionate to known sources of income, etc. (including trap cases), CVC (2004: 81–82) shows that 1,193 cases with 2,046 public servants were registered during the year 2004. The figures of earlier years show that in around 60 percent cases, prosecution sanctions are granted and nearly two-third end up with convictions. The report mentions that 6,614 cases were pending trial in various courts. However, considering the large number of employees of the central government and its subordinate bodies and the general perception of a high prevalence of corruption, which has been corroborated through CMS survey, these figures are extremely insignificant. Therefore, the authors conclude that the working environment in the country provides "low-risk high-gain" opportunities to corrupt individuals.

Means to combat corruption

Caiden (2001: 19) infers that as long as the underlying causes persist, corruption is unlikely to be eliminated altogether; so long as human beings remain greedy, corruption will persist. Anticorruption measures need to address major areas of governance by reducing its scope, lessening its occurrence and implementing fail-safe devices to detect and punish those who are indulging in it. The authors endorse the World Bank's (1997: 105) inference that a multi-pronged strategy is needed to combat corruption. The measures must address the concerns on various fronts and be sustained over a long period of time for tangible outcomes. The Asian Development Bank (ADB) and the Organization for Economic Co-operation and Development (OECD) have jointly issued an anticorruption plan with three pillars: developing effective and transparent systems, strengthening anti-bribery action (i.e. accountability), and supporting active public involvement (i.e. participation) (see Bhargava and Bolongaita 2004: 28–32). This essay recommends approaches suitable to local conditions to deal with corruption in India.

Since independence, India's public services have been reformed at different times. Most recently, the Second Administrative Reforms Commission (established in August 2005) is working on reforming the governance system in the country. The authors believe that this Commission could consider recommending an objective and merit-oriented system of officers' postings and transfers; there is also a need for including ethical cases and morality in the training of officials. Indian bureaucracy is excellent in preparing plans but rather weak when it comes to implementation. Perhaps a result-based but ethically oriented policy-process is required. The prime minister of India stated at the Conference of Heads of Anticorruption/Vigilance Bureau of States, held on 17 November 2006, that the government plans to introduce a new Public Service Bill before Parliament which will have provisions for protection of whistleblowers and aim at developing public services as professional, politically neutral, merit-based and accountable instruments for promoting good governance (CBI Bulletin 2006b: 12). This may provide the opportunity for honest civil servants to expose corrupt colleagues/bosses.

DARPG (2006: 11) argues for a paradigm shift from "lack of trust" of the colonial legacy to "trust in citizens" in redesigning government services. A climate of trust and confidence would change the style of governance, and systems can be designed to identify the exceptions, i.e. rule-breakers. This change may help in re-engineering the processes to remove the complex web of responsibilities, replacing them with specific/ individual duties. This not only improves accountability but acts as a motivating force for efficient and honest officials. Furthermore, with a reduction in the layers of decision-making, the scope for corruption would be reduced.

The *Economist* report on India's "Babu Raj" mentions that, on coming to power, politicians transfer scores of senior officers who are seen as being too close to the policies and programs of the previous government: for example, when Uma Bhararti came to power in Madhya Pradesh province in 2003, she transferred 240 of the province's 296 senior officers (*Economist* 2008: 30). Because of constitutional protection, it is very difficult for politicians to dismiss officers; instead, they transfer them to some ineffective or powerless posts. That is why many bureaucrats "tend to attach themselves to politicians for enrichment and advancement" (*Economist* 2008: 30). Such an entanglement is not without mutual benefits, as rent-seeking is a part of that involvement. This has resulted in a political culture which has corrupted the democracy as well as the state machinery: how can there be a clean administration if the country's leaders and politicians are themselves not free from corrupt practices (Dwivedi and Jain, 1988: 207)? Dhar (2003: 69) argues that political and social domains supervene the administrative and economic domains; therefore, unless the political system is cleaned, the hope of quick and effective economic or administrative reforms is difficult to realize. He further mentions that often it is elections that either slow the reforms wagon or derail it. Therefore, electoral reforms promoting a contest by honest individuals may go a long way to creating clean polity.

In a liberal democratic system, politicians guide and steer the systems of governance, and are expected to show a high degree of honesty and integrity through their conduct. In the case of India, all candidates for national and provincial elections are required to declare their assets and criminal records;

however, once the election is over, no efforts are made to update and track their records. Moreover, when a legislator has a question related to an ethical aspect of his action, he has nowhere to seek an official opinion on the matter. Such an office is needed for India too, akin to the office of Parliamentary Ethics Commissioner in Canada (which has a low level of corruption) who acts as an officer of Parliament and advises the Speaker concerning any case on ethical issues. The office also keeps a track of property holdings based on annual returns of the parliamentarians, keeping the information confidential.

Many civil servants are known to misuse government facilities, which is a form of corruption. Because of the perception that their salaries are low as compared to the private sector, they resort to corrupt practices. To some extent this could be tackled if their perks were monetized and their remuneration made competitive with what is being offered by the business and commercial sectors in the country.

Despite large-scale corruption, there are many dedicated and well-meaning officials in the government who represent "islands of integrity." If the contributions of such honest officials were recognized, these persons might become role-models for others, especially for the fence-sitters. That is why Davis (2004: 67) mentions that a strategy of "shame and pride" is well suited for strongly hierarchical institutions of a country like India. Public assessment of individuals in group staff meetings with superiors and open-air sessions with customers of the Hyderabad Metropolitan Water Supply and Sewage Board helped in improving performance through this strategy. Lahiri (2007: 26) suggests "naming and shaming" as a strategy for improving the work performance of public delivery in the country. The strategy helps in identifying those who are doing their job honestly and sincerely, and giving them public recognition, and at the same time naming the most corrupt officials and holding them up to public disrespect. Jankins and Goetz (1999: 619–20) outline how the instrument of *Jan Sunwai* (conducting impromptu public hearings in villages and small urban centers) ensures transparency and accountability in government services in dealing with poor people. The World Bank also advocates strengthening the "voice" of the public to ensure accountability. The authors infer that if officers are made to answer to the common people and confront their actual work on site, it will force them to be more honest.

Organizations today are suffering not only from corruption but from the paralyzing venom of negative thinking and a fatalistic resignation to corruption as an entirely incurable disease. The antidote is to identify best practices and success stories and replicate these. For example, if emphasis is given to public servants' dedication, loyalty, patriotism and sense of calling/mission, rather than harping on their corrupt, lazy and venal practices, they may be motivated to follow these values and accept their duty with a sense of devotion and honesty. There is great potential for using the Appreciative Inquiry (AI) approach in identifying success stories, analyzing the reasons for their success and replicating these rather than spending time and resources on analyzing failure to check corruption. In the government and allied organizations, the tendency is to focus on what went wrong. AI as a technique requires a paradigm shift in the way organizations work; it requires the gaze to shift from the wrong to the right, from failure to success. This helps in identifying the positive elements which could be reinforced for a multiplier effect.

Delay in taking disciplinary action has dual disadvantages: (1) the real culprits manage to escape punishment because of dilution; and (2) the innocent unnecessarily suffer on account of systems inefficiency. Even though CVC and the government have given directives on time-bound completion of proceedings, the procedures are so elaborate that the charged officers are able to manipulate the delay to their advantage. These procedures need to be revisited and simplified so that the whole process may be concluded in not more than one year in the worst case. Also, considering the large number of cases pending and causing delay in the disposal of criminal cases, judicial reforms are overdue. Justice delayed is justice denied. The corrupt are able to beat the system by delaying action through various ingenious legal battles. The cases dealing with corruption need to be handled on a fast track so that exemplary action may provide deterrents to others. This will inspire and encourage the fence-sitters (who constitute nearly 60–80 percent of the entire public service) to shift towards honesty.

World Bank (2006: 28–31) cites the success of e-governance in the Stamps and Registration Department of Maharashtra in combating corruption through business processes re-engineering (BPR) by setting standards for transactions and the calculation of stamp duty, and improving transparency and accountability in the functioning of the field offices. By revisiting the processes and procedures the system may be redesigned in such a way that decisions are consistent, partiality is removed, the need for personal contact is eliminated, and accountability is ascertained.

Mishra (2007: 361–75) argues that information and communication technology offers a powerful tool which can assist change and create new, efficient, consistent, transparent and accountable systems with no scope for arbitrary discretion, and empowers people by enabling them to check the status of their cases online and provide feedback/ complaints without fear. However, the effectiveness of this instrument depends on how it is designed and implemented; nothing is automatic. Experiences over decades confirm that a successful e-governance requires business process re-engineering, sustained dedication of resources, and strong political will to combat corruption (Konana 2007: 10). A citizen-centric rather than techno-centric approach will bring the desired outcome (Saxena 2005: 512; Brown 2005: 247–48). Finger and Pecoud (2003: 5) visualize the use of information and communication technology for service delivery, monitoring and policy-making as a three-step model: *e-government*, i.e. providing better quality and efficient delivery of services, maybe in partnership with private sector or civil society organizations; *e-regulation*, i.e. regulating price, quality and accessibility; and *e-democracy*, i.e. making policy by taking feedback from public and other stakeholders. Therefore, by leveraging technology, a corruption-free environment can be created.

The Right to Information Act, 2005, has emerged as a strong tool for improving transparency; however, it will take time before the public becomes fully conversant with its provisions and is able to use it judiciously. Subsequent to this Act, the Corruption Perception Index (CPI), published by Transparency International, improved for India from 2.9 in 2005 to 3.5 in 2007. By empowering citizens through awareness campaigns and providing them with requisite information regarding the services delivered by the government, accountability is enhanced. Simplification of forms and procedures further eliminates the role of middlemen or touts, who act as conduits for perpetuating corruption. Further, civil society organizations (CSOs) may keep a watch on public servants in terms of consistency in their dealings, and this may reduce the scope for corruption (World Bank 1997: 9). The Act provides the opportunity for CSOs to seek information from public officials wherever they have doubt about honest functioning. The media may play an important role in making citizens aware of their rights and propagating the value of a clean system; for this they will have to come out of their comfort zone, as has been discussed by Khare (2007: 10).

It is common knowledge in India that when requesting a permit, license or permission to start a business, a person may face a host of file-clearances by various government offices which provide opportunities for delay, harassment and corruption. Davis (2004: 63) and Caseley (2006: 531) conclude that the Single Window Cell (SWC) of the Hyderabad Metropolitan Water Supply and Sewage Board helped in curbing corruption to a great extent. Before the opening of SWC, an individual had to seek a "no objection certificate" (NOC) from fourteen different offices in order to get a new water connection; all these points were potential sources of corruption.

Since the *World Development Report 1997*, the World Bank has been emphasizing a greater role of markets in the provision of infrastructure and other civic services. The competition and choice reduces the scope for corruption. Even the regulatory functions of the government can be so designed that the individual monopoly of the government officials are reduced; instead, the system may allow various players to offer those regulations, with government setting the standards and providing oversight. Furthermore, many government departments have developed and uploaded "citizens' charters" on their websites. What is required is to make these charters more focused by laying down norms for the delivery of services, and to disseminate these standards and procedures widely to ensure their adherence by public agencies. Jain (1998: 361) discusses how effective usage of this instrument ushers in good governance.

The Santhanam Committee Report concludes with the sentence: "the lack of moral earnestness, which has been a conspicuous feature of recent years, is perhaps the greatest single factor which hampers the growth of strong traditions of integrity and efficiency" (Santhanam Committee 1964: 109). Such "lack of moral earnestness" has now engulfed the entire system. What should be done to reduce it? Can spirituality play a role as countervailing software to control greed, exploitation, abuse of power and corruption? Various studies have demonstrated that spirituality plays an important part in the happiness and well-being of people; it can also play a crucial role in keeping the system of governance honest and transparent (Bruce and Novinson 1999; Dwivedi 2007: 276–91; Leland and Denhardt 2005). Dwivedi (2007: 276–91) suggests that it would help instill self-discipline, a sense of public good and service, and absence of arrogance in holding public office; it can serve as both ethical code and operational strategy for the transformation of human character by strengthening the genuine and substantial will to serve ordinary people. Although many believe that spirituality is an integral part of various religious traditions and beliefs, its impact on secular public institutions (e.g. Weber's treatment of the Protestant ethic) is crucial in establishing a strategy for good governance. Spirituality in governance requires belief in *Dharma* (the concept of righteousness) and actively doing good *Karma* (the concept of cause and effect of any activity performed by an individual).

Ultimately, public services, being a subset of the society, reflect the prevalent values and norms. If the society at large has become tolerant to corruption, then it will be very difficult to expect honest dealings by the civil servants. Therefore, all-out efforts should be made to improve the educational system to inculcate strong values, ethical conduct and commitment towards the welfare of the society at large. Attitudes are easier formed than changed. So reaching out to younger people during the adolescent years, when they are forming their attitudes, is critical. Didacticism does not work with this age group, but exposing them to people who embody strong virtues and calling charismatic guest lecturers can be effective. It is important to make honesty a fundamental and basic prerequisite virtue for young minds. The former president of India, A.P.J. Abdul Kalam, presents India Vision 2020, to become a developed nation as an inspiring goal to citizens (Kalam and Rajan 1998: 1–25). Such a vision, if it is materialized, may help not only the government but the civil society and the public at large.

The above listed measures to combat and control corruption in the public domain indicate that serious efforts are needed by all stakeholders to work together in getting rid of this ailment. It is equally true that by simply enacting ethics laws, corruption cannot be reduced. That is why the authors suggest that along with strengthening the institutions of accountability, it is crucial that emphasis be laid on character-building, moral reasoning and promoting good behavior. For this, training programs should be modified to include ethical and spiritual aspects.

Concluding observations

The Indian economy is growing faster than those of many industrialized nations, and that resurgence is experiencing a high rate of growth since the liberalization introduced in early 1990s with a series of reforms, deregulation and privatization. In the budget speech 2007–08, the finance minister of the government of India quoted an estimated growth rate of 9.2 percent in the 2006–07 GDP, and expressed the hope that the 8 percent growth target set for the Tenth Plan will be nearly achieved, despite a poor start in 2002–03 (Chidambaram 2007: 1). India's economic performance is rooted in its indigenous enterprise and funds. The important question is whether this growth can translate into the commensurate well-being of the public without corruption being controlled. All developmental goals, such as poverty alleviation, access to safe drinking water and sanitation, education for all, regular supply of electricity, good roads, and quality health-care, may not materialize unless corruption, which eats away a major portion of public expenditure, is checked. Growth without ethical practices may endanger delivery and work against the interests of the have-nots.

If we agree with the statement of a former CBI director, Joginder Singh, that the rot is so deep that it cannot be solved by speeches or by any one single political party (quoted by Narasimhan 1997), then an all-out effort will have to be made. Towards that end, the authors have given a set of suggestions. We feel that with visionary leadership, motivated youth, empowered communities, and enlightened champions, corruption can be checked. The late prime minister Rajiv Gandhi once said that only 15 percent of every Rupee spent on development reaches the real beneficiaries. Sustained and all-out efforts rather than ad hoc and short-lived campaigns, which not only send wrong signals but develop cynicism (Bardhan 1997: 1338), will be needed to alter this. The Right to Information Act, 2005, has provided an important tool in the hands of civil society and the public in making this dream come true. An interactive dynamic approach, taking care of various reactions, nuances, implications and road bumps, rather than a linear approach could be more effective in achieving these objectives (Grindle and Thomas 1991: 149–50). Accordingly, the promoters of ethical conduct in governance must be aware of a possible backlash by *corruption entrepreneurs*, who could be strong initially because of their amassed wealth and influence but would soon become weak in the face of public and international agencies' outcry against corruption.

Notes

1 Indian currency is called the Rupee (Rs); and as of 1 June 2008, 1 US$ was equal to about 42.50 Rupees.
2 Posts where opportunities abound for making illicit money.

References

Bardhan, P. (1997) "Corruption and development: a review of issues," *Journal of Economic Literature*, 35(3): 1320–46.
Basu, K. (2007) "Let the cream percolate," *Outlook Special Issue: State of the Nation*, New Delhi, 47(15): 28.

Bhargava, V. and Bolongaita, E.P. (2004) "An analytical framework for improving the effectiveness of anticorruption policies and programmes," in World Bank (ed.) *Challenging Corruption in Asia: Case Studies and a Framework for Action*, Washington, DC: World Bank.

Brown, D. (2005) "Electronic government and public administration," *International Review of Administrative Sciences*, 71(2): 241–54.

Bruce, W. and Novinson, J. (2009) "Spirituality in public service: a dialogue," *Public Administration Review*, 59(2): 163–69.

Caiden, G.E. (2001) "Corruption and governance," in G.E. Caiden, O.P. Dwivedi, and J. G. Jabbra (eds.) *Where Corruption Lives*, Bloomfield, CT: Kumarian Press.

Caseley, J. (2006) "Multiple accountability relationships and improved service delivery performance in Hyderabad City, Southern India," *International Review of Administrative Sciences*, 72(4): 531–46.

CBI Bulletin (2006a) "Prime Minister Dr Manmohan Singh delivering speech on the occasion of foundation stone laying ceremony," January.

—— (2006b) "PM's key note address to the biennial conference of heads of anti-corruption/vigilance bureaux of states, UTs and Officers of the CBIs, New Delhi on 17 November 2006," June–December.

Chidambaram, P. (2007) "Budget 2007–8 speech of P. Chidambaram, Minister of Finance, 28-02-2007," in Taxmann (ed.) *Taxmann the Budget 2007–08*, New Delhi: Taxmann Publications.

CMS (2005) "India Corruption Study 2005 to improve governance," New Delhi: Centre for Media Studies, online. Available at www.cmsindia.org/cms/events/publications.htm (accessed 14 July 2007).

CVC (2001) "The Indian Administrative Service: a study of the current state of punitive and preventive vigilance mechanisms," online. Available at www.cvc.nic.in (accessed 28 June 2007).

—— (2004) "Central Vigilance Commission annual report 2004," online. Available at www.cvc.nic.in (accessed 28 June 2007).

DARPG (2006) "Background note: improving public service delivery—management aspects and technology applications," online. Available at http://darpg.nic.in/arpg-website/conference/chiefsecyconf/csc.doc (accessed 8 June 2007).

Das, A. (2007) "81 percent NRIs had to bribe in India," *Hindustan Times* (New Delhi edition), 15 July.

Davis, J. (2004) "Corruption in public service delivery: experience from South Asia water and sanitation sector," *World Development*, 32(1): 53–71.

Dhar, T.N. (2003) "Governance: action, innovations and ethics," in C.P. Barthwal (ed.) *Good Governance in India*, New Delhi: Deep Publications.

Dwivedi, O.P. (1967) "Bureaucratic corruption in developing countries," *Asian Survey*, 7(4): 245–53.

—— (2007) "Spirituality in public administration: a challenge for the well-being of nations," in D. Argyriades, O.P. Dwivedi, and J. G. Jabbra (eds) *Public Administration in Transition*, London: Vallentine Mitchell.

Dwivedi, O.P. and Jain, R.B. (1988) "Bureaucratic morality in India," *International Political Science Review*, 9(3): 205–14.

Dwivedi, O.P. and Mishra, D.S. (2007) "A good governance model for India: search from within," in A. Farazmand and J. Pinkowski (eds) *Handbook of Globalization, Governance and Public Administration*, New York: Taylor & Francis.

Economist (2008) "Battling the babu raj," *The Economist*, 6 March.

Finger, M. and Pecoud, G. (2003) "From e-government to e-governance? Towards a model of e-governance," *Electronic Journal of e-Government*, 1(1): 1–10.

Grindle, M.S. and Thomas, J.W. (1991) *Public Choice and Policy Change: The Political Economy of Reform in Developing Countries*, Baltimore: Johns Hopkins University Press.

Jain, R.B. (1998) "An instrument of public accountability: problems and perspectives in India," *Indian Journal of Public Administration*, 44(3): 354–61.

Jankins, R. and Goetz, A.M. (1999) "Accounts and accountability: theoretical implication of the right to information movement in India," *Third World Quarterly*, 20 (3): 603–22.

Kalam, A.P.J. and Rajan, Y.S. (1998) *India 2020: A Vision for the New Millennium*, New Delhi: Viking Penguin India.

Khare, H. (2007) "Reclaiming the power of disapproval," *The Hindu* (New Delhi Edition), 15 March.

Konana, P. (2007) "Can IT enabled services lower corruption?," *The Hindu* (Thiruvanathpuram Edition), 29 January.

Lahiri, A. (2007) "Deliverance from deprivation: reforms have to chase expenses to see if they are producing results," *Outlook Special Issue: State of the Nation*, 9 April, New Delhi, 47(15): 26

Leland, P.J. and Denhardt, K.G. (2005) "Incorporating spirituality into the MPA curriculum: framing the discussion," *Journal of Public Affairs Education*, 11(2): 121–31.

Maheshwari, S.R. (2002) *Administrative Reforms in India*, New Delhi: Macmillan.

Mishra, D.S. (2007) "E-governance as a reform strategy for combating corruption in delivery of public services," *Indian Journal of Public Administration*, 53(3): 351–75.

Narasimhan, C.V. (1997) "Prevention of corruption: towards effective enforcement," in S. Guhan and S. Paul (eds) *Corruption in India: Agenda for Action*, New Delhi: Vision Books.

Panchu, S. (2007) "What hangs on the lamp post?" *The Hindu* (New Delhi Edition), 15 March.

Raj, M.S. (1984) "Priorities in administrative reforms," in T.N. Chaturvedi and S. Maheshwari (eds) *Selected Articles: Administrative Reforms*, New Delhi: Indian Institute of Public Administration.

Santhanam Committee (India) (1964) *Report of the Committee on Prevention of Corruption*, New Delhi: Ministry of Home Affairs, Government of India.

Saxena, K.B.C. (2005) "Towards excellence in e-governance," *International Journal of Public Sector Management*, 18(6): 498–513.

Srinivas, A. and Nayar, L. (2007) "Elephant must remember: growth story, yes, but there are over 300 millions yet to see it," *Outlook Special Issue: State of the Nation*, 9 April, New Delhi, 47(15): 20–22.

Srivastava, C.P. (2001) *Corruption: India's Enemy Within*, New Delhi: Macmillan.

TI (2007) "Transparency International," online. Available at www.transparency.org (accessed 29 May 2008).

Varma, P.K. (2004) *Being Indian*, New Delhi: Penguin Books.

Vittal, N. (1999) "Applying zero tolerance to corruption," online. Available at www.cvc.nic.in/vscvc/note.html (accessed 28 June 2007).

World Bank (1997) *World Development Report: The State in the Changing World*, New York: Oxford University Press.

—— (2006) *Reforming Public Services in India: Drawing Lessons from Success*, New Delhi: Sage Publications India.

11 Preventing corruption in Turkey

Issues, instruments and institutions

Muhittin Acar and Uğur Emek

Introduction

The existence of corruption in Turkish political-bureaucratic system as a pervasive, entrenched, and enduring problem has long been an "open secret" for anybody involved even scantly in the public affairs of the country. While it is not an easy task to get consensus in Turkey among neither the elites nor the electorate as to the exact causes of and likely cures for the endemic corruption, there is nonetheless an emerging sense of agreement among people from different walks of life that corruption indeed poses a serious threat to development, democracy, and security in the country.

It is safe to suggest that the need for a series of strong, sustained and synchronized policies and actions to promote public integrity, transparency, and accountability and to prevent and punish corrupt practices in public life has become even more significant and urgent in the most recent decades, if not years. Certainly, the existence of a relatively free, open, and competitive media, the ascendance of civil society organizations, the country's aspirations to become a full member of European Union, and near-periodic eruptions of corruption scandals and severe economic crises help the corruption-related issues publicly discussed, which then leads to putting such problems on the agenda of political discourses and debates. However, exposing corruption is not sufficient to prevent it: the actions and measures taken in this direction should match the political rhetoric, which has so far hardly been the case.

While discussing the reasons behind this sore yet simple reality might constitute an interesting topic for a lengthy study, our focus in the current chapter is on something else. We are interested in: a) pointing out the need for creating a coalition among the clean (politicians), the competent (bureaucrats), and the competitive (businesspersons) to wage an effective and enduring war against corruption in the country; b) explaining how juxtaposing three members of such a coalition with the three core issues, namely, political financing regime, public personnel regime, and public expenditure and procurement regime is both possible and plausible; and c) describing major characteristics of the three core issues, along with relevant instruments and institutions, as they relate to the efforts toward creating and/or maintaining "free and fair competition" within and across those sectors. In the following section we focus on items (a), and (b), while we deal with item (c) in the third, fourth, and fifth sections. The chapter ends with a brief concluding section.

The arguments and the issues

Preventing corruption requires, among other things, the primacy and prominence of effective policies and programs envisioned through a good analysis of ideologies and interests involved, on one hand; and of issues, instruments, and institutions, on the other. While a good grasp of the phenomena and problem calls for a solid understanding of the actors and factors involved in both categories, this has rarely been the case lately in the writings of those contemplating about the subject of preventing corruption in different national and/or sectoral contexts. One might speculate, for instance, that studying the relations and interactions between the elements of the first group (i.e. ideologies and interests) was deemed more suitable for those researchers coming from a political-economy tradition flavored with a critical perspective,[1] while policy-oriented researchers tend to focus more on the intricacies and interactions associated with the elements categorized in the second group (i.e. issues, instruments, and institutions).[2]

Briefly told, the approach taken here can be best described as falling into the latter category, although one of our main purposes here is to shed light on the intertwinement of corruption with political, bureaucratic, and economic issues and institutions in Turkey. Notwithstanding the ideas and positions advanced therein, we extend and refine one of our arguments presented in an earlier work (Acar and Emek 2008: 200–01). Succinctly summarized, we have postulated that future success of the efforts aiming to prevent, prosecute, and punish corruption in Turkey would depend to a considerable extent on whether and how a strong coalition among the clean (politicians), the competent (bureaucrats), and the competitive (businesspersons) is stylized, secured, and sustained. We have reasoned that while the spectrum of the stakeholders to be included in any such coalition is inevitably wider than these three groups, the trio represents the chief segments or sectors of the society. In addition, the choosing of these three groups is also in line with the idea that any cleaning operation should start where the dirt of corruption has accumulated most: the shining sword of the anticorruption princess should cut first where it hurts most. We have therefore concluded that:

> Most effective and indispensable measures to be taken against corruption in Turkey should involve: incentives for politicians to play and stay clean; personnel policies to recruit, retain, and reward the best of professionals in the service of public; and to improve the conditions for creating a competitive market economy, especially focusing on betterments regarding state-market interactions. Increased transparency and

accountability on these three areas would inevitably encourage the three groups of people to become or stay clean, competent, and competitive.

(Acar and Emek 2008: 201)

We thus posit that one of the best ways to prevent corruption in Turkey is to focus on improvements regarding issues and instruments that are highly likely to contribute most to the establishment and/or enhancement of transparency, accountability, integrity, and performance in politics, bureaucracy, and business. In a sense, our position regarding the complexity and connectedness of the actors and factors involved in anticorruption efforts is inspired in large part by holistic approaches to the phenomena, underlying the encompassment of key issues, sectors, and institutions that contribute to transparency, accountability, and integrity in a society.[3]

The point of departure for us, however, lies with the juxtaposition of three sectors or segments of a possible anticorruption coalition, consisting of politicians, public professionals, and businesspeople, with the three core issues: the political financing regime, the public personnel regime, and the public expenditure and procurement regime. The selection of these three issues can hardly be considered as arbitrary. First of all, the trio, sometimes separately but often times jointly, has been high on the agenda not only of international organizations but also of academics musing persistently about preventing corruption in various contexts across the globe (e.g. Bedirhanoğlu 2007a; Gençkaya 2008; Huther and Shah 2000; Larbi 2007; Ma and Ni 2008; OECD 2007; Pope 2000; SIGMA 2007; Sun 2008; Walecki 2007). Furthermore, compared to some possible alternative issues and sectors (e.g. the media, judiciary, civil society, and internal auditing), where the establishment of a direct and exclusive correspondence within and across is difficult, the three issues examined here can easily be associated, even identified with, one of these three sectors or segments. Thus, it is plausible to look deeper into these three issues as rough proxies representing to a certain extent the major policies and practices prevailing in political, bureaucratic, and business segments of the society.

Maybe more importantly, based on a review of the relevant literature as well as our own familiarity with the context, we postulate that it is worth debating in depth the nexus between these three issues and the existence (or lack) of "free and fair competition" among politicians, public professionals, and businesspeople in Turkey. We thus argue that policy makers and public at large better concentrate their energies and efforts on improving policy capacity and institutional design in these and other relevant issue areas so as to contribute to improving conditions for "free and fair competition"[4] in politics, bureaucracy, and the business world,[5] rather than limiting their focus to popular, yet not-so-practical "campaign-style anticorruption drives," reflecting an outdated "fight corruption by fighting corruption"[6] rhetoric.

At the core of our analysis and assessment that follows is thus the question of how and to what extent the major policy instruments and institutions currently in use in these three issue areas are contributing to or constraining the efforts toward preventing corruption in the country. At this point, it is imperative upon us to state that it is neither feasible nor desirable to fully engage in these three issues, given the space limits and other constraints facing us. Thus, in the remainder of this section we select to cover some key aspects of political financing regime, public personnel regime, and public expenditure and procurement regime as they most relate to the notion of "free and fair competition" within and across political, bureaucratic, and business worlds. Having said this, we can now turn first to the issue of the financing of political parties and elections.

Political financing

Needless to say, the existence of "free and fair elections" has long been a defining characteristic of the democratic system of government. We should clearly state at the outset that the people of Turkey have been enjoying at least since 1950 a competitive, multi-party political system where regular elections are held to determine the ruling cadre of national and local officials. Thus, we need not to spend too much time and effort to make the case for the "freeness" of political-electoral competition in Turkey, which has been rated strongly[7] in terms of the practice of the citizen's right to vote, participation in politics, and overall election integrity.[8] We do need, however, to spare a certain amount of space and attention for elaborating on some of the issues and instruments pertaining to the "fairness" (or lack there of) of political-electoral competitions, especially those related to regulations and practices concerning political financing and subsidies in the country.

The financing of political life has recently been at the forefront of the debate concerning contemporary challenges to democratic governance. Among the major issues brought to the light that are more relevant here are the links between political financing and political competition, equity in politics, and political corruption (Alt and Lassen 2003; Gençkaya 2008; Hopkin 2004; Pinto-Duschinsky 2002; Scarrow 2004; van Biezen and Kopecky 2007; Walecki 2007). Although a broad definition of political financing goes beyond the financing of political parties and campaigns so as to include, among others, the costs of political lobbying and political litigations as well as the expenses associated with newspapers and media that are created and paid to promote a partisan line, a narrower definition focuses almost exclusively on financing of political parties and political campaigns (Pinto-Duschinsky 2002: 70).

Even when narrowly defined as "*money for electioneering*" (ibid.), political financing "is one of the most troublesome regulatory areas for electoral democracies ... (in part) because it raises questions of how to ensure minimal political equality when wealth is unequally distributed" (Scarrow 2004: 653). Similarly, van Biezen and Kopecky (2007: 239) forward that the state has assumed even more significance in terms of party financing in the newer democracies of Southern and East-Central Europe in part "because public funding is seen as a key mechanism for achieving equality of competition and hence as an important instrument for the establishment of effective multiparty democracy." Finally, Hopkin (2004: 636) maintains that: "The question of political equality lies at the heart of how populistic democratic theories view party finance" mainly "because a completely unregulated system of funding allows economic inequalities ... to be translated directly into political inequalities."[9]

As for the link between political financing and political corruption, it suffices to note here that, more often than not, major corruption scandals involving political actors were also read as cases of illicit, or at least irregular, financing of political institutions and/or individuals.[10], [11] In short, "In addition to being a source of scandal and corruption, the ways in which political activity is financed may lead to severe inequalities" (Pinto-Duschinsky 2002: 70).[12], [13] That is why there is an ever-growing interest in political financing, not only among academic researchers and political analysts, but also in policy communities across different national and international contexts.[14] Turkey should not be and is not an exception: In most recent years, there has been a growing sense of awareness and attention regarding the link between anticorruption efforts and the need for reforms concerning political financing and political-administrative ethics in the country.[15]

While the scope, content, and classification of such reforms would inevitably be a subject of different debates and interpretations in the country, for the sake of convenience and clarity our focus will be restricted here to the following three categories:

- Regulations regarding incomes and expenses of political parties and candidates.
- Direct and indirect state subsidies to political parties and candidates.
- Issues and instruments providing cross-checks and additional control.

Articles 67–69 of the Turkish Constitution provide the essentials of the main legal-institutional framework regarding political financing in the country. For instance, according to the Turkish Constitution (Article 67) election laws shall be crafted in such a way that they reconcile the principles of fair representation and stability in administration. On the other hand, Article 67 of the Constitution stipulates that the state should provide political parties with financial aid adequately and fairly. More to the point, Article 69 of the Constitution prohibits political parties from engaging in commercial activities, and stipulates that the revenues and expenditures of political parties shall be consistent with their objectives. It also lays out the basic parameters regarding the financing and auditing of political parties.[16] Then, Articles 61–77 of the Law on Governing Political Parties (Act 2820) regulate political financing in accordance with those constitutionally-set parameters.[17]

Briefly told, despite the fact that this constitutional-legal framework involves a series of essential and useful provisions concerning contemporary political financing in Turkey (e.g. the listing, registering, and restricting of revenues, including donations; articulating trading and borrowing prohibitions; and laying the ground for auditing and investigation of the accounts and transactions of political parties by the Constitutional Court), there exist a number of loopholes and inadequacies in the current system that inhibit the fairness of political competition in the country. Chief among them are the following:

- Coupled with the fact that a large informal/unregistered economy exists in the country, the current legal-institutional framework paves the way for illegal–informal contributions to the political parties and candidates. In other words, the so-called soft money controls and corrupts to a certain extent the processes and outcomes of political competition in the country. For instance, although there are a number of provisions aiming to limit and register donations to political parties, "the campaign spending of political parties is not regulated by law. In other words, there is no restriction on campaign spending" (Gençkaya, 2008: 74). Furthermore, individual political candidates are not subject to any campaign finance regulation or restriction. There is a widely shared belief in the country that a considerable amount of donations to political parties and candidates are made covertly, in part because of the lack of ceilings on political campaign expenditures. Together with the fact that the costs of running for an office have increased tremendously, the lack of regulations and restrictions on the political expenditures of political parties and candidates significantly hurts the fairness of the election processes (Global Integrity, 2007).
- The existing legal-institutional framework and political practices contribute to the unfairness of the political system in a number of other ways, not the least of which are inefficiencies, irregularities, and illegalities manifested in the recording, disclosing, assessing, and auditing of revenues and expenditures of political parties and candidates. For example, there are no standardized procedures for presenting and auditing political party accounts. According to Gençkaya (2008: 74):

> The Constitutional Court examines the parties' accounts according to "whatever political parties return, and information and documents that are available" ... In general, the examination of the accounts of party organizations are [sic] far from being systematic and rigorous ... Due to the heavy workload of its primary duty to review the constitutionality of laws adopted by the parliament, and the insufficient number of experts, the Court's auditing remains superficial and ineffective.[18]

A somewhat similarly disheartening, mixed-feeling story involves state subsidies to political parties. On one hand, the first in-kind state subsidies to political parties in the country go back to 1949, when qualified political parties were allocated fifteen-minute speech times each on the state radio on the eve of the general elections.[19] Today, all lawfully registered parties that enter general elections are allocated radio and television time in the general elections (but not in local elections). Similarly, "the state aid to political parties was introduced [in 1965] by Law No. 648 on Political Parties."[20] Today, "qualified" political parties receive state aid.

On the other hand, the existing legal-institutional system involves certain provisions that hamper the functioning of political competition in the country on a fair, transparent basis. Examples include, but are not limited to, the unequal allocation among parties of propaganda time between and before the elections (favoring the governing party or parties), and unequal distribution of the political subsidies among parties (favoring the already existing parties, as opposed to newcomers).[21]

The Turkish Constitution (Article 83) provides Turkish parliamentarians with parliamentary immunity compatible with the rationale used in the EU member states: members of the Turkish Grand National Assembly (TGNA) shall not be liable for their votes and statements concerning parliamentary functions, for the views they express before the Assembly. Parliamentarians are also protected against any arrest and court cases during their entire time in the parliament for all crimes (including alleged corruption cases), whether those crimes are committed while they are in power or before election.[22] The existing constitutional-legal framework concerning immunities granted to members of parliament, especially parliamentary immunity in the form of inviolability, has been one of the most hotly debated and sharply criticized issues in the country, especially in the last decade or so (Acar and Emek 2008: 189–90; Gençkaya 2008: 74–76; GRECO 2006: 17–19; SIGMA 2005a: 13).[23]

In Turkey, there is no specific law that can be considered an equivalent of a single, written version of a parliamentary code of conduct. However, the Turkish Constitution, the Rules of Procedure of the TGNA, and some other laws have provisions regarding assets declaration, incompatibility, and conflicts of interest. For instance, Article 82 of the Constitution lists the activities incompatible with membership. In compliance with the requirements and restrictions provided therein, the Law on Activities Incompatible with Membership of Parliament (Act 3069) lists the guiding principles and prohibitions.[24] On the other hand, the Law on Asset Declaration, Struggle against Corruption and Unlawful Actions (Act 3628) obligates MPs to declare all assets they hold or control. The existing framework vis-à-vis asset declarations by elected officials exhibits many weaknesses, especially in terms of its scope and coverage (e.g. political personalities in the management boards of political parties and their close relatives are not included), confidentiality (hence lack of transparency and accountability) besetting the declaration process, and too long a time interval required between subsequent declarations (five years) (cf. SIGMA 2005a: 11–12).[25]

All in all, Turkey needs to improve its legislative-institutional framework as well as its public ethics infrastructure regarding the financing, auditing, and integrity of political parties and candidates to enhance the integrity, transparency, and accountability of its political systems and actors.[26]

Public personnel regime

Before anything else, a civil service of competence and integrity is essential to assist the duly constituted government in formulating policies, carrying out decisions and administering public services for which they are responsible (Pope 2000). That's why civil service legislation is considered the main reform area for addressing such problems as politicization, patronage, and irregularity. In this respect, merit-based recruitment is a necessary (though not sufficient) condition for improving (curbing) bureaucratic performance (corruption), while promotion, accountability and salary scheme are seen complementary tools (Rubin and Andrew 2006). An empirical study using data gathered from 35 developing countries shows, for instance, that the merit-based recruitment and promotion of civil servants is a good (and positive) determinant of the degree of integrity exhibited in public personnel regime (Rauch and Evans 2000).

Merit could be defined as "the selection of the best person for any given job" (McCourt 2007). This definition necessitates the practice of merit principles at every stage of a public professional's career, including recruitment, advancement and promotion. As such, the most able among a number of candidates should be recruited, the appointment should be open to all,[27] and appointment decisions should be systematic, transparent and challengeable.

In terms of providing "free competition," especially "free entries into the market for the jobs in public administration," in theory the main characteristics and policies of Turkish public services are quite comparable and compatible with contemporary perspectives and practices: There are few or no restrictions to the entry of law-abiding Turkish citizens into competition for job openings in government ministries and departments. When it comes to establishing and/or maintaining in practice "fair competition" among potential and present civil servants, however, the Turkish public personnel regime has significant challenges, if not deep-rooted problems, especially in terms of promotion, motivation, and accountability at the middle and upper echelons of bureaucracy.

Recruitment for the civil service in Turkey is in principle carried out through merit-based competition. A major recruitment scheme was introduced into the public personnel regime in 1999: a general examination called the Public Personnel Selection Exam (KPSS),[28] which is organized and administered by the Student Selection and Placement Center (ÖSYM). Those successfully passing this exam usually go through further selection processes organized and managed independently by ministries or other public authorities. These selection procedures generally consist of a written in-house examination and an interview. However, these in-administration procedures, especially the interview stage, do not guarantee objectivity and impartiality in the recruitment process. On the contrary, they are most prone to practices reflecting nepotism, cronyism, and patronage (cf. SIGMA 2005b). On the other hand, in many public organizations there are few or no clear rules for promotion, which means moving up to higher positions in the rank. It is not infrequent for party loyalists to receive quid pro quo appointments to high-level government positions. Therefore, the objectivity and impartiality of the promotion scheme is very much in doubt: more often than not, the advancement and promotion of many public employees is based on discretionary (and discriminatory) decisions of the managers and politicians (Özgür 2004).

Besides, Turkish public administration has many elements that are required to promote and maintain a professional civil service (SIGMA 2005b). For instance, impartiality and political neutrality in public services are legal obligations for civil servants. Meanwhile, in carrying out their duties, public officials should be loyal to the state, the constitution and the law. On the other hand, they have to disclose their assets, withdraw from the decision-making processes that affect them and their relatives, and not perform any activity related to their responsibility while in office for three years after leaving their offices.[29] To fulfill these obligations, they have the right to professional stability, administrative resource, tenure, retirement, protection against imputations and aspersions. If they fail to respect their obligations, they can be sanctioned by both the State Employees Law (Act 657)[30] and the general Penal Code. Besides, the Law on the Declaration of Assets and Combating Bribery and Corruption explicitly criminalizes such acts as bribery, malversation, embezzlement and corruption, and specifies that public servants accused of corruption-related offences cannot benefit from the immunity and immunity-lifting procedure established for other crimes.[31]

Assuming for a while that a proper legal-institutional framework for merit, service orientation, and accountability is in place, we still have to take into account the lack of motivational elements that are also inhibitive for career development and for betterment of bureaucratic performance. SIGMA (2005b) argues that causes of unfavorable staff motivation are twofold: first, the civil service system offers to good performers few or no real prospects for promotion. Put differently, the links between the performance of civil servants and their promotion and pay are very weak, to say the least (Acar and Özgür 2004: 209). Second, politicians tend to negatively influence decision-making mechanisms and manipulate bureaucratic decisions excessively for obtaining their own narrowly defined interests. Having said that, SIGMA concluded that "the political manipulation is at the origin of distributional problems and imbalances across administration." The second issue has also something to do with the tense (and tenacious) balance between the demands and desires for a merit-based bureaucracy and the need to abide by policy mandates spelled out by elected representatives of the citizenry. On one hand, increased professionalism among different ranks of civil servants in the country is essential to ensure the professional conduct of the public's business. On the other hand, the enduring question posed to identify and analyze the relationship between politics and administration in democracies is also very relevant in Turkey: How can governments bring expertise to bear on public policy development and implementation while retaining the supremacy of political values and elected representatives? (See Klingner 2001, cited in Acar and Özgür 2004: 210). We should thus reiterate that the merit and equality should be diligently respected to increase motivation in career development and enhance quality in bureaucratic functions.

Some of the existing deficiencies of the public personnel regime have also been recognized by scholarly studies as well as by international and domestic official reports. Among others,[32] the reasoning of the draft Public Administration Fundamental Law[33] states that a merit-based recruitment system in the Turkish civil service could not be set up and operated, and thus a relationship between civil service and politicians could not be established. Accordingly, on one hand, politicians have been trying to influence the day-to-day duties and decisions of bureaucrats (read as attempts at micromanaging) while, on the other hand, bureaucracy has worked on the strategies and policies for which politicians are naturally responsible, without taking inputs from politics.

After pointing out that the public personnel regime must be changed, because it is the root cause of the such administrative problems as inefficiencies, irregularities, and opaqueness, the Justice and Development Party (AKP) Government in its Urgent Action Plan of 2003 asserted that "although many governments that have taken office since the 1980s have committed to reform, nothing has been done, because changes laying the groundwork for reforming the state can only be achieved by a strong government and political will behind it" (Prime Ministry 2003). It is not possible to unsubscribe to this view. However, after five years of being at the helm, AKP governments have achieved only limited progress in terms of reforming the overall system of the civil service.[34] Moreover, subsequent AKP governments have been accused of "excessive staffing" in the civil service based on patronage and cronyism.[35]

Of course, civil service reform is not the only means of preventing corruption in public service. An effective penal code containing provisions concerning bribery, trading in influence, abuse of power and embezzlement; a right to access to information for transparency in public services; and a code of ethics providing benchmarks such as integrity, impartiality, honesty, respect, and conflict of interest are all necessary supplementary legislations to detect and curb corruption. In recent years, Turkey has adopted a new Penal Code, Law on Access to Information, and Law on the Establishment of the Public Servants' Ethics Board, in line with internationally accepted standards.

As is the case for law enforcement in general, the administrative capacity to effectively enforce laws and regulations regarding the public personnel regime is also crucial to attain expected outcomes. The Ethical Board for Public Servants, which was established in 2004, is responsible for supervising public officials to ensure that ethical standards are met. Nevertheless, the Board is not operating effectively because of the lack of human and financial resources. The Board needs to be strengthened in order to be able to carry out its tasks of monitoring respect for ethical principles and investigating complaints (EC 2006b). We think that the lack of power and resources for the Board to operate effectively provides yet another example as to how present-day politicians and bureaucrats value the protection of ethical standards. As argued by Klitgaard (2006), in the case of "systemic corruption" in which politicians and bureaucrats act closely together, there are few official incentives to discover and prosecute corruption, but strong political influences not to do so. In this respect, if ethical standards were their priority, they would appropriate sufficient resources to the Board, because, in the end, priorities for allocation of public funds in budgeting process are solely determined by politicians and bureaucrats.

Public expenditure and procurement

Better performance in the public expenditure program is essential for good quality provision of public services and sustainable economic development. Better performance mainly means, among other things, higher expenditure efficiency, improved policy outcomes, and a more effective accountability to the parliament and the public at large (ODI 2003). Shleifer and Vishny (1993) show that, for a given budgetary activity at the same level of spending, public expenditures are less efficient in countries experiencing a high level of corruption, mainly because corrupt public officials in those countries have a tendency to favor investment projects generating higher bribes, instead of choosing the most efficient ones. Especially in developing country contexts, corruption hampers efforts toward maintaining a balanced budget, distorts policies concerning efficient allocation of limited budget resources among different government programs and departments, and diminishes the quality of public services (Delavallade 2006).[36]

A growing concern is thus to ensure that issues and instruments related to public procurement are conceived and designed as an integral part of the overall schemes concerning public financial management (OECD 2007). In other words, it is generally believed that anticorruption efforts at legislative level necessitate a comprehensive procurement law in line with such internationally accepted criteria as competition, transparency, non-discrimination, accountability, and supervision. In this vein, it is safe to say that the Turkish public procurement system has gone through a significant reform process after 2002, as part of a comprehensive budgetary reform framework[37] developed in line with the aforementioned international standards, especially pursuant to the rules and standards promulgated by the European Union (EU). The previous legal framework concerning public procurement had many outdated provisions, unsuitable for the requirements of a modern public procurement system designed for providing competition, transparency, non-discrimination, confidentiality, and efficiency. As raised by Turkish public officials interviewed for a report prepared for the World Bank (World Bank 2001: 25), the old procurement system had many weaknesses, including the lack of clear-cut procedures and transparency in the procurement methods used, excessive discretionary power exerted by procurement officials, undue political influences, and the lack of a regulatory and supervisory structure to ensure effective implementation that have been conspired to provide a fertile ground for corruption through entrapments and enactments of irregularities, infringements and illegalities.[38]

Although public procurement has long been singled out by the public and its officials as one of the most corruption-prone areas in need of an urgent and comprehensive reform,[39] not much progress was achieved until 2002. Arguably, the EU decision to grant Turkey candidate status during the Helsinki Summit in 1999 and the economic reform program "Strengthening the Turkish Economy," which was put into implementation right after the 2000–2001 financial crisis, significantly contributed to the hand of reformers desiring to enhance anticorruption efforts, including the preparation and adaptation of a new Public Procurement Law (PPL) (Acar and Emek 2008). As stated in the Ninth Development Plan: "new procurement law with competitive and transparent tender rules and in conformity with international norms aims, among others, to increase effectiveness and to prevent corruption" (State Planning Organization (SPO) 2006: 28).

Fully in operation since 2003, the PPL was closely modeled after EU public procurement legislation.[40] It gave way to the creation of the Public Procurement Agency (PPA) as an independent agency charged with overseeing public procurement in Turkey, ensuring the effective enforcement of the new, more transparent and competitive procurement rules. In addition to public supervision, the principles of reliability, confidentiality and accountability in procurement have been emphasized in the new legal framework.[41]

Despite some important improvements it brought to the existing procurement regime, a number of significant deficiencies still exist in the new PPL in comparison to international norms and practices. Chief among them are:

- significant exemptions in terms of the scope and coverage provided by the law;
- insufficient justifications for exceptional procurement procedures, which unduly restrict competition; and
- incomplete/ambiguous definitions for technical specifications, qualification criteria, and tender evolution which could lead to discrimination between tenderers.

These and other deficiencies in the PPL and secondary legislation have become even worse over time, thanks to the numerous amendments made to it since its inception, resulting in the dilution of the (originally tight) policies and rules. Adding insult to injury, not-so-infrequent attacks by politicians and businessmen directed at the practitioners in charge of implementing even such diluted legal-institutional framework have further weakened the enforcement capacity of public supervision, which contributed to the fertile ground for corruption in and through the public procurement regime.

Since the very beginning of the changes brought to life through the new PPL, its stakeholders, both in the private sector and on the government side, have expressed their discontent about the new, more competitive and transparent procurement procedures, and have had difficulty in coming to terms with the review and remedy authorities of the PPA.[42], [43] The PPL has thus been amended fifteen times since its inception. More often than not, these amendments have adversely affected its stated purposes and functions.[44] Maybe more importantly, new exemptions have been introduced into the PPL on an ad hoc basis. Particularly, politically important "big ticket" projects in such areas as culture, education, sports, and energy have been exempted from the scope of the PPL. Put differently, it has been made possible for a significant amount of goods, services, and works to be procured without going through a competitive and transparent tendering process. Interestingly enough, with the exception of those coming mainly from the EU, not many complaints were heard about such broad-based, not-so-justified exemptions.[45]

In theory, the preferred method of procurement is a competitive open procedure. In practice, however, the share of negotiated procedures in total procurement is high compared to the EU equivalent (SIGMA 2007). The justifications for granting the exceptional procurement procedures, such as negotiated procedure and direct procurement, are ill-designed. The conditions under which the application of these procedures is warranted are ambiguous at best, arbitrary at worst. Then, it is not surprising to see in procurement statistics provided by the PPA itself that the use of exceptional procedures restricting competition and providing opportunities for discrimination between tenderers has been on the rise.[46] As a corollary to this, the Turkish Court of Accounts identified in an Annual Consolidated Report the excessive use of direct procurement and negotiated procedure as the main problem continuing to beset the current public procurement regime (SIGMA 2006a).

It is thus safe to conclude that the existence of a comprehensive legal-institutional framework is an essential but not sufficient condition for enhancing integrity and preventing corruption in and through the public procurement regime. Government officials in Turkey should recognize that effective enforcement of rules and regulations should also be ensured to obtain satisfactory outcomes. Although key personnel of the main purchasing departments across the public sector have in general the necessary procurement experience and skills, municipalities and smaller contracting entities still suffer from capacity problems (SIGMA 2006a) and thus are more vulnerable to undue influence, easy manipulation and frequent bribery in public procurement. That's why we think more attention should be paid to the procurement organizations, administrative systems and procedures of the implementing institutions. In this respect, procurement specialists responsible for both implementation and supervision of the PPL should be provided with the much-needed knowledge and training to understand how the policies and rules promulgated can be implemented and enforced effectively and evenly.[47]

Conclusion

We began the chapter by briefly emphasizing the seriousness, pervasiveness, and recalcitrance of corruption problem in Turkey, highlighting the increased need in recent years for policies and actions to prevent, prosecute, and punish corrupt practices in public life. We then moved to succinctly explain and justify the main arguments we have advanced in the chapter. We have discussed, albeit with varying degrees of detail, depth, and success, why and how political financing regimes, the public personnel regime, and the public expenditure and procurement regime in Turkey involve certain risks and challenges in terms of establishing and/or sustaining "free and fair competition" among politicians, public professionals, and businesspeople in the country. In doing so, we have also speculated about possibilities for, and some ingredients of, achieving progress in preventing corruption in those areas.

In so far as the specific issues, instruments and institutions are concerned, our focus has been near-exclusively on Turkey, although the existing challenges and the prospective changes we have touched upon might have relevance to many other countries facing similar conditions and constraints. We also should state at this junction that while the quest for purity and justice in the system of democratic governance may turn out to be a challenging endeavor, if not a fruitless odyssey, some methods known to contribute to the establishment of "free and fair competition" in different sectors of a society have quietly been accepted over the years in different parts of the world. There is enough experience and expertise available inside and outside the country for envisioning, enacting, and enforcing effective legal-institutional frameworks supporting "free and fair competition" in the issues examined so far in the chapter. In other words, those who want to focus on 'free and fairer competition' in politics, bureaucracy and business in Turkey do not have to start from scratch. Nor do they need to reinvent the wheel locally and alone.

The legal-administrative frameworks and the accompanying instruments and institutions designated for preventing corruption should target, first and foremost, enhancing "competition on merit." Although "competition on merit" is a popular notion, especially in the antitrust literature, it does not have a commonly agreed-upon definition (OECD 2007). However, it is widely accepted that the purpose of a public policy related to "free and fair competition" in any area of societal life should aim to protect "competition," not "competitors." Competitors should compete equally on a level playing-field not distorted by such external factors as unfair governmental intervention, conflicts of interest, breach of rules for private gain, undue influence of decisions by bribery, and so on. Of course, it is much easier to be said than done, given the challenges stemming not only from forming and functioning a coalition of the clean, competent, and competitive, but also from effective and equal enforcing of the enacted rules and regulations in a country context that is fairly well known for the laxity and lateness in the implementation stage of certain public policies and programs.

While there has been not enough substance provided for a genuine debate, neither in the general public nor in this chapter, about the former, there has been much more ado about the effective implementation of enacted legislative frameworks in international circles lately. More specially, it has dawned on such international organizations as the EU, IMF, OECD, and the World Bank that even legislations enacted in line with internationally accepted standards may still hamper, at least partially, the effective functioning of the national integrity system unless and until they are effectively and equally implemented by strong institutions.[48]

Finally, we should reiterate our strongly held belief, revived and revised throughout the preceding pages: there is a growing need for building a system of clear governance in Turkey to enhance prospects for its people's struggle toward attaining a high level of prosperity, peace, and security. One of the best ways to meet such a need is to focus on the policies and programs that are more likely to contribute not only to effective functioning of political, economic, and bureaucratic institutions in the country, but also to the establishing and/or sustaining of "free and fair competition" in politics, bureaucracy, and the business world. Envisioning, enacting, and enforcing such policies and programs requires, among other things, a strong and sustainable coalition bringing on board the clean (politicians), the competent (bureaucrats), and the competitive (businesspeople). The debate on the nuts and bolts of such a challenging yet rewarding task is left for another work, at a different time.

Notes

1 See, for instance, Bedirhanoğlu (2007b) and some of the works she cites therein.
2 See, for example, Pope (2000).
3 Chief among them are Transparency International's National Integrity System (NIS), SIGMA's Public Integrity System (PIS), and Global Integrity's country profiles, as well as some other studies pondering on "ethics regime," "ethics infrastructure," and "integrity regime." For more on this, see Acar and Emek (2008: 189) and Sampford et al. (2006).
4 On one hand, we certainly do not claim that "competition" is at all times and under all circumstances the only way, or the best criterion to determine the "winners" or "best outcomes." On the other hand, these days, the idea of constantly questioning and checking the nature of competition in these and other areas of societal life to make it more bearable, at least freer and fairer, should be foreign to few people, given the speedy spread of ideas and ideologies promoting constant and continuous competition in economic, political, and social dimensions of our lives.
5 Careful readers will easily recall Klitgaard's (1988) widely cited formula somewhere here:
Corruption = Official Monopoly Power + Official Discretion - Accountability
Huther and Shah (2000: 12), for example, explicitly state that: "Successful anticorruption programs are those which address the underlying governance failures, resulting in lower opportunities for gain and a greater likelihood of sanctions."
6 See Kaufmann (2005: 88), who explains the concept as follows:

A fallacy promoted by some in the field of anticorruption, and at times also by the international community, is that the best way to fight corruption is by fighting corruption—that is, by means of yet another anticorruption commissions and ethic agencies, and the incessant drafting of new laws, decrees, and codes of conduct. Moreover, in some settings, the disproportionate emphasis on prosecutions—typically of a few corporations or individuals, and often of the political opposition—at the expense of a focus on prevention and incentives for integrity has reduced the effectiveness of anticorruption efforts.

7 For more on this, see Global Integrity (2007), especially information provided through pp. 19–30.

8 We do not mean to suggest, however, that there is no room for improvements on this front. On the contrary, politicians and ordinary citizens alike should start paying their long-overdue attention and tribute to the question of democratic character and quality of political representation in the country. Such a quest would include, but not be limited to, such issues as under-representation in national and especially in local politics of certain groups (e.g. the young, the working class, the unemployed, the poor, and women); the undue interventions at almost periodic intervals of the military forces into the political-administrative affairs of the country; the not-so-exceptional investigations and decisions of the judiciary vis-à-vis political parties and elected representatives which in the end can be treated as the instances of the restrictions and tensions put into the "free and fair competition" in the political arena. Examples of the latter point are the two most recent cases brought before the Constitutional Court, one against the Democratic Society Party (DTP) on the grounds of protecting the state and society against separatist actions and deeds, the other against the Justice and Development Party (AKP), the current ruling party, which received 47 percent of the popular vote in the last general election, on 22 July 2007, on the grounds that the party has become the focus-center of deeds and actions against secularism. It suffices to say here that even in countries like Turkey that have been enjoying a middle-aged, moderately mature democracy, there is still a long way to go before stating with confidence that the "freeness" of the political competition does not need any significant improvements any more.

9 Citing others, Hopkin (2004: 637) neatly explains the significance of creating a level playing-field for political competition that is worth quoting here:

> First, the inequality of resources between candidates undermines the fairness of the electoral contest itself, because better-funded parties (those backed by moneyed interests) are better equipped to win the electorate over, while voters may even remain relatively unaware of other (less well-funded) options available to them ... Second, and perhaps more seriously, in a polity where no alternatives to the elite parties emerge voters will have no option but to vote for candidates whose ability to represent them has already been mortgaged to narrow wealthy interests ... Finally, information asymmetries (which themselves may stem from economic inequality, and which in any case narrow interests have more incentives to overcome) can prevent voters from finding out about the policy implications of parties' funding arrangements.

10 See Pinto-Duschinsky (2002: 73) for a sampling of campaign financing scandals involving different countries from around the world, ranging from Papua New Guinea to the United Kingdom. For brief, selective, and chronological information on the events and cases related to political corruption in Turkey, see Global Integrity (2007).

11 Van Biezen and Kopecky (2007) employ an analytical framework that distin-
   guishes between three basic dimensions of the state–party relationship: a) the
   extent to which parties depend on the state; b) the extent to which parties are
   managed by the state; and c) the extent to which parties themselves control the
   state. More to the point, they define the third dimension as "the extent to which
   parties penetrate and control the state and use public offices for their own
   advantage, as opposed to the general public good" (p. 240), and further divide
   this dimension into three components: party patronage; party clientelism, and
   corruption. They conclude that:

> All three forms of party rent-seeking can potentially distort and corrupt the
> ideal type of representative relationship in a democratic system because they
> are based on particularistic rather than universalistic exchanges and because
> they exploit the resources of the state for private rather than public purposes.
>
> (p. 241)

   We can add nothing to this elegantly elaborate expression other than saying that
   there are plenty of examples reflecting all three forms of party rent-seeking in
   Turkey and that building a clean politics and government requires an equal
   attention to and awareness of the consequences and costs of them for democratic
   governance in the country.
12 Pinto-Duschinsky (2002: 71–72) exemplifies and briefly explains "corrupt" political financing practices as follows: political contributions that contravene existing
   laws on political financing; the use for campaign or party objectives of money that
   a political officeholder has received from a corrupt transaction; unauthorized use
   of state resources for partisan political purposes; acceptance of money in return
   for an unauthorized favor or the promise of a favor in the event of election to an
   office; contributions from disreputable sources; and spending money on banned
   purposes such as vote-buying. A person moderately knowledgeable about the
   Turkish political-administrative context might easily claim that finding examples
   in the Turkish political system for each and every type of "corrupt practice of
   political financing" listed above should not be a challenging task after all.
13 In his paper, entitled "The *Europeanization* of political parties: influencing the
   regulations on political finance" (original emphasis), Walecki (2007: 14) stipulates
   that those working on the issue of political party funding talk about at least four
   different motivations for regulating political finance: preventing abuse; enhancing
   fair political competition; empowering voters; and strengthening parties as effective democratic actors. He further speculates that the EU focused only on the first
   two—preventing abuse and limiting party-related corruption (ibid.).
14 According to Walecki (2007: 3),

> Illicit party financing is certainly not a recent development and it has long been
> a common challenge throughout European democracies. Yet, it has started to
> be perceived by major international organizations such as Transparency Inter-
> national, the World Bank, the Council of Europe, the United Nations, and
> the European Union, as a major issue in a global fight against corruption.

   One might speculate by saying that it is good to see that international organizations have learned their lessons regarding the link between corruption and political financing, which has been touted by some academics for years, as illustrated
   in the following sentences taken from Pinto-Duschinsky (2002: 84):

> There is a lesson for bodies such as the World Bank and the International
> Monetary Fund, which have been prominent in the campaign against corruption

but which have been reluctant to enter the thicket of political financing. The links between political financing and political corruption are so common and so important that these organizations cannot reasonably expect to tackle corruption if they turn a blind eye to the issue of political funding.

We can only hope to see that a large majority of the electorate as well as the members of our hypothesized coalition in Turkey would learn a similar lesson before it is too late.

15 It also explains in part why we have chosen political financing as one of the three thematic issues of the current chapter. It is also important to note that, as argued by Walecki (2007: 10), "The issue of political party funding was considered by the European Union to be particularly relevant for the democratization process and anticorruption reforms in Turkey. Since 2005 the EU has consistently pressured Ankara to reform its party funding system." Among the short-term priorities designated in the Turkey 2007 Accession Partnership is anticorruption policy involving the following three items: a) developing a comprehensive anticorruption strategy, including the fight against high-level corruption, and a central body to oversee and monitor its implementation, including through establishing statistical data; improving coordination between all institutions involved; b) ensuring implementation of the Regulation on Principles of Ethical Behavior for Civil Servants and extending its provisions to elected officials, judiciary, academics and military personnel; c) limiting the immunities granted to politicians and public officials in line with European best practices and improving legislation on transparency in political party and election campaign financing (EC 2008: 7).

16 For instance, it states that political parties cannot accept material or non-material foreign aid: the receiving of any financial or in-kind aid from foreign states, international organizations, and individuals and legal persons constitutes a reason for the permanent banning of that party by the Constitutional Court.

17 For a detailed analysis of the related provisions and policies embedded in the Constitution and Act 2820, see Gençkaya (2008: 2000).

18 In June 2008, Turkish newspapers were all carrying the news about the outcomes of the Constitutional Court's auditing of the accounts of People's Republican Party (CHP). According to these newspaper accounts, the Court had completed the financial-legal auditing of CHP's accounts, and had come across irregularities in the party's expenditures, in total approximately 1 million New Turkish Liras (YTL) (around 800,000 US dollars) for the years 1998, 2004, 2005, and 2006. The vividly and widely reported details of the news might be interpreted in at least three different ways. First, given the fact that CHP is the oldest and the second-biggest party in the country (according to the outcomes of the most recent elections in 2007), it seems reasonable to speculate that irregularities are not so uncommon throughout the political party system. Second, the fact that the auditing in 2008 involved the accounts belonging to 1998 indicates the laxity—at least lateness—in the system. Third, although obviously the available framework functions too little, too late, it is possible to conclude on a more optimistic note: the system still detects at least some deficiencies, and awareness is still high: there is still a room for policy entrepreneurs to craft something better and more effective out of all these.

19 Gençkaya (2000: 172). The source just cited contains a substantial amount of useful, systematic, and chronological information and analysis on different aspects of political financing in Turkey.

20 Gençkaya (2008: 71).

21 Seemingly, these types of problems are not peculiar to Turkey, as is illustrated by the following quotation:

> Most systems of state funding do seem to favor the status quo, in particular by their neglect of emerging political forces. State funding almost always

> gives a significant advantage to parties which have been successful in the past and are already present in the elective institutions. To this extent, state funding provides a level playing field, but only to those who have already played before.
>
> (Hopkin 2004: 645)

22 This provision does not apply to cases where a member is caught in the act of committing a crime punishable by a heavy penalty, nor does it apply if an investigation has been initiated before the parliamentary election. However, in such situations the relevant authority should immediately notify parliament (GRECO 2006: 17).

23 According to Gençkaya (2008: 76),

> Since 1983, the Assembly has lifted the immunities of 18 deputies among hundreds of cases. As a gentlemen's agreement, the GNA postpones the immunity files until the end of the legislative term ... [This and other practices have been] eroding the public's confidence in justice and the accountability of elected public officials.

AKP governments have been reluctant to act on changing the status quo vis-à-vis parliamentary immunity, in part because they have been arguing that the immunity issue should be considered for all public servants, not just parliamentarians (Acar and Emek 2008: 189).

24 For more information and discussion on this, see Gençkaya, (2008: 74–75). In essence, members of TGNA are legally prohibited from holding offices in the governmental agencies, state-supported/tax-exempt enterprises, the executive and supervisory organs of labor unions and professional organizations.

25 According to Gençkaya (2008: 79),

> The scope of asset declarations should be extended to include political personalities on the executive boards of political parties, their provincial and local organizations, and their relatives. The principal of confidentiality of asset declaration is an obstacle to transparency, which could otherwise be enhanced through asset declaration.

26 For more information and discussion about past and present problems associated with political financing, as well as the prospects and proposals for developing a more effective and fair system of political financing and competition in Turkey, see Dülger 2002, Gençkaya 2002, and Tacar 2002.

27 Of course, public personnel regimes may legitimately develop a number of exceptions to the rule of merit, including the so-called "positive discrimination policies" (e.g. affirmative action programs designed to create equal opportunities for previously disadvantaged groups), appointments to politically sensitive posts (e.g. the creation of exceptions for political appointees), and internal appointments to reduce transaction costs. However, even these and similar other exceptions should be limited in number and scope, and should be determined and designed through transparent means and ways.

28 Around one million candidates who have at least a four-year college degree took a two-day exam held on 29 June 2008. Another million or so government job-seekers, who hold a high school diploma or an associate degree from a two-year college, took a similar exam on September 21, 2008.

29 The lack of transparency and laxity of enforcement besetting regulations vis-à-vis asset declarations as well as conflicts of interest and post-government private-sector employment should be the subject of a brief, sore note here.

30 Promulgated in 1965, Act 657 continues to provide the main legal-administrative framework for the public personnel regime in Turkey. It covers all major aspects of the public personnel system, including recruitment, training, advancement, and disciplinary processes and sanctions. Due in part to the hundreds of changes made over the years to the Act and/or related regulations, the framework itself has become complicated and confusing and thus a serious roadblock in the way toward ensuring "free and fair competition" in and through the public personnel regime.

31 A recent report prepared by a GRECO Evaluation Team (GET) provides some remarks on the issue that can be a good basis for offering a different perspective on the issue. It is thus worth quoting at length here:

> The GET found that the system of administrative preliminary investigation and permission for prosecution, although in theory not applied in corruption cases, in principle could affect the capacity of the law enforcement and prosecutorial authorities to investigate and prosecute criminal offences which may be committed in connection with corruption. Therefore, the GET recommends to analyze the effects of the administrative authorization for prosecution on the effectiveness of the criminal proceedings and to consider reforming the system of preliminary administrative investigation and administrative authorization for prosecution, in order to reduce the categories of public officials who *de facto* benefit from immunities from criminal proceedings.
>
> (GRECO 2006: 20)

32 For example, see SIGMA (2006b), State Planning Organization (SPO) (2000) and Prime Ministry (2003) for policy instruments such as norm cadres, meritocracy, and equal pay for equal work to enhance the public personnel regime prescribed therein.

33 The law was adopted in 2004 but was returned to the parliament by the president to be revised and resubmitted; it is still pending on the agenda of the parliament.

34 Interestingly, in its Urgent Action Plan of 2008, the AKP government excludes personnel regime reform from its agenda (Prime Ministry 2008).

35 The prime minister describes the situation as recruitment and promotion of those understanding well his "body language" in response to allegations of "excessive staffing" on a patronage basis (Sağlam 2006). In the meantime, some scholars of Turkish political economy assert that the patrimonial state tradition in Turkey is a key element of the political culture, where the government centrally sustains its authority via a patrimonial bureaucrat class whose personal fate depends on the government. Therefore, the patrimonial bureaucratic class take their legitimacy from their loyalty to the government rather than their merits (Heper 1985). In this vein, it could be argued that staffing based on loyalty in Turkey has a long tradition and there is not enough political desire to overhaul it.

36 For more on why and how budget reform is an important instrument for preventing corruption in a developing country context, see Ma and Ni (2008).

37 For a detailed evaluation of the Turkish public expenditure reforms, see Gönenç et al. 2005, SIGMA 2006a, and World Bank 2006.

38 The Ministry of Construction in Turkey was quoted as saying in an OECD study that

> Until the enactment of the new PPL in 2003, Turkey has suffered exceptionally high construction costs by international comparison. For instance, the cost of construction for 1 km of highway was US$ 10 million in Turkey, compared to international reference price of a US$ 4 million.
>
> (Gönenç et al. 2005)

39 For example, the Seventh Development Plan envisioned in 1995 that "public procurement legislation would be changed to provide competition and transparency ... and would be harmonized with EU Directives" (State Planning Organization (SPO) 1995).

40 Public procurement is the main subject of the one of the 35 chapters to be covered during accession negotiations between Turkey and EU, which started on 3 October 2005.

41 For a detailed assessment of the main features of the PPL, see SIGMA 2005a.

42 The PPA can determine the corrective action, terminate procedure, or reject the complaint as invalid, after investigating any illegality on its own initiative *sua sponte* or through complaints received from those who incurred damages from the breach of tendering rules.

43 For example, in a newspaper article, entitled "Institutions and companies are having difficulty in adapting to new public procurement law," Ağaç (2004) talks about the dissatisfaction of private companies with "long" (45-day) deadlines required in requests for tender. Such a time lag between the public announcement of the tenders and the deadlines for full submissions is set to provide contractors with sufficient tender preparation time so that the competition among them is played out more rationally and fairly. As such, private companies should enjoy and support these kinds of policies. Contrary to "normal expectations," some private companies seemingly complain about the rules aiming to create a level playing-field in the tendering process. On the other hand, Kıvanç (2008) informs the public that current government is intending to narrow down the review and remedy authority of the PPA. If the draft legislation is enacted as speculated, the PPA will not be able to investigate illegalities on its own initiative or when the contracting entity has cancelled the complained tender, even if the tender process was lawful and the re-tendering was just beneficial to the losing parties rather than value for money. Actually, the prime minister signaled his discontent with the PPA long ago when he complained about the status and remedies of the PPA by asserting that "while we try to speed up investments, the PPA slows down them because of the long review process stemming from formalities of the PPL. We will change their legal status and set them in order" (http://webarsiv.hurriyet.com.tr/2004/12/30/577042.asp, accessed 11 June 2008). Not surprisingly, the prime minister's words were interpreted by some as: "Public Procurement Agency in Turkey is at risk of government obstruction" (Economist Intelligence Unit 2003: 81).

44 Münir (2008) explains these changes as "honeycombing the rules of the new procurement system that protect public procurements from stains and corruptions."

45 In its Screening Report for Public Procurement, the EU states that the "PPL's scope remains too narrow and still differs from EU legislation in various aspects ... and exemptions are not in line with the EU Directives" (EC 2006a).

46 Collusive behaviors among tenderers are also crucial to mention in terms of infringement of competition law, but we ignore them in this chapter for reasons of brevity.

47 For misunderstanding of implementation of the PPL, a statement from the president of the PPA provides a striking example: in responding to some criticisms he was on record as saying that "we do not have the mission to fight against corruption and should just investigate legality" (www.turkishdailynews.com.tr/article.php?enewsid = 104831, accessed 11 June 2008). Needless to say, a legality investigation is a precondition to detecting the occurrence of corrupt acts or threats declared unlawful by the PPL. Besides, both the PPL and the Penal Code clearly prohibit fraud, bribery and corruption in public procurement, and the PPA is in charge of making the PPL effectively enforced.

48 For example, the EU developed the "administrative capacity criterion" for (prospective) EU membership in the Copenhagen European Council Summit Conclusions in 1993 (Kellermann 2007).

References

Acar, M. and Emek, U. (2008) "Building a clean government in Turkey: pillars, perils, and prospects," *Crime, Law, and Social Change*, 49(3): 185–203.

Acar, M. and Özgür, H. (2004) "Training of civil servants in Turkey: progress, problems, and prospects," *International Journal of Public Administration*, 30(3–4): 197–218.

Ağaç, F. (2004) "Kurumlar ve firmalar, kamu ihale yasası'na uyumda zorlanıyor" (Institutions and companies are in difficulty over adopting new public procurement law), online. Available at www.telepati.com.tr/ocak04/konu9.htm (accessed 11 June 2008).

Alt, J.E. and Lassen, D.D. (2003) "The political economy of institutions and corruption in American states," *Journal of Theoretical Politics*, 15(3): 341–65.

Bedirhanoğlu, P. (2007a) "Sermayenin bir birikim ve rekabet stratejisi olarak yolsuzluk ve neoliberal yolsuzlukla mücadele gündemi" (Corruption as a accumulation and competition strategy of capital and the neoliberal anticorruption agenda), *Eğitim, Bilim, Toplum*, 5(17): 30–44.

—— (2007b) "The neoliberal discourse on corruption as a means of consent building: reflections from post-crisis Turkey," *Third World Quarterly*, 28(7): 1239–54.

Delavallade, C. (2006) "Corruption and distribution of public spending in developing countries," *Journal of Economics and Finance*, 30(2): 222–39.

Dülger, M. (2002) "Siyasetin finansmanı: çerçeve ve ilkeler" (Political financing: framework and principles), in *Political Financing*, Ankara: TESEV and National Democratic Institute.

EC (2006a) "Screening report Turkey: Chapter 5—public procurement," online. Available at http://ec.europa.eu/enlargement/pdf/turkey/screening_reports/screening _report_05_tr_internet_en.pdf (accessed 11 June 2008).

—— (2006b) *Turkey 2006 Progress Report*, SEC (2006) 1390, Brussels: EC.

Economist Intelligence Unit (2003) "Europe enlarged: understanding the impact," online. Available at www.export.gov.il/_Uploads/589Europeenlarged.pdf (accessed 19 June 2008).

—— (2008) "Council decision of 18 February 2008 on the principles, priorities and conditions contained in the Accession Partnerships with the Republic of Turkey and repealing Decision" 2006/35/EC (2008/157/EC), online. Available at www.dtm. gov.tr/dtmadmin/upload/AB/ABKurumsalDb/2007kob.pdf (accessed June 2008).

Gençkaya, Ö.F. (2000) "Siyasi partilere ve adaylara devlet desteği, bağı?lar ve seçim giderlerinin sınırlandırılması—karşılaştırmalı bir inceleme ve Türkiye için öneriler" (State aid to political parties and candidates, donations, and limitations on electoral expenditures—a comparative study and proposals for Turkey), in A. Çarkoğlu (ed.) *Siyasi Partilerde Reform* (*Reform in Political Parties*), Istanbul: TESEV, 127–234.

—— (2001) "Priorities for political ethics in Turkey," *Insight Turkey*, 3(2): 37–44.

—— (2002) "Siyasetin finansmanı, sınırlamalar ve denetim: karşılaştırmalı uygulamalar" (Political financing, limitations, and control: comparative practices), in *Political Financing*, Ankara: TESEV and National Democratic Institute.

—— (2008) "Political finance, conflict of interest and accountability in Turkey: implications for democracy," in Council of Europe (ed.) *Corruption and Democracy*, Strasbourg: Council of Europe Publishing.

Global Integrity (2007) "Global Integrity report: Turkey," online. Available at http://report.globalintegrity.org/reportPDFS/Turkey.pdf (accessed June 2008).

Gönenç, R., Leibfritz, W. and Yılmaz, E. (2005) "Reforming Turkey's public expenditure management," OECD Economics Department Working Papers No. 418.

GRECO (2006) "Joint first and second evaluation round: evaluation report on Turkey," online. Available at www.coe.int/t/Dg1/Greco/evaluations/round2/GrecoEval1-2(2005)3_Turkey_EN.pdf (accessed 11 June 2008).

Heper, M. (1985) *The State Tradition in Turkey*, North Humberside: Eothen Press.

Hopkin, J. (2004) " The problem with party finance—theoretical perspectives on the funding party politics," *Party Politics*, 10(6): 627–51.

Huther, J. and Shah, A. (2000) "Anticorruption policies and programs—a framework for evaluation," World Bank policy research working paper.

Kaufmann, D. (2005) "Myths and realities of governance and corruption," online. Available at www.worldbank.org/wbi/governance/pdf/2-1_GCR_Kaufmann.pdf (accessed 11 June 2008).

Kellerman, Alfred E. (2007) "The impact of EU accession on the development of administrative capacities in the states in Central and Eastern Europe: similar developments in Russia?" *Romanian Journal of European Affairs*, online. Available at http://ssrn.com/abstract = 963284.

Kıvanç, A. (2008) "Hükümet Kamu İhale Kanunu'nda AB'yi takmadı, yine bildiğini okuyor" (Government doesn't care about EU negotiations and does what it still wants), online. Available at www.radikal.com.tr/Default.aspx?aType = HaberDetay &ArticleID = 882329&Date = 09.06.2008&CategoryID = 101 (accessed 12 June 2008).

Klingner, D.E. (2001) "Strengthening personnel management in developing countries: lessons learned, lessons forgotten, and an agenda for action," *Public Personnel Management*, 30(1): 1–16.

Klitgaard, R. (1988) *Controlling Corruption*, Los Angeles: University of California Press.

—— (2006) "Introduction: subverting corruption," *Global Crime*, 7(3–4): 299–307.

Larbi, G.A. (2007) "Editorial: symposium on political corruption," *Public Administration and Development*, 27: 189–90.

Ma, J. and Ni, X. (2008) "Toward a clean government in China: does the budget reform provide a hope?" *Crime Law and Social Change*, 49: 119–38.

McCourt, W. (2007) "The merit system and integrity in the public service," paper presented at Conference on Public Integrity and Anticorruption in the Public Service, Bucharest, 29–30 May.

Münir, M. (2008) "AKP neden kamu ihale yasasını elli defa değiştirdi" (Why AKP changed public procurement law by numerous times), online. Available at www.milliyet.com.tr/Default.aspx?aType = YazarDetay&ArticleID = 758221&AuthorID = 57&Date = 23.05.2008 (accessed 12 June 2008).

Ngo, T. (2008) "Rent-seeking and economic governance in the structural nexus of corruption in China," *Crime Law and Social Change*, 49: 27–44.

ODI (2003) "Results-oriented public expenditure management: will it reduce poverty faster?" ODI Briefing Paper, April, online. Available at www.odi.org.uk/Publications/working_papers/wp203.pdf (accessed 11 June 2008).

OECD (2007) *Integrity in Public Procurement: Good Practice from A to Z*, Paris: OECD.

Özgür, B. (2004) "Kamu yönetiminde yönetici çıkmazı" (Manager deadlock in public administration), *Maliye Dergisi* (Journal of Public Finance), 145, online. Available at http://portal1.sgb.gov.tr/calismalar/maliye_dergisi/maliyedergisi.asp?link = 2 (accessed 11 June 2008).

Özsemerci, K. (2003) *Türk kamu yönetiminde yolsuzluklar, nedenleri, zararları ve çözüm önerileri* (Corruption in Turkish Public Administration, Its Causes, Consequences, and Solutions), Ankara: Sayıştay Başkanlığı.

Palmer, D. and Maher, M.W. (2006) "Developing the process model of collective corruption," *Journal of Management Inquiry*, 15(4): 363–70.

Pinto-Duschinsky, M. (2002) "Financing politics: a global view", *Journal of Democracy*, 13(4): 69–86.

Pope, J. (2000) *Confronting Corruption: The Elements of a National Integrity System*, Berlin: Transparency International.

Prime Ministry (2003) "58. Hükümetin acil eylem planı" (Urgent action plan of 58th government), online. Available at http://ekutup.dpt.gov.tr/plan/aep.pdf (accessed 11 June 2008).

—— (2008) "60. Hükümetin acil eylem planı" (Urgent action plan of 60th government), online. Available at http://ekutup.dpt.gov.tr/plan/ep2008.pdf (accessed 11 June 2008).

Rauch, J.E. and Evans, P.B. (2000) "Bureaucratic structure and bureaucratic performance in less developed countries," *Journal of Public Economics*, 75: 49–71.

Rubin, E. and Andrew, W.B. (2006) "Effects of the institutional design of the civil service: evidence from corruption," online. Available at http://papers.ssrn.com/sol3/papers.cfm?abstract_id = 894035 (accessed 14 June 2008).

Sağlam, E. (2006) "Merkez Bankası başkanının vücut dili bilmesi gerekmiyor" (The governor of the Central Bank doesn't need to know body language), online Available at http://hurarsiv.hurriyet.com.tr/goster/haber.aspx?id = 4088139&yazarid = 8 (accessed 11 June 2008).

Sampford, C.J.G., Shacklock, A., Connors, C., and Galtung, F. (eds) (2006) *Measuring Corruption*, Hampshire, England: Ashgate Publishing.

Scarrow, S. E. (2004) "Explaining political finance reforms—competition and context," *Party Politics*, 10(6): 653–75.

Shleifer, A. and Vishny, R.W. (1993) "Corruption," *Quarterly Journal of Economics*, 108(3): 599–617.

SIGMA (2005a) "Turkey public procurement system assessment," online. Available at www.sigmaweb.org (accessed 12 June 2008).

—— (2005b) "Turkey public service and the administrative framework assessment," online. Available at www.sigmaweb.org (accessed 12 June 2008).

—— (2006a) "Turkey public expenditure management system assessment," *Publishing on the Internet*. Online. Available at www.sigmaweb.org (accessed 12 June 2008).

—— (2006b) "Turkey public service assessment," online. Available at www.sigmaweb.org (accessed 12 June 2008).

—— (2007) "Turkey public procurement system assessment June 2007," online. Available at http:www.sigmaweb.org (accessed 12 June 2008).

State Planning Organization (SPO) (1995) *Seventh Five Year Development Plan: 1996–2000*, Ankara: SPO

—— (2000) *Long-term Strategy and Eighth Five-Year Development Plan 2001–2005*, Ankara: SPO.

—— (2006) *Ninth Development Plan: 2007–2013*, Ankara: SPO

Sun, Y. (2008) "Cadre recruitment and corruption: what goes wrong?" *Crime Law and Social Change*, 49: 61–79.

188   *Muhittin Acar and Uğur Emek*

Tacar, P. (2002) "Siyasetin finansmanı konusunda reform önerileri" (Reform proposals on political financing), in *Political Financing*, Ankara: TESEV and National Democratic Institute.
van Biezen, I. and Kopecky, P. (2007) " The state and the parties—public funding, public regulation and rent-seeking in contemporary democracies," *Party Politics*, 13(2): 235–54.
Walecki, M. (2007) "The *Europeanization* of political parties: influencing the regulations on political finance," EUI Working Papers MWP 2007/29.
World Bank (2001) *Turkey Country Procurement Assessment Report*, Washington, DC: World Bank, Europe and Central Asia Region.
—— (2006) *Public Expenditure Review*, Washington, DC: World Bank.

12 Evolving perceptions of government integrity and changing anticorruption measures in Taiwan

Chilik Yu, Chun-Ming Chen, Lung-Teng Hu, and Wen-Jong Juang

After its retreat from mainland China to Taiwan in 1949, the Nationalist Party (the Kuomintang or KMT) controlled almost every aspect of the country, making Taiwan a single-party authoritarian regime. Although the fight against this authoritarian regime never ceased, not until 1986 was the opposition force strong enough to form an opposition party, the Democratic Progressive Party (DPP), to mobilize a nationwide challenge to the KMT. In 1987, one year after the DPP's birth, President Chiang Ching-kuo lifted martial law, and the process of democratic transformation began in Taiwan.

During the democratic transformation period, corruption issues were more visible and salient in election propaganda than any other political issue (Fell 2002). In fact, the DPP's anticorruption campaigns of the 1990s were a critical factor in terminating the single-party authoritarian regime controlled by the KMT for over fifty years. In May 2000, when the KMT peacefully turned over the presidency to the DPP, Taiwan was considered a "best case" among "third-wave" democratizations. As Rigger (2004: 285) argues:

> Taiwan's transformation from single-party authoritarianism to multi-party democracy came about with very little violence or bloodshed. Nor did it require wrenching economic or social upheavals. In fact, one might describe Taiwan's experience as a "best-case" democratization.

Has this best-case democratization created a clean government? Does democracy always breed integrity? Based on past experience, the answer is, not necessarily. In reviewing the case of Italy, Colazingari and Rose-Ackerman (1998: 469) indicate that democracy is not necessarily an antidote to corruption:

> A shift from authoritarian to democratic rule does not necessarily reduce payoffs. Rather it redefines the country's norms of public behavior. A country that democratizes without also creating and enforcing laws governing conflict of interest, financial enrichment, and bribery risks undermining its fragile new institutions through private wealth seeking.

Does the above argument apply to Taiwan? More specifically, has democratic transformation in Taiwan, especially the party turnover in the central government, created a clean government, or has it made the state more corrupt? This chapter seeks to answer this question by using corruption measurement data from various sources. It also discusses new anticorruption policies for the new government in Taiwan. The chapter is divided into five sections. The first section discusses the measurement of corruption and integrity. Section two discusses data from the Governance Indicators with a focus on Taiwanese data, and compares this with data from other countries and territories in East Asia.[1] Section three presents and discusses data from the Taiwan Integrity Survey, while also illustrating salient corruption issues in Taiwan covered by the mass media in 2006. Section four introduces policy designs proposed by the new government, the so-called President's Public Integrity Agenda. The concluding section argues that Taiwan needs to work toward a strong democracy, a vital civil society, and good governance to maintain its reputation as the best case among the third-wave democratizations in the world.

Measurement of corruption and integrity

Is talk of governmental integrity mere rhetoric or reality? Since corruption undermines a country's democratic, economic, and social development, opposing corruption has become a worldwide movement aligning the public, private, and third sectors. With such awareness, strategies and initiatives for fighting corruption have been developed. One tool for combating corruption is the continuous monitoring of a government's integrity as well as society's as a whole. But how to measure integrity and corruption has been a longstanding concern of scholars and practitioners alike. Effectively measuring the extent of integrity has never been an easy task, since corruption always accompanies multifaceted structural problems, such as political decay, institutional unhealthiness, and judicial failure. But despite these difficulties in measuring corruption and integrity, researchers have conducted numerous studies and collected empirical evidence for improving measurement techniques.

Some researchers define integrity as "individuals upholding the obligation of office by implementing public programs in accordance with laws and rules, as well as in support of the public intent or the collective interest" (van Blijswijk et al. 2004: 719). Along this line, public officials and politicians who hold public authority are responsible and accountable for performing duties in accordance with norms, laws, rules, and ethical standards as they pursue the public interest rather than private gain. Moreover, for individual public servants, the notion of integrity serves as "an internal moral compass that guides the behavior of public professionals" (van Blijswijk et al. 2004: 719). Therefore, at some level, integrity can be regarded as a measure of a public servant's professionalism.

Corruption is a major cause of public distrust in governments (Eigen 2002). Using data from the East Asia Barometer, Chang and Chu (2006) found a strong link between political corruption and the decline of institutional trust in Asian democracies. Thus, combating corruption and enhancing the integrity of civil servants has become critical for restoring public trust in government (van Blijswijk et al. 2004). Corruption undermines both a country's democratic development and economic competitiveness (Velkova and Georgievski 2004). Public corruption has been defined as "the abuse of public office for private gain" (Boylan and Long 2003: 421). Although opposing corruption has become a top policy priority in many countries in the twenty-first century, successfully fighting corruption and enhancing integrity has no quick solution. One possibility might be to continuously investigate and measure the degree of corruption and expose it to the public.

The most prominent contribution to developing a diagnostic tool for measuring public integrity is the result of the efforts of a number of international organizations; these efforts have led to developing several cross-national indicators for measuring corruption: that is, the opposite of integrity. For instance, the Global Competitiveness Report of the World Economic Forum (WEF), a leading assessment of the competitive condition of economies worldwide, is composed of the Growth Competitiveness Index and the Business Competitiveness Index. Public integrity, in particular, is considered a perceptual measure of the competitiveness of public institutions (World Economic Forum 2007). The World Bank is also developing a new set of Governance Indicators (GI), which measure six critical dimensions of governance, one of which is the degree of effort in controlling corruption in a given country (Kaufmann et al. 2007).

On the business side, the Business Environment and Enterprise Performance Survey (BEEPS), a joint effort of the European Bank for Reconstruction and Development (EBRD) and the World Bank, scrutinizes the extent to which governmental policies both facilitate and constrain business investment activities (Fries et al. 2003). BEEPS not only inspects administrative corruption by public officials, but also examines the intent of firms that try to influence government policies and regulations by illegal means (Fries et al. 2003).

In addition, Transparency International (TI), an anticorruption nongovernmental organization based in Berlin, first published its Corruption Perceptions Index (CPI) in 1995 and has released survey results annually ever since. The CPI demonstrates a cross-national study of corruption that aggregates multiple expert and business surveys. One can take a snapshot of the views of business people and country analysts for the current or recent years from the index. Another corruption measurement tool developed by TI is the Global Corruption Barometer (GCB), which is a worldwide public opinion survey conducted for TI by Gallup International. Initiated in 2003, the GCB assesses the tendencies toward corruption worldwide by surveying people's perceptions of corruption and experiences with bribery in selected countries each year.[2]

In addition to all the integrity and corruption measures published by international organizations, a great number of institutions in Taiwan have also conducted various surveys to monitor the government's integrity and corruption. These include central and local government agencies, academic institutions, the mass media, and nongovernmental organizations. Among these surveys, a longitudinal research project—the Taiwan Integrity Survey (TIS)—conducted by TI's chapter in Taiwan on behalf of the Ministry of Justice since 2003, is probably the most systematic measure of governmental integrity and corruption in Taiwan.

Most analyses of integrity and corruption are based partly upon perceptual surveys. But survey-based and perceptual measures of corruption have been criticized as being weak in reliability, since respondents involved in corruption may not report the whole experience, while those not involved can only report perceptions rather than provide accurate information (Golden and Picci 2005; Ivkovic 2003). For example, regarding the CPI, which is drawn from worldwide data, scholars argue that the index is more reliable and accurate for developed countries than for less developed ones (Golden and Picci 2005). Responding to this critique, Kaufmann et al. (2005: 16–19) argue that researchers who investigate governance issues such as corruption may find that valid direct measures and objective data are unavailable; examining the public's and/or the elite's subjective perceptions may be an alternative approach, even if it is not problem-free.

Accordingly, this chapter uses data from the GI and the TIS to demonstrate current governmental integrity and corruption in Taiwan. While the GI is concerned with the extent to which public corruption exists across countries based on expert views, the TIS investigates the public's attitudes toward and experiences with corruption.

Results from the Governance Indicators (GI)

The Governance Indicators by Kaufmann, Kraay and Mastruzzi (2007) presents updated aggregate governance research indicators for 212 countries and territories from 1996 to 2006. This study includes six dimensions of governance: (1) voice and accountability, (2) political stability and absence of violence, (3) government effectiveness, (4) regulatory quality, (5) rule of law, and (6) control of corruption. The six governance indicators are measured in units ranging from about -2.5 to 2.5, with higher values corresponding to better quality of governance. The indicators are constructed using data given by a large number of business, citizen, and expert survey respondents in industrial and developing countries, as reported by a number of survey institutes, think-tanks, nongovernmental organizations, and international organizations. Table 12.1 shows the scores from the control of corruption for the seven countries and territories in East Asia over the period 1996 to 2006.

Figure 12.1 shows the trend of this measurement. Significantly, the downward trend in this figure is quite congruent with public perceptions in Taiwan.

Table 12.1 GI control of corruption scores for countries and territories in East Asia, 1996–2006

	1996	1998	2000	2002	2003	2004	2005	2006
Singapore	2.25	2.29	2.25	2.33	2.36	2.44	2.25	2.30
Hong Kong	1.53	1.30	1.31	1.45	1.50	1.59	1.69	1.71
Japan	1.21	1.10	1.24	1.13	1.07	1.16	1.25	1.31
Taiwan	0.74	0.83	0.79	0.71	0.66	0.67	0.64	0.53
Macao	N/A	0.48	0.45	-0.06	0.82	1.35	0.55	0.41
South Korea	0.52	0.07	0.14	0.33	0.40	0.22	0.47	0.31
China	-0.09	-0.22	-0.36	-0.40	-0.49	-0.57	-0.68	-0.53

Source: http://info.worldbank.org/governance/wgi2007/pdf/2006WorldwideGovernance Indicators.xls.

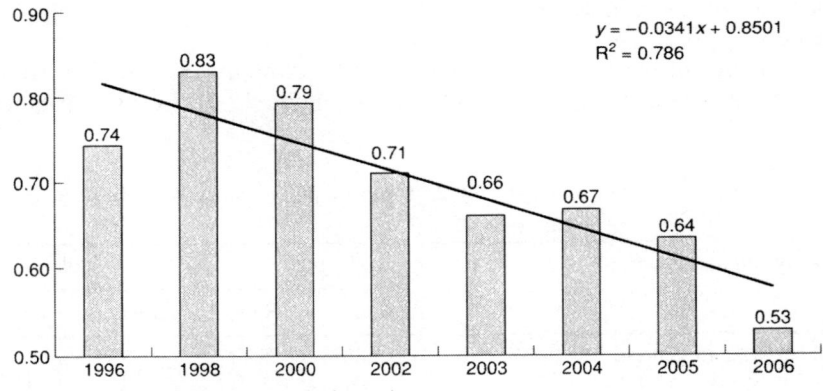

$y = -0.0341x + 0.8501$
$R^2 = 0.786$

Note: a lower score indicates greater levels of corruption

Figure 12.1 GI control of corruption scores for Taiwan, 1996–2006.
Source: http://info.worldbank.org/governance/wgi2007/pdf/2006WorldwideGovernance Indicators.xls.
Note: A lower score indicates greater levels of corruption.

Citizen perceptions of government integrity—evidence from the Taiwan Integrity Survey (TIS)

The TIS is a longitudinal research project initiated by the Ministry of Justice in 1997. So far thirteen nationwide surveys have been conducted. Starting in 2003, the TI's chapter in Taiwan has conducted five surveys on behalf of the Ministry of Justice to investigate public perceptions of the integrity of public officials. For the 2005 and 2006 data, a telephone survey was administered from 1 July to 5 July both years and covered 1,616 and 1,604 residents in Taiwan, respectively.

Similar to the GCB, the TIS investigates the public's perception of the integrity of 21 types of public officials in Taiwan. The measurement scale ranges from 0 to 10, with 10 representing high integrity and 0 representing high corruption. Table 12.2 shows the results of the 2005 and 2006 surveys.

Overall, these results show that people see the problem of corruption worsening, with an average score of 4.92 in 2005 dropping to an average of 4.79 in 2006. Thus, there is a widespread perception that elected officials and political appointees, who ought to represent the public interest, are in fact more likely to abuse their power for private gain. According to the 2006 data, legislators (rank 20 with a score of 3.65), cabinet ministers/executives (rank 18 with a score of 3.82), city/county councilors (rank 17 with a score of 3.91), town/township/city council members (rank 16 with a score of 4.27), town/township/city chiefs (rank 15 with a score of 4.35), and city/county heads/directors (rank 14 with a score of 4.44) are considered relatively corrupt as compared with most career civil servants. This result is consistent with that from the 2006 GCB, in which people expressed great concern about the role of political parties and elected politicians in the corruption equation.

The change in the ranking and score of cabinet ministers/executives from 2005 to 2006 deserves special attention (see Figure 12.2). In 2005, cabinet

Table 12.2 Perceptions of integrity for 21 types of public officials in Taiwan, 2005 and 2006, TIS

Types of public officials	2005		2006	
	Mean	*Rank*	*Mean*	*Rank*
Civil servants in general	5.83	2	5.83	1
Public medical treatment staff	6.04	1	5.81	2
Division of motor vehicles officers	5.69	3	5.71	3
Environmental protection inspectors	5.55	5	5.68	4
Fire brigade inspectors	5.58	4	5.50	5
Tax collectors	5.54	6	5.48	6
Prosecutors	5.49	7	5.33	7
Judges	5.28	8	5.14	8
Funeral-burial staff	5.03	10	4.96	9/10
Customs officers	4.91	11	4.96	9/10
Prison and detention center staff	4.68	14	4.93	11
Police officers	5.09	9	4.88	12
Commerce-industry inspectors	4.53	15	4.49	13
City/county heads/directors	4.78	12	4.44	14
Town/township/city chiefs	4.46	16	4.35	15
Town/township/city council members	4.32	17	4.27	16
City/county councilors	4.07	18	3.91	17
Cabinet ministers/executives	4.73	13	3.82	18
Procurement or construction staff	4.00	19	3.77	19
Legislators	3.95	20	3.65	20
River and gravel inspectors	3.77	21	3.61	21
Average	4.92		4.79	

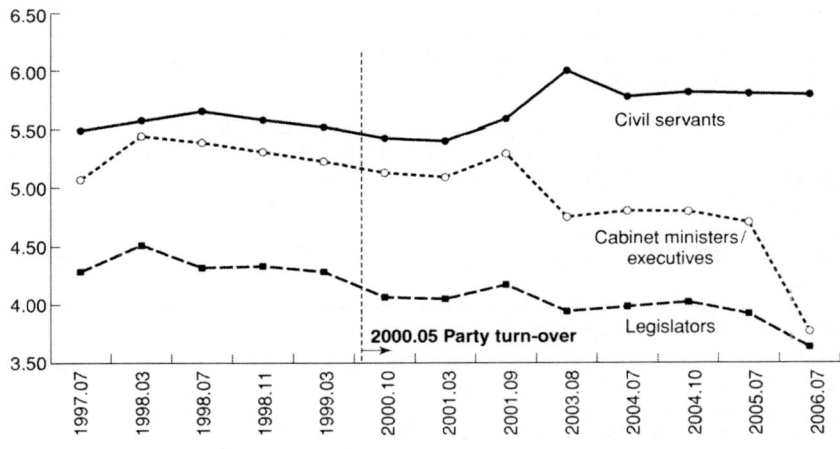

Note: a higher score indicates higher perceived levels of integrity

Figure 12.2 Perceptions of integrity for three types of public officials, 1997–2006 TIS.
Source: www.ti-taiwan.org/ch.files/doc.files/news061213.doc.
Note: A lower score indicates greater levels of corruption.

ministers/executives were ranked 13th with a score of 4.73, while in 2006 the public gave them a score of 3.82 and a ranking of 18, demonstrating a significant drop from the previous year. Taking a longer view, Table 12.3 and Figure 12.2 show changes in perception regarding cabinet ministers/executives' integrity during the period 1997 to 2006. Corruption among civil servants is relatively less of a problem. Scores of the perceived integrity of civil servants in Taiwan climbed from 5.47 in 1997 to 5.83 in 2006. However, legislators and cabinet ministers/executives were a different story. Perceptions of legislators' integrity slipped consistently from 4.27 in 1997 to 3.65 in 2006, while the perceived integrity of cabinet ministers/executives dropped sharply from 5.07 in 1997 to 3.83 in 2006. In contrast to the public's long-standing negative attitude toward legislators, cabinet ministers/executives have suffered a substantial loss of people's respect in the past decade. In addition, the perceived integrity of both legislators and cabinet ministers/executives after the party turnover in May 2000 was on average much lower than before.

Why have the cabinet ministers/executives lost the respect and trust of the people? A number of corruption scandals widely covered by the mass media in recent years might account for this change in the public's perception.

- In January 2006, a former Fair Trade Commission vice chairman was accused of defrauding the Ministry of Economic Affairs of more than NT $ 500 million (US$ 15.7 million).
- In March 2006, Taipei prosecutors indicted a political official of the Ministry of Transportation and Communications and a businessman for

Table 12.3 Perceptions of integrity for three types of public officials, 1997–2006

Types of public officials	1997 Jul	1998 Mar	1998 Jul	1998 Nov	1999 Mar	2000 Oct	2001 Mar	2001 Sep	2003 Aug	2004 Jul	2004 Oct	2005 Jul	2006 Jul
Legislators	4.27	4.50	4.32	4.34	4.30	4.07	4.07	4.20	3.97	4.01	4.04	3.95	3.65
Cabinet ministers/ executives	5.07	5.45	5.40	5.31	5.24	5.14	5.10	5.31	4.79	4.83	4.83	4.73	3.83
Civil servants	5.47	5.58	5.66	5.59	5.53	5.43	5.42	5.60	6.02	5.81	5.84	5.83	5.83

Source: http://www.ti-taiwan.org/ch.files/doc.files/news061213.doc

bribery in connection with the installment of an electronic toll collection system for freeways.

- In April 2006, a National Science Council deputy minister was accused of unlawfully awarding an NT$ 8.05 billion (US$ 252 million) contract for a vibration-reduction project for the Southern Taiwan Science Park.
- In April 2006, a deputy secretary-general to the president was arrested on charges of bribery. He was convicted of corruption and sentenced to twelve years in prison on 13 December.
- In June 2006, the director-general of inspection at the Financial Supervisory Commission was subpoenaed for questioning by prosecutors for involvement in a stock market scandal.
- In August 2006, Taipei district prosecutors indicted a former chairman of the Financial Supervisory Commission for breach of trust in connection with his previous capacity as board chairman of the state-run Taiwan Sugar Company.
- In November 2006, a former vice-minister of the interior was indicted for bribery in connection with the construction of a cable car system at Yangmingshan.
- In February 2007, a former Financial Supervisory Commission member was indicted on corruption charges. He was suspected of accepting bribes and lobbying illegally for several companies.
- In March 2007, a former minister of transportation and communications who owned stakes in resorts, aquariums, and freeway rest areas around the country was accused of accepting a US$ 20,000 bribe, which was stuffed in a tea container.
- In May 2007, the director general of the state-funded National Space Organization was detained on suspicion of "passing favors" to an international broker.

All these corruption cases involved cabinet ministers and executives, who were higher in rank than those involved in similar scandals in previous years. In addition, more scandals exploded in 2006 and 2007 than ever before, and the press covered these scandals more intensely. Figure 12.3 shows the news reports on corruption in Taiwan from the United Daily News Group, one of biggest news groups in Taiwan. The increase in news reports on corruption in 2006 was dramatic. Given the mass media's strong agenda-setting effect on public perceptions (Protess and McCombs 1991), the public now has a much worse perception of corruption with respect to cabinet ministers and executives.

The low trust in cabinet ministers/executives fuels skepticism and cynicism toward government. Although skepticism and cynicism are a worldwide phenomenon, the Taiwan government's image of fighting corruption is quite weak, with 25 percent of the people in Taiwan believing that their government actually encourages corruption rather than fighting it. The TIS used three questions to investigate the public's assessment of the government's performance in fighting corruption and promoting integrity in Taiwan. Figures 12.4, 12.5, and 12.6 present the results of these questions over a three-year period.

In 2004, regarding the government's performance in fighting corruption and black-gold politics, about 46 percent of respondents were dissatisfied while about 44 percent were satisfied.[3] In 2005, the degree of dissatisfaction rose to 61 percent, while the percentage of satisfied respondents fell to 33 percent. In 2006, the gap between the dissatisfied and the satisfied grew even wider, 72 and 23 percent respectively. By the same token, the public's satisfaction with the government's performance in investigating vote-buying also decreased. In 2004, the percentage of satisfied respondents was only 5 percent lower than the dissatisfied rate (42 vs 47 percent), but the gap grew wider in 2005 (40 vs 54 percent) and changed dramatically in 2006 (31 vs 64 percent). When respondents were asked about the future in the 2004 survey, 43 percent still felt optimistic about improving government integrity, which was higher than the 35 percent of respondents who felt pessimistic. But the

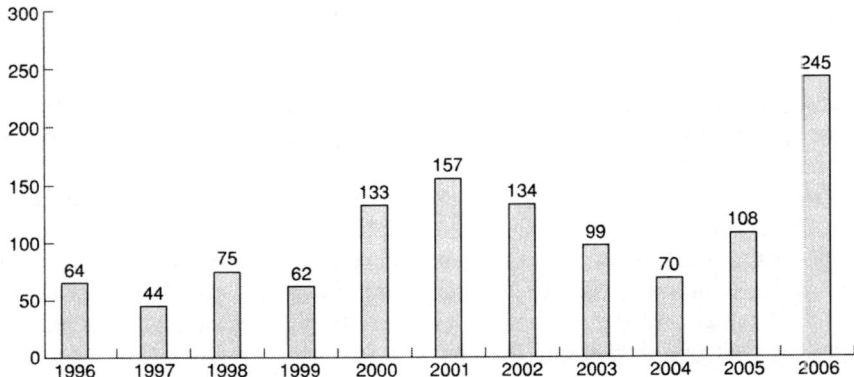

Figure 12.3 Numbers of news reports on corruption in Taiwan.
Source: http://udndata.com/.

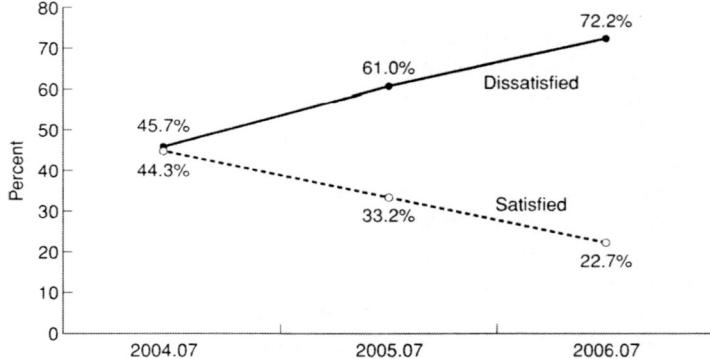

Figure 12.4 Assessing the government's performance fighting corruption and black-gold politics, 2004–2006.

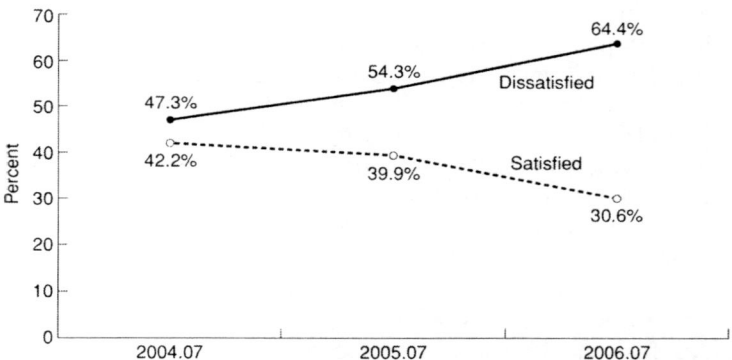

Figure 12.5 Assessing the government's performance investigating vote-buying, 2004–2006.

Source: www.ti-taiwan.org/ch.files/doc.files/news061213.doc.

feeling has shifted in recent years. Feelings of pessimism about the future have grown stronger, as the results from 2005 and 2006 show (roughly 39 percent being optimistic vs 47 percent pessimistic).

One partial explanation for the results may be information asymmetry. Though people may read headlines of scandals over and over, rarely are the daily anticorruption efforts by various government agencies recognized. But another partial explanation is the public's increasing awareness about the essence of political power and human nature, as raised by the democratization process over the past two decades in Taiwan.

In the late nineteenth century, historian Lord Acton issued an epic warning that the most serious threat to liberty is political power. In a letter to Bishop Mandell Creighton in 1887, he famously wrote: "All power corrupts,

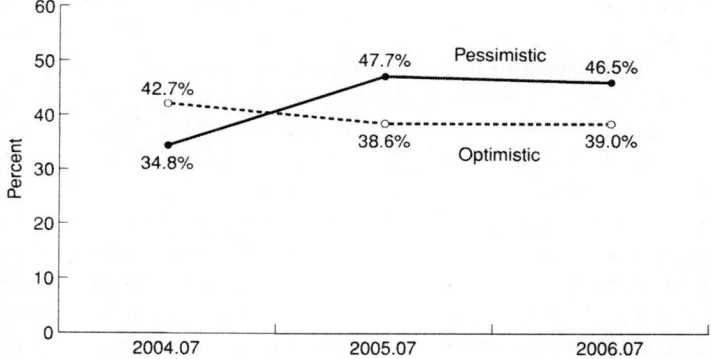

Figure 12.6 Assessing the improvement of government integrity in the future, 2004–2006.
Source: www.ti-taiwan.org/ch.files/doc.files/news061213.doc.

and absolute power corrupts absolutely. Great men are almost always bad men." A sudden surge in and revelation of corruption in Taiwanese politics have put Lord Acton's commentary on political power and human nature on display. As politicians climb the ladder of power, they attract fraud and vice, and eventually envelop themselves in corruption and scandal driven by personal greed and selfish ambitions. It may be that powerful people, whether small-time officials in rural towns or the president and the first family, cannot refuse the temptations that come with their political titles. Whether this is due to the nature of political power or to human nature, is it the price of democratic transformation? The answer should be negative.

A step forward: the President's Public Integrity Agenda

In past years, people in Taiwan have experienced some setbacks that have frequently been witnessed throughout most democratic transformations. Scandals in the then ruling DPP government as well as the first family have reduced citizen trust in politicians, public officials, and the government as a whole. Surveys conducted by the United Daily News reveal that citizen satisfaction with the DPP government dropped from 79 percent on 19 June 2000 to 21 percent on 19 May 2008. Meanwhile, only 18 percent of respondents said they were satisfied with the general performance of the DPP government over the past eight years, while about 70 percent were unsatisfied. Thus, eight years of turmoil have lowered people's trust in Taiwan's democratization.

Recently, the Taiwanese people elected a new president, Mr. Ma Ying-jeou, to take over the government. Three issues that the new president should address foremost are (1) how to restore people's confidence by rebuilding the value of integrity in the bureaucratic system and the government, (2) how to accelerate the progress of improvement in public integrity, and (3) how to make Taiwan worthy of being called the best case of the third-wave democratizations.

Undoubtedly, the task of coping with integrity issues is not easy. Because the Chen administration was criticized as being corrupt, President Ma has set out an integrity policy, called the President's Public Integrity Agenda, which is regarded as a guideline and policy directive for the new government in anticorruption reform. The President's Public Integrity Agenda highlights the most important agendas, including establishing the Central Integrity and Ethics Commission at the cabinet level, preventing improper political interventions in independent agencies, adjusting punishments for buying votes in political party elections, remaking anticorruption laws, inflicting penalties on officials who declare properties dishonestly, penalizing the crime of unknown sources of huge-sum properties, aggravating charges upon imposturous entrepreneurs, and opening decision-making processes to prevent conflicts of interest.

As new cabinet members are taking their offices, the most imperative missions regarding anticorruption in President Ma's government are twofold: First, the Ma administration must initiate institutional reforms by which laws with flaws are revised or new laws are legislated. Second, since both the executive and legislative branches are under the KMT's control, the Ma administration should leverage cross-branch synergy into concrete actions. These imperative anticorruption missions are elaborated as follows.

Initiating institutional reforms

Generally speaking, the existing rules and laws associated with government ethics have flaws. Thus, the first imperative of the new government should be to remake the anticorruption laws in the present legal system. The following rules, laws, and reform directions are those that the new government should take into account:

1   Remaking ineffective and outdated laws and regulations. Those picky rules and complicated laws, which make it difficult deal with government agencies and may misguide people with ill intentions into going to the back door, must be simplified and rationalized. Some deregulation, along with openness in government information, is needed to make government smaller and more transparent.
2   Penalizing the crime of unknown sources of huge-sum properties. According to the United Nations Conventions against Corruption Article 20, a public official should be penalized if he or she has gained a significant property increase relative to his or her lawful income but cannot offer reasonable explanation. Related legislation was established in Singapore in 1988, in Hong Kong in 1971, and in China in 1988. In Taiwan, legislation regarding the crime of illicit enrichment was made by revising the Law on Property-Declaration by Public Servants in March 2007,

through the advocacy of the TI-Taiwan, the Judicial Reform Foundation, the Prosecutorial Reform Committee, and the National Clean Election Promotion Association. However, if one is found guilty of this crime, the punishment is a fine, and the penalty's effectiveness is questionable. In this respect, the Ma administration is planning to amend the Anticorruption Statute and criminalize illicit enrichment.

3 Establishing a cumulative penalty on dishonest property declaration. A public official in Taiwan who declares assets dishonestly will be punished by a fine based upon the present Law on Property-Declaration by Public Servants. However, the virtue of this administrative penalty is uncertain. This law needs to be amended, and a cumulative penalty on the behavior of dishonest property declaration needs to be established. In the President's Public Integrity Agenda, a public official guilty of dishonest property declaration will be punished the first time by a fine, but repeated offences will be handled as criminal behavior.

Taking concrete actions

The new laws must be enforced for the system to work. Hence, the first priority of the President's Public Integrity Agenda is to establish a Central Integrity and Ethics Commission at the cabinet level as the supervisory mechanism of anticorruption performance, and to coordinate governmental energy in combating corruption. In the Commission, the premier will serve as the chief commissioner, the minister of justice will serve as the chief executive, and related ministers and experts will also sit on the commission. A regular meeting will be held once a month. While the Ma administration has proposed to examine the effectiveness of the Commission's operation after two years, there is a group of policy analysts who would like to see an independent bureau established like the Independent Commission Against Corruption in Hong Kong and Singapore.

Conclusion: searching for a strong democracy, a vital civil society, and good governance

Information about public perceptions of and experience with corruption is vital to anticorruption efforts. People's perceptions are an indicator of the success or failure of anticorruption policies and initiatives. In addition, it would be helpful in assigning priorities to policy initiatives, managerial action, and anticorruption efforts to make data available showing which sectors, institutions, or public officials are considered most corrupt.

The data presented in this chapter show that the Taiwanese people doubt the integrity of their government. This is especially true of elected officials and political appointees. Why has this happened? The message from the data is clear: Taiwan's democratic transformation has not improved, but rather has injured, the government's integrity. Democratic transformation has not been sufficient to control corruption, especially political corruption. If political corruption arises in connection with democratic transformation, it will undermine the legitimacy of democracy. People will miss "the good old days," and even wish for "more bureaucracy and less democracy." As Chang and Chu (2006: 256) succinctly point out:

> Political corruption is considered one of the most destructive yet unresolved problems common to most societies. Importantly, political corruption represents a direct and brutal betrayal of public trust placed in institutions, since political corruption revolves around situations where governmental officials entrusted by the public engage in malfeasance for private enrichment (Bardhan, 1997). Because corruption recklessly violates the fundamental principles of democracy—such as accountability, equality, and openness—recent studies have suggested that corruption causes political distrust among citizens, thus leading to legitimacy crises in political systems (Anderson and Tverdova 2003; Seligson 2002).

One certainly could argue that the increase in corruption cases does indeed result from the democratic transformation. However, in Taiwan the charges against corrupt high-ranking officials have been possible because of the independence of the judicial system, the strength of civil society, and the freedom of the press. These three elements usually do not exist in authoritarian regimes. But though this may be true, we must also be aware that, for a number of democratic countries in the world that possess all three elements, the number of corruption cases has been lower than those in Taiwan in recent years. As such, Taiwan needs to make a greater effort to promote integrity, fight corruption, and rebuild public trust in government.

The prospective achievements of the President's Public Integrity Agenda proposed by the Ma administration need more observation. Yet, the fundamental issue that must be taken into account is the need of the new government to bring civil society back in this agenda; it also needs to make the spirit of integrity and honesty the basis of elementary and secondary education. Relying on the government per se will be never sufficient to establish a clean government. Leveraging grassroots power in both the public and private sectors in order to prevent corruption is an imperative for the new government. Unfortunately, we do not see it in the President's Public Integrity Agenda.

Along with the democratization process, an abundance of non-profit organizations have been established in Taiwan. For instance, to prevent legislators from abusing power, the Coalition for Citizen Watch (CCW) has formed to raise citizen awareness of the push for transparency in the legislative process. In addition, tens of thousands of ordinary people are involved in volunteer work as well. The new government cannot ignore the power of ordinary people; on the contrary, it is expected that the Ma administration will use wisely the vital energy embedded in civil society. In this regard,

Transparency International's Chapter in Taiwan (TI-Taiwan) has been devoted to curbing and combating corruption in Taiwan by promoting consciousness against corruption; strengthening local research on and understanding of bribery; aligning with governmental institutions, business corporations, and civil society; monitoring the public and private sectors' unethical behaviors; and attempting to create a culture of transparency and integrity in Taiwan. The National Clean Election Promotion Association has been dedicated to promoting the importance of clean elections and raising strategies to prevent vote-buying in elections as well. In addition, more non-profit organizations and volunteers have become involved in the Citizen Anticorruption Networks initiated by the Ministry of Justice.

Furthermore, some good programs use the collective power of citizens in support of governmental forces. For example, the program of the Citizen Supervision of Public Construction, initiated by the Public Construction Commission at the Executive Yuan, empowers citizens to notify government via the Internet if they see any suspected problems concerning corruption in ongoing or finished public works and construction projects (Chen and Huang 2008). Accordingly, the new government should involve societal power in the anticorruption movement and cultivate a clean-state grassroots volunteer program.

In addition to involving civil society in the anticorruption movement, a government with foresight will foster citizen integrity through education. The new government could develop a systematic curriculum plan to educate students regarding the virtues of integrity in elementary and secondary schools. This is undoubtedly the best strategy for fostering honest citizens from childhood.

In Taiwan, the challenge remains for political leaders to prove that they are not actually fueling corrupt practices but are doing the best they can to enhance transparency, accountability, and integrity. But in addition to expecting political leaders to exercise self-control, refrain from corruption, and show a strong commitment to integrity, a much stronger civil society is needed, and citizens must play a more active and aggressive role in building a system of integrity and ensuring good democratic governance. The search for strong democracy and good governance is an indispensable step for Taiwan to maintain its reputation as the best case of third-wave democratizations in the world.

Notes

1 For the purposes of this chapter, East Asia includes China, Hong Kong, Japan, Macau, Singapore, South Korea, and Taiwan.
2 For information regarding the CPI and GCB, please refer to http://www.transparency.org/tools/measurement
3 Taiwanese democracy has been criticized for certain political organizations and politicians making connections with gangsters (black) and obtaining money interests (gold) through inappropriate means.

References

Anderson, C. and Tverdova, Y. (2003) "Corruption, political allegiances, and attitudes toward government in contemporary democracies," *American Journal of Political Science*, 47(1): 91–109.

Bardhan, P. (1997) "Corruption and development: a review of issues," *Journal of Economics Literature*, 35(3): 1320–46.

Boylan, R.T. and Long, C.X. (2003) "Measuring public corruption in the American states: a survey of state house reporters," *State Politics and Policy Quarterly*, 3(4): 420–38.

Chang, E.C.C. and Chu, Y. (2006) "Corruption and trust: exceptionalism in Asian democracies," *The Journal of Politics*, 68(2): 259–71.

Chen, D.Y. and Huang, T.Y. (2008) "Accountability through participation: a case study of the designing and implementing of the Citizen Supervision on Public Construction (CSPC) in Taiwan," paper presented at the Accountability and Public Governance International Conference, Taipei, Taiwan.

Colazingari, S. and Rose-Ackerman, S. (1998) "Corruption in a paternalistic democracy: lessons from Italy for Latin America," *Political Science Quarterly*, 113(3): 447–70.

Eigen, P. (2002) "Measuring and combating corruption," *Policy Reform*, 5(4): 187–201.

Fell, D. (2002) "Party platform change in Taiwan's 1990's elections," *Issues and Studies*, 38(2): 31–60.

Fries, S., Lysenko, T., and Polanec, S. (2003) "The 2002 business environment and enterprise performance survey: results from a survey of 6,100 firms," online. Available at www.ebrd.com/pubs/econo/wp0084.pdf (accessed 10 February 2006).

Golden, M.A. and Picci, L. (2005) "Proposal for a new measure of corruption, illustrated with Italian data," *Economics and Politics*, 17(1): 37–75.

Ivkovic, S.K. (2003) "To serve and collect: measuring police corruption," *Journal of Criminal Law and Criminology*, 93(2): 593–649.

Kaufmann, D., Kraay, A., and Mastruzzi, M. (2005) "Measuring governance using cross-country perceptions data," online. Available at www.worldbank.org/wbi/governance/pdf/MeasuringGovernancewithPerceptionsData.pdf (accessed 10 February 2006).

—— (2007) "Governance matters VI: governance indicators for 1996–2006," online. Available at http://papers.ssrn.com/sol3/papers.cfm?abstract_id = 999979#PaperDownload (accessed 10 February 2006).

Manion, M. (2004) *Corruption by Design: Building Clean Government in Mainland China and Hong Kong*, Cambridge, MA: Harvard University Press.

Protess, D.L. and McCombs, M. (1991) *Agenda Setting: Reading on Media, Public Opinion, and Policymaking*, New York: Lawrence Erlbaum Associates.

Rigger, S. (2004) "Taiwan's best-case democratization," *Orbis*, 48(2): 285–92.

Seligson, M. (2002) "The impact of corruption on regime legitimacy: a comparative study of four Latin American countries," *Journal of Politics*, 64(2): 408–33.

Transparency International (2005) *Report on the Transparency International Global Corruption Barometer 2005*, Berlin, Germany: Transparency International.

—— (2006) *Report on the Transparency International Global Corruption Barometer 2006*, Berlin, Germany: Transparency International.

van Blijswijk, J.A.M., Breukelen, R.C.J., Franklin, A.L., Raadschelders, J.C.N., and Slump, P. (2004) "Beyond ethical codes: the management of integrity in the

Netherlands tax and customs administration," *Public Administration Review*, 64(6): 718–27.

Velkova, E. and Georgievski, S. (2004) "Fighting transborder organized crime in southeast Europe through fighting corruption in customs agencies," *Southeast European and Black Sea Studies*, 4(2): 280–93.

World Economic Forum (2007) "The Global Competitiveness Report 2007–2008," online. Available at www.weforum.org/en/initiatives/gcp/index.htm (accessed June 2008).

13 Corruption, culture and institutions

Evidence from the Pacific Islands

Peter Larmour

Ideas about "culture" have often been used to explain, or excuse, acts of corruption. Gift giving, it is sometimes said, is "part of our culture." Outsiders should not confuse it with bribery or corruption. Such a relativistic approach has been strongly criticized by academic writers on corruption, such as Sayed Alatas in his classic *Sociology of Corruption*, and by activists, such as Transparency International.

Alatas saw cultural relativism as another kind of Western naiveté and condescension towards non-Western societies. The West, he argued, imagined them to be incapable of telling right from wrong. Alatas provided copious evidence of concern about abuse of public office in different periods (ancient Rome) and cultural traditions (Muslim and Chinese). Just because leaders violated local norms, he argued, did not mean those norms did not exist. "Cultural practices are used for the purposes of corruption rather than being the cause of corruption" (Alatas 1968: 96–97).

More recently, Transparency International (TI) takes a robust stand against what it calls the "myth" or "excuse" of culture. Its influential *Source Book* quotes one of the organization's founding fathers, who went on to be elected president of Nigeria. Talking of the distinction between gifts and bribes, Olusegun Obasanjo says,

> I shudder at how an integral aspect of our culture could be taken as the basis for rationalizing otherwise despicable behavior. In the African concept of appreciation and hospitality, the gift is usually a token. It is not demanded. The value is usually in the spirit rather than in the material worth. It is usually done in the open, and never in secret. Where it is excessive, it becomes an embarrassment and it is returned. If anything, corruption has perverted and destroyed this aspect of our culture.
>
> (quoted in Transparency International 2000: 8)

Nevertheless, ideas about culture and corruption won't go away easily. Transparency International is an international organization and, whatever its universalistic beliefs, has in practice to defer to claims of national difference.

Meanwhile, ideas about culture have become more and more influential in the social sciences, particularly in the burgeoning field of Cultural Studies.

This chapter draws for empirical evidence on a series of reports on National Integrity Systems in the Pacific Islands. The reports followed a standard template provided by TI, which asked about the existence and performance of various aspects of each country's "National Integrity System"—the executive, the legislature, the auditor general, civil society and so on (Larmour and Barcham 2006). The authors of the reports were also asked to comment generally on the corruption situation in each country. The authors of twelve of the fourteen reports were specifically asked to comment on the role played by culture (and the authors of the two earlier reports discussed culture without being prompted).

The Pacific Islands consist of fourteen small countries, ranging in population from about six million to about 1,600 (with a median of about 100,000). It is typically divided up into three main "culture areas": Micronesia, to the northwest; Melanesia, to the southwest; and Polynesia to the east (see Table 13.1). All but two of these fourteen countries are parliamentary democracies. The two exceptions are Tonga, where the government is still responsible to a hereditary monarch rather than the legislature, and Fiji, ruled by a military

Table 13.1 Pacific Islands population and political status

	Population (mid-year 2004 estimate)	Political status
Melanesia		
Fiji Islands	836,000	Independent 1970
Papua New Guinea	5,695,300	Independent 1975
Solomon Islands	460,000	Independent 1979
Vanuatu	215,000	Independent 1980
Micronesia		
Federated States of Micronesia	112,700	Free association with USA
Kiribati	93,100	Independent 1979
Marshall Islands	55,400	Free association with USA
Nauru	10,100	Independent 1968
Palau	20,700	Free association with USA
Polynesia		
Cook Islands	14,000	Free association with New Zealand
Niue	1,600	Free association with New Zealand
Samoa	182,700	Independent 1962
Tonga	98,300	Never colonized
Tuvalu	9,600	Independent 1978

Source: South Pacific Commission.

government since a coup in December 2006. The region has also been a cradle for the Western study of Anthropology, providing evidence, for example, for Marcel Mauss's classic study of *The Gift*. In each country arguments about the role of custom and tradition are an important part of everyday life and politics, including discussions about corruption.

The concept of "culture"

"Culture" according to Raymond Williams is "one of the two or three most complicated words in the English language" (Williams 1985 [1976]). In his influential book *Keywords* he distinguished three broad usages. The first describes a process of intellectual spiritual and aesthetic development, related to the idea of civilization. The second applies to particular ways of life. It was the mainstream anthropological approach and includes the practical and material aspects of a way of life, as well the signifying and symbolic ones (Kuper 1999). The third applied more narrowly to artistic and intellectual endeavor: theatre, dance, music and film.

The first usage applied to spiritual and intellectual development, rather than the economic development that concerns the development banks and aid donors who have become interested in corruption since the 1990s (Kaufmann et al. 1999).

The second of Williams's usages of "culture" seems most relevant to the possibility that something regarded as corrupt in one particular culture, or sub-culture, might not be regarded as corrupt in another: the issue of "cultural relativism."

The third usage, to do with the expressive arts, is particularly relevant in the Pacific Islands: Collective performances cost money and other resources, and participation in cultural events is part of the role of leaders, and hard to distinguish from the politics of alliances, and democratic electioneering. The Samoa report, for example, talks about "pressure to contribute to cultural functions" (So'o et al. 2004: 5).

A recent update of Williams's *Keywords* begins by warning "there is now a good deal of hesitancy over the value of the word 'culture'" (Bennett et al. 2005, but see Sahlins 1999). It notes the gradual triumph of Williams's second, anthropological meaning—culture as a way of life—but a parallel rejection of the idea that these ways of life might be fixed, uncontested from within, or clearly distinct, as colonial governments in the Pacific Islands are said to have made them.

Two dominant approaches to social science—Marxism and rational choice—have tended to deal with "culture" indirectly. Marxism tended to treat it as an effect of more fundamental economic processes, while rational choice theories try to grasp it through individual attitudes and dispositions. Writing in a Marxist tradition, Colin Leys wondered in the 1960s "What is the problem with corruption?" reminding us that corruption was the foundation of what is now regarded as prestigious "old money" in the US (Leys 2002).

Johann Lambsdorff, the inventor of TI's influential Corruption Perceptions Index, has reviewed what he calls empirical research on cultural determinants of corruption (Lambsdorff 1999). It tends to be concerned with individual attitudes and dispositions. In a survey of 33 countries, La Porta et al. (1997: 333–8) find that trust has a significant negative impact on corruption. The same survey also found some correlation between membership of a hierarchical religion (Catholic, Orthodox or Muslim) and corruption. Protestantism also seems to be negatively correlated with corruption. Lambsdorff concludes his review:

> Culture can only explain a certain fraction of the level of corruption and there remains sufficient room for improvements of a country's integrity. Moreover cultural attitudes can also be a reflection of the organizational patterns that led to their formation.
>
> (Lambsdorff 1999: 2)

Believing that "culture matters," Thompson et al. concede that "the trouble with taking explicit account of culture is that explanation tends to go out of the window" (Thompson et al. 2006: 32). They identify three typical misuses of the concept that seem relevant to understanding corruption. First, culture is invoked as an "uncaused cause." We might hear that someone acted corruptly "because of her culture." But what caused her culture to be like that? Second, culture is invoked as "an explanation of the last resort." Having exhausted other more favored explanations for corruption—political, economic, ethical, etc.— we turn to culture as a kind of residual category, or noise. Third, culture is invoked as a "veto on comparison." You can't compare, say, corruption in Australia with corruption in China because each can only be understood in its own terms. Some statements about culture in the Pacific have that blocking and checking character. For example, when the Papua New Guinea (PNG) prime minister once said, in reply to a question about a payment made to another MP in exchange for political support, "Corruption is part of a culture," he may simply have been saying: "Back off: this is none of your business."

The concept of "institution"

If "culture" is a complicated idea, then so is the idea of an "institution," and there is some overlap between the two. A common image from institutional economics is of institutions as "rules of the game," framing and constraining individual action (North 1990: 4). Their "institutional" quality lies in their being "stable valued and recurring" (Goodin 1996: 21). A dictionary of sociology offers a definition of "institution" as "An enduring set of ideas about how to accomplish goals generally recognized as important in society" (Johnson 2000).

It gives as an example the state and the family. The chapters on China in this book would typically add "the Party" to these two examples, while (as we shall see) in the Pacific Island cases discussed below we would need to add "the gift" as an institution.

The idea that institutions can be designed, rather than inherited or treated as given, is a feature of two theories of corruption prevention that are now influential in the international community (Larmour 2006). The first, propagated by TI, is of the National Integrity System. It was originally proposed by a constitutional lawyer, Jeremy Pope, and draws on the Madisonian idea of checks and balances embodied in the American and Westminster constitutions. It is open to adjustment, like a watch, by a skilled designer. The second, influential in the World Bank, was invented by Robert Klitgaard (1988), who argued that corruption could be designed out of institutions by reducing discretion, eliminating government monopolies, and increasing accountability.

The word "policy" is not simple either. Here we will use a framework from the study of public policy—the policy cycle—to sort and re-analyze empirical material from TI-sponsored studies of National Integrity Systems in the Pacific Islands. The re-analysis suggests various points at which governments might do more to prevent corruption. Then we will turn to the underlying institutional dualism, or pluralism, that the studies reveal.

Culture in the NIS Pacific reports

Each of the National Integrity System (NIS) reports makes some general points about culture and corruption. The authors' discussions typically express tension, contradiction or dilemma around the relationship. The Solomon Islands report remarked that for some village people impartial treatment from an official to whom they were related would be regarded as "culturally unacceptable," even "an insult" (Roughan 2004: 9). But others, more familiar with relatives in professional positions, would not.

The Fiji report talks of the "cultural dilemma, in which the official roles of public servants are interwoven with and often compromised by their traditional obligations" (Singh and Dakunivosa 2001: 9). In Nauru "it may be that tradition and culture also causes corruption" (Kun et al. 2004). Both the Tonga and Vanuatu reports use the phrase "hide" or "hiding behind the culture" (Newton Cain and Jowitt 2004: 23; James and Tufui 2004: 5). The Vanuatu report stresses that "Melanesian culture does not cause corruption—it does not condone behavior that benefits an individual at the expense of the community. Instead there is a mismatch between introduced notions of corruption and local culture" (Newton Cain and Jowitt 2004: 12). The PNG report finds "certain aspects of the culture which seem to be more compatible with corruption" but is quick to say "this does not mean that PNG has a corrupt culture" (Mellam and Aloi 2003: 8). In a similar zigzag way the Samoa report says, "Although Samoan culture does not necessarily teach corrupt behavior, the propensity to use public resources and misuse entrusted power have sometimes been associated with the pressure to contribute to cultural functions" (So'o et al. 2004: 5).

Two reports use the positive phrase "caring and sharing" to describe the local culture (Nauru, PNG). In PNG, "sharing and caring is synonymous with leadership in Melanesian culture" while "mobilization and distribution of wealth is an essential component" of a leader's responsibilities (Mellam and Aloi 2003: 11). The Fiji report also talks about "the friendly and forgiving nature and extreme tolerance inherent in the culture" (Singh and Dakunivosa 2001: 12).

The Tuvalu report listed important values: "reciprocity, status, gift giving, family ties, and community" (Taafaki 2004: 4). Kiribati culture was characterized as egalitarian. In Cook Islands, by contrast there was a predisposition to obey superiors. Marshall Islands culture was described as being overridden by "American ideologies and materialism" (Pollock 2004: 12), while the Tuvalu report also contrasts the "confrontational" style, adopted by ministers and associated with the Westminster system, contrasts with the "Tuvaluan search for agreement, consensus, value for respect and cooperation."

Some reports did identify differences within countries. The report on PNG pointed to its cultural diversity, and noted, for example, two provincial exceptions to its statement that traditional leadership had little impact (these were in Milne Bay and New Ireland.) The report on Micronesia (FSM) also found strong cultural differences between states, and different levels of corruption between them (highest in Chuuk).

Culture was not always regarded as a factor mitigating or softening accusations of corruption. In Kiribati, particularly, local councils of elders deployed "the force of culture as the informal anticorruption system" (Mackenzie 2004: 19). Similarly village councils in Samoa (called *fono*) deployed sometimes-draconian punishments as part of the "traditional integrity system." It bore heavily on the consciences of men in Palau. "Strong traditional awareness of right and wrong brings its own pressures, as some suicides of middle-aged men may have resulted from the heavy conscience burden resulting from involvement in corrupt practices that generated quiet, but powerful scorn" (Schuster 2004: 8).

The structure of their task forced the authors to treat culture as something of a residual category, outside the framework of the questionnaire, and literally added on to it. They tended to treat it as an uncaused cause—one of the misuses of the concept identified above. However, four of the reports offer the "smallness" as an explanation for these cultural characteristics (Samoa, Palau, Tuvalu) (see Larmour and Barcham 2006). Smallness led to "lack of anonymity" (James and Tufui 2004: 43), the prominence of particular personalities (Taafaki 2004), and the fact that people were "bound to be related" (So'o et al. 2004: 12).

The reports also use culture in two more specific senses. First, culture was seen as something attached to particular institutions, for example a "civil service culture." This corresponds to Raymond Williams's second usage of culture as a "way of life" in relatively closed and total institutions like the police or the civil service. Similarly, the Solomon Islands report talks of a public service "ethos of procedure" which (the report argues) was the object of "active subversion" by politicians like Solomon Mamaloni (Roughan 2004: 10). (The Tuvalu report also suggested that civil servants' reluctance to be frank with ministers might reflect a "cultural problem": Taafaki 2004: 9).

Second, it was seen as something pervasive and entrenched, such as a "culture of corruption" in the forestry industry in Solomon Islands (Roughan 2004: 28), a "culture of permissiveness" in Solomon Islands or a "culture of welfare" in Marshall Islands. The Fiji report quotes the Ombudsman's remark about a "culture of silence" that inhibits complaints (Singh and Dakunivosa 2001: 21). Here the socialized aspect of culture is being emphasized, inviting questions about how that culture was learned or could be unlearned. Culture was also a professional role for the "cultural officer" in Kiribati, where the job presumably dealt with the organizing of dancing and cultural shows— Williams's third sense.

Points of entry for cultural factors

Culture can be a little broad as an explanation. To narrow it, it helps to think about points at which cultural factors might matter in different ways. The academic study of Public Policy often has recourse to the idea of a "policy cycle," in which problems move through stages of identification, definition, legislation and implementation. A similar framework helps identify the points at which culture seems to matter in the Pacific Islands.

In a general suspicion of corruption

Gunnar Myrdal (1968), writing about South Asia, talked of the "folklore of corruption." The Samoan report talks of a general public suspicion of corruption, not based on particular evidence, but a result of the government's "secure grip on power" and its track record in the 1990s which included constitutional amendments to increase the size of the cabinet and to reduce the term of office of the auditor, and the assassination of a minister named in the auditor's reports (So'o et al. 2004: 11). This suspicion was hard to shake off.

Similarly, the Solomon Islands report coins the phrase "insidious tolerance" in which "people express suspicion of corrupt activity at the slightest indication, but at the same time are willing to accept inaction concerning that suspicion" (Roughan 2004: 9).

The culture here may be a culture of suspicion, which may be exaggerated or well founded. Its opposite might be the "trust" that writers on social capital give importance to.

In the identification of particular people or behavior as corrupt

This is the point at which people have to consider whether they think a particular action—or inaction—is corrupt, or not. They may also consider it bad for other reasons, but not corruption. It looks like a solitary decision, but it is in fact a social event. It involves language, and in practice is likely to involve the to-ing and fro-ing of discussion with colleagues or friends or family (or some kind of internal dialogue reproducing these interactions). This process may refer to what others have done before, or would do—and involves role models, childhood injunctions, and the examples set by characters in folktales, literature or film.

In Vanuatu and Nauru, for example, it seems that only the givers, not the receivers, of bribes are perceived as acting corruptly. In Vanuatu "ordinary people who receive bribes are not 'corrupt'. Chiefs who tell individuals how to vote after receiving bribes or goods for their villages are sometimes perceived as corrupt, but not always. The person offering the bribe is, however, acting corruptly" (Newton Cain and Jowitt 2004: 10). Similarly in Nauru, people encouraging or benefiting from corruption tend not to be regarded as corrupt themselves. Where people are paid to vote one way or another, "The blame attaches to the person who offers the temptation rather than the person who accepts it" (Kun et al. 2004: 9).

In the seriousness with which it is taken

Corruption may be taken less seriously than it is (now) by donors. Epeli Hau'ofa created several tales around the fun of fooling donors in an imaginary Pacific Island country very like Tonga (Hau'ofa 2004). NGOs now imbue any discussion of corruption with a deadly earnestness. Some assessment of seriousness is going to be necessary for any practical action, which will have costs in fractured social relationships and police time. Assessment of seriousness is an important part of anticorruption policy. It is easy for an agency or campaign to get bogged down in trivial examples and miss the more serious manifestations.

In FSM people don't see that misappropriated money is "taken out of the pockets of citizens" (Hill 2004: 12). In Nauru carelessness may have been higher when people thought "resources were in abundance" (Kun et al. 2004: 11). In Vanuatu "grassroots" people saw the activities of law and government as "irrelevant to their everyday life," and as a consequence "did not place any burden of expectation on their leaders" (Newton Cain and Jowitt 2004: 5). People only got concerned when they saw their own money was at stake, as in the riots that followed revelations about National Provident Fund money (yet the perpetrator of the equivalent abuse in PNG got a heroes' welcome). In Vanuatu the Ombudsman found that while 33,000 people were members of NPF, there were only 784 applications for housing loans, of which 150 were successful. "The majority of these were Ministers, members of parliament, Vanuatu Provident Fund Board members and staff, UMP party supporters, political appointees and families of these groups." Many of the favored groups had loans approved without even submitting applications, while many applications were never considered (Newton Cain and Jowitt 2004: 14).

In willingness to criticize and report

The Cook Islands report talks of "fear of reprisal: people would rather live with the consequences of corrupt politicians than face losing their jobs" (Ingram 2004: 12). In Palau "people find it difficult to correct or discipline or even report that a friend, relative or co-worker is behaving in a corrupt manner" (Schuster 2004: 9). In Tonga people won't report others because of "shame to the family involved, damage to the social fabric, and the breaking of relationships" (James and Tufui 2004: 10). In FSM "it is very improper to question or openly criticize others or cause someone to lose face" (Hill 2004: 11). In Palau "quiet and subtle scorn" was preferred to overt rebuke, and "indirectness" was a virtue.

In Solomon Islands there has been "lack of public or institutional pressure to redress blatant corruption acts." The report points to "a marked unwillingness of leading individuals" in the relevant institutions (Roughan 2004: 11). The Fiji report argues that in small societies with strong cultural ties "everyone knowing each other makes the act of ignoring illegal practices" easier than "blowing the whistle" (Singh and Dakunivosa 2001).

The Cook Islands report talks of "the traditional practice of respect for elders and leaders that leads to reluctance to question their actions" (Ingram 2004: 5, 12). In FSM there is "reluctance to openly criticize others, particularly chiefs" (Hill 2004: 8). Similarly the Nauru report: "traditionally, Nauruans do not question the actions and behavior of their chiefs out of respect or fear or both" (Kun et al. 2004: 12). The "welfare and cohesion of the extended family" is held more dearly than the putative cost to the country (ibid.). And in Vanuatu "tradition discourages the criticism of leaders" (Newton Cain and Jowitt 2004: 5). In FSM "traditional deference," for example, might make a customs officer "unlikely to closely question or search a chief arriving in the country from abroad" (Hill 2004: 12).

However, in FSM it was suggested that people were reluctant to report less from fear of reprisal than from the expectation that they will "get their chance" to benefit corruptly next (Hill 2004: 12).

In reaching authoritative judgments

The report on Tonga found that people can "hide behind the culture" because there were no authoritative guidelines to "distinguish between cultural practice and corruption" though a planned Code of Conduct for Public Servants might help (James and Tufui 2004: 5). The courts in Kiribati have been particularly engaged in drawing lines between appropriate and inappropriate gift giving in Kiribati. The courts are required to take custom into account in deciding cases (Mackenzie 2004: 6). Following a series of cases involving ministers and campaigns (Larmour 1997) the Kiribati electoral ordinance was amended as follows in 1997.

Any person making a customary offering to a Maneaba [meeting house] referred to in i-Kiribati as "Mweaka," "Moanei," or "Ririwete," with the sole intention of showing respect for the customs and traditions of Kiribati shall not be guilty of bribery.

(Mackenzie 2004: 9)

The courts have also become involved in distinguishing between "respect for customs and tradition" and "intention to influence voters." For example, "in the custom of *bubuti* it is acceptable for someone lacking in [certain] resources to make a specific request to another who is better endowed" (Mackenzie 2004: 9, quoting Chief Justice Williams). Such requests were being made in the form of a fine demanded of a candidate visiting a *Maneaba*, and had involved (for example) a chainsaw or a video set. The court decided the issue depended on the intention of the giver. In the case before them the High Court found the gifts "were made because of custom. The candidates had no choice" (Mackenzie 2004: 9).

In a similar case in Tuvalu—that the candidate had provided chiefs with food and drink prior to a by-election, and that chiefs had promised the votes of their villagers in return—the High Court found the feasting to be in accordance with custom rather than "corrupt practices" (Taafaki 2004: 15).

In implementing authoritative decisions

Most countries in the region have laws prohibiting bribery and other instances of corruption. They are often part of the criminal code, and a responsibility of the police to enforce. Police typically have a great deal of discretion as to whether or not they investigate and—later—go on to prosecute offences. Police may be corrupt themselves, though the complaints in the NIS studies tended to be more about competence and professionalism than corruption. However, police were not implementing the law against relatives in FSM, and in PNG police performance was "watered down by lack of capacity, political influence and regionalism" (Mellam and Aloi 2003: 27).

In punishment

The Cook Islands report notes a recent successful prosecution for Secret Commissions that "public attitudes are often sympathetic" to the person found guilty. It rehearses what people often said: "We feel sorry for his children," "How much did the community lose from his criminal actions?" and "The community did not suffer any loss" (Ingram 2004: 12). There are no obvious victims, so the principles of restorative justice might suggest leniency. In Nauru, as in PNG, people who are the subject of headlines or gossip "continue to be re-elected" (Kun et al. 2004: 9). In FSM there was "a willingness to ignore or forget transgressions by leaders" (Hill 2004: 8). In Vanuatu, people who have been damned in Ombudsman Commission reports "continue to get elected"

(Newton Cain and Jowitt 2004: 10). And in Nauru, every time a new president is elected, there is a batch of presidential pardons (Kun et al. 2004: 18).

In Kiribati, however, a decline in cultural sanctions—in this case ostracism of those involved in theft—was contributing to the rise of petty corruption among junior officials (Mackenzie 2004: 10).

State institutions have a different role at each point of the policy cycle set out above. For example, at the point at which behavior is identified as corrupt, the law might be changed to penalize receivers of bribes as well as those offering them. Increased penalties might signal the seriousness with which corruption is taken. Whistleblower protection might overcome citizens' reluctance to report. The Pacific Islands evidence also points to capacity issues: in the courts, reaching authoritative judgments, and among the police, in implementing them. However, the analysis also suggests the difficulty of moving too far ahead of public opinion which (as we have seen) sometimes treats corruption lightly, is reluctant to report it, and is forgiving of those convicted. And at the first point in the policy cycle, a "general suspicion of corruption" may make popular opinion cynical about the motives of any state action, even—or especially—action taken in the name of anticorruption. There may be suspicion that such action is politically motivated, avoiding the big fish, and only done for show.

The policy cycle rotates through state and society, like a paddle wheel, describing a massive feedback loop between state action and the demands that citizens make in response to it. The Pacific Islands evidence also suggests strongly that "the state" is not the only institution this cycle encounters. The dictionary definition above proposed "family" as another, and some kinds of corruption—in particular, nepotism—seem to arise when family responsibilities conflict with the responsibilities of office. This institutional conflict is experienced as an ethical dilemma, in which an official may be pulled in two equally valued directions—for example, to do her job properly and appoint the best-qualified candidate, or to be a good family member and appoint a relative. The Pacific Islands evidence, and the anthropology of "potlatch", also suggest the importance of another institution, conceived of as "an enduring set of ideas about how to accomplish goals generally recognized as important in society": that is, the gift or gift giving.

Gifts and bribes

Olusegun Obasanjo, quoted from TI's sourcebook at the start of this chapter, argued that it was simple to distinguish a gift from a bribe. Samoa's prime minister—interviewed by the authors of that country's NIS study—argued similarly. "What determines an acceptable gift is 5 percent policy/law and 95 percent common sense." He gave as an example "a bottle of whisky or ten *tala* [US$ 3.60] would be regarded as an acceptable gift while a gift of say 3,000 *tala* [US$ 1,080] would certainly be regarded as unacceptable and there would be seen as a bribe" (So'o et al. 2004: 10).

This argument seems a little disingenuous. "Gift giving," says the Samoa report "has always been a means of obtaining and maintaining political support in Samoa's traditional society" (So'o et al. 2004: 5). It talks of "the quality and quantity" of gift giving driving the recipient to follow the donor's wishes (ibid.: 10). "It is quite normal for a customer to give the employee who is serving him/her during normal duty hours a small amount of money" (ibid.: 10). Similarly, in Tonga, for example, relations of respect "require the presentation of a gift when making a request of another person, especially a social superior" (James and Tufui 2004: 5), and "educated people are well aware that gifts act as bribery" (ibid.: 25), though "the point at which a traditional gift becomes a bribe is hazy" (ibid.: 10). Churches also engage in fundraising through "annual public displays of free gifting" (ibid.: 22). "Under the cover of 'tradition'" in FSM politicians may make "strategic donations to leaders and customary chiefs, sometimes in relation to a wedding or funeral" (Hill 2004: 5).

Marcel Mauss's anthropological classic *The Gift* uses anthropological evidence from Melanesia and Polynesia (as well as North America and India) to understand social systems based on systematic and repeated exchanges between collectivities—clans, tribes and families, often acting through chiefs—rather than individuals. The most extended form is the famous Kula Ring in what is now Papua New Guinea where various prestigious forms of shell money are given and received in expeditions around a ring of islands—bracelets moving from west to east and necklaces from east to west (Mauss 1990: 27–39).

The most intense form of gift giving did not take place in the Pacific Islands, but in the north west of what is now America. In "potlatch," chiefs engage in intensely competitive gift giving. Prestige and honor depend on how much you can give, and on the repayment (with interest) of gifts received. At the extreme, valuable goods are publicly destroyed to demonstrate one's wealth and humble one's rivals. The point—as Mary Douglas sums it up in her introduction to a recent edition of Mauss's classic–is that there is no such thing as a free gift. Gifts create obligations—that's the point of giving them, and a reason one might want to refuse them. They may look voluntary but are in practice compulsory, if one is to survive with honor intact. A milder Western version might be birthday presents.

Mauss sums up the three obligations that underpin a gift economy:

1 The obligation to give. Leaders are always at every moment obliged to invite their friends, share their food, and so on.
2 The obligation to accept. Refusal offends, even if it means an added burden.
3 The obligation to reciprocate, often with interest. Objects must be passed on, not hoarded. A gift of one blanket must be reciprocated with two.

(Mauss 1990: 50–55)

For economists, Mauss estimated rates of interest of "30–100 percent per year" in potlatch (ibid.: 53).

Some of the features of this "war of property" between competitive chiefs seem to be continued and reproduced in election campaigns throughout the Pacific region. In Samoa, politicians are expected to provide gifts of "food money and school fees" to voters. They also pay fine mats and money. In Niue candidates make "donations" (Talagi 2004). More generally, in Marshall Islands, "chiefs and elites are expected to offer services and gifts when available" (Pollock 2004). Ministers also give gifts between elections, for example when a minister visits an outer island in Tuvalu, local people might offer a feast and expect one of their "pet projects" to be funded or shipping schedules be altered in their favor in return (Taafaki 2004: 14).

These gifts are hardly token, spiritual or undemanded in Olusegun Obasanjo's sense of the African gift, above. The politician who has to make them often feels them excessive. And there are no examples in the reports of gifts deemed so excessive that the recipient returns them. The gifts are also transparent, felt to be legitimate and sometimes quite legal. In Fiji gifts to voters and chiefs are "an integral part of election campaigns," and in Nauru a "legitimate part of the electoral system" (Kun et al. 2004). They may involve traditional items—like the fine mats in Samoa—but also non-traditional ones, like "fairy lights, stereo and small car" (Pollock 2004) in the example from Marshall Islands.

The third obligation of gift giving is to pass it on, and this is an understudied aspect of corruption. It tends to be assumed that corrupt payments are wasted, consumed (or sent overseas to buy real estate, or hidden away in a Swiss bank). It is true that conspicuous waste is part of the north-west American potlatch culture. It may also be that the money exchanged is usefully invested. The logging company bribes a politician who builds a road— though it may be "in the wrong place," according to planners. Or the politician pays the school fees of the child that then goes to university. We don't yet know enough about the grey or black economy in this region.

The "potlatch" aspect is especially obvious in gift giving beyond government. The Tonga report worries about public ceremonies of "free gifting" to churches. The Tuvalu report worries about competition between villages over the size of gifts to retiring church ministers.

Conclusions

We have seen how popular opinion about corruption in the Pacific Islands is often suspicious, confused about what counts as corruption, reluctant to get involved, and forgiving of those accused. These recalcitrant and feckless opinions are seen as obstacles, in need of correction, by anticorruption campaigners inside and outside government. State elites in the Pacific Islands, as elsewhere, are often quick to recommend "political education" to align popular views more closely with their own. The influential ICAC model includes "Education" among its three prongs. But the state is not the only form of social glue, and other institutions, like the family and kinship, may make legitimate contradictory claims on individuals. The Pacific Islands evidence also suggests that institutions of giving, receiving and passing on of gifts also need to be taken seriously if corruption is to be reduced, rather than simply denounced.

Acknowledgements

I am grateful for comments on earlier versions by Geoff White, Raymond Apthorpe, Manu Barcham, Michael Goldsmith, and Ashwin Raj, while I remain responsible for the final result.

References

Alatas, S. (1968) *The Sociology of Corruption: The Nature, Function, Causes and Prevention of Corruption*, Singapore: D. Moore Press.

Bennett, T., Grossberg, L., and Morris, M. (eds) (2005) *New Keywords: A Revised Vocabulary of Culture and Society*, London: Wiley-Blackwell.

Crocombe, R. (2001) *The South Pacific* (3rd edn), Suva: University of the South Pacific.

Elias, N. (ed.) (1998) *On Civilization, Power and Knowledge: Selected Writings*, Chicago and London: University of Chicago Press.

Evers, H. and Mehmet, O. (1994) "The management of risk: informal trade in Indonesia," *World Development*, 22(1): 1–9

Goodin, R. (1996) "Institutions and their design," in R. Goodin (ed.) *The Theory of Institutional Design*, New York and Melbourne: Cambridge University Press.

Gupta, A. (1995) "Blurred boundaries: the discourse of corruption, the culture of politics, and the imagined state," *American Ethnologist*, 22(2): 375–402

Harrison, E. (2004) "The 'cancer of corruption'," in I. Pardo (ed.) *Between Morality and Law: Corruption, Anthropology and Comparative Society*, Aldershot: Ashgate, 135–54.

Hau'ofa, E. (1994) *Tales of the Tikongs*, Honolulu: University of Hawaii Press

Hill, E. (2004) "Federated States of Micronesia," in Transparency International (ed.) *Transparency International Country Study Report*, online. Available at www.transparency.org.

Ingram, T. (2004) "Cook Islands," in Transparency International (ed.) *Transparency International Country Study Report*, online. Available at www.transparency.org.

James, K. and Tufui, T. (2004) "Tonga," in Transparency International (ed.) *Transparency International Country Study Report*, online. Available at www.transparency.org.

Johnson, Allan G. (ed.) (1990) *Blackwell Dictionary of Sociology* (2nd edn), Oxford: Blackwell.

Kaufmann, D., Kraay, A., and Zoido-Loban, P. (1999) "Governance matters," Policy Research Working Paper 2196, Washington, DC: World Bank Institute.

Klitgaard, R. (1988) *Controlling Corruption*, Los Angeles: University of California Press.

Kun, R., Togomae, W., and Kun, R. (2004) "Nauru," in Transparency International (ed.) *Transparency International Country Study Report*, online. Available at www.transparency.org.

Kuper, A. (1999) *Culture: The Anthropologists' Account*, Cambridge, MA: Harvard University Press.

La Porta, R., Lopez-de-Silanes, F., Shleifer, A., and Vishny, R.W. (1997) "Trust in large organizations," *American Economic Review, Papers and Proceedings*, 137(2): 333–8.

Lambsdorff, J. (1999) "Corruption in empirical research—a review," online. Available at www.transparency.org.

Larmour, P. (1997) "Corruption and governance in the South Pacific," *Pacific Studies*, 20(3): 1–17.

—— (2006) "Civilizing techniques: Transparency International and the spread of anticorruption," in L. Seabrooke and B. Bowden (eds) *Global Standards of Market Civilisation*, London: Routledge, 97–106.

Larmour, P. and Barcham, M. (2006) "National integrity systems in small Pacific island states," *Public Administration and Development*, 26: 176–84.

Ledeneva, A. (1998) *Russia's Economy of Favours: Blat, Networking and Informal Exchange*, Cambridge: Cambridge University Press.

Leys, C. (2002) "What is the problem with corruption?" in A. Heidenheimer and M. Johnston (eds) *Political Corruption: Concepts and Contexts*, New Brunswick: Transaction, 59–76.

Mackenzie, U. (2004) "Kiribati," in *National Integrity Systems Country Study Report*, online. Available at www.transparency.org.

Mauss, M. (1990) *The Gift*, London: Routledge.

Mellam, A. and Aloi, D. (2003) "Papua New Guinea," in Transparency International (ed.) *Transparency International Country Study Report*, online. Available at www.transparency.org.

Myrdal, G. (1968) *Asian Drama: An Inquiry into the Poverty of Nations*, New York: Atheneum.

Newton Cain, T. and Jowitt, A. (2004) "Vanuatu," in Transparency International (ed.) *Transparency International Country Study Report*, online. Available at www.transparency.org.

North, D. (1990) *Institutions, Institutional Change and Economic Performance*, Cambridge: Cambridge University Press.

Pollock, N. (2004) "Republic of the Marshall Islands," in Transparency International (ed.) *Transparency International Country Study Report*, online. Available at www.transparency.org.

Reid, B. (1990) "Weighing up the factors: moral reasoning and culture change in a Samoan community," *Ethos*, 18(1): 48–71.

Roughan, P. (2004) "Solomon Islands," in Transparency International (ed.) *Transparency International Country Study Report*, online. Available at www.transparency.org.

Sahlins, M. (1999) "Two or three things I know about culture," *Journal of the Royal Anthropological Institute*, 5(3): 399–421.

Schuster, D. (2004) "Republic of Palau," in *National Integrity Systems Country Study Report*, online. Available at www.transparency.org.

Singh and Dakunivosa (2001) "Fiji," in *National Integrity Systems Country Study Report*, online. Available at www.transparency.org.

So'o, A. et al. (2004) "Samoa," in Transparency International (ed.) *Transparency International Country Study Report*, online. Available at www.transparency.org.

Taafaki, T. (2004) "Tuvalu," in Transparency International (ed.) *Transparency International Country Study Report*, online. Available www.transparency.org.

Talagi, M. (2004) "Niue," in Transparency International (ed.) *Transparency International Country Study Report*, online. Available at www.transparency.org.

Thompson, M., Verweij, M., and Ellis, R. (2006) "Why and how culture matters," in R. Goodin and C. Tilly (eds) *The Oxford Handbook of Contextual Political Analysis*, Oxford: Oxford University Press, 319–40.

Transparency International, (2000) "Source Book," online. Available at www.transparency.org.

Williams, R. (1985 [1976]) *Keywords* (revised edn), New York: Oxford University Press.

14 Concluding remarks

Toward cleaner governance?

Gerald E. Caiden

China, among many other countries in Asia and the Pacific, and probably around the globe, appears to be failing in its anticorruption efforts. Corruption, however defined, seems to be on the rise according to the increased international attention it is receiving. But this may be more of the function of wider publicity than reality on the ground. Before the twentieth century, little was known about the inner workings of government except to insiders who kept very quiet, whereas the revolution in information technology and communications enables the populace to know much more almost instantaneously, certainly about public misconduct. Perhaps people are more vocal today about their unwillingness to tolerate corrupt practices which victimize them and fritter away scarce resources that go into conspicuous consumption or secret foreign bank accounts instead of societal development locally.

Some of the blame can be attributed to globalization and the impact of internationally induced or outside corruption spread by defective international organizations, particularly global business corporations richer and possibly more powerful in the economy of poor countries than their own governments. In some, the continuance of post-colonial repressive governance in authoritarian kleptocracies is more to blame as elites exploit powerless masses unable to do anything about the former's corrupt practices. Elsewhere, the fault lies with corrupt institutions and corrupt individuals within cleaner organizations able to secrete their improper conduct. Another explanation is the size of the underground economy, the existence of black markets, and the presence of well-connected organized crime that together exploit local scarcity and promote unfair rent-seeking. And, of course, there is the simple explanation offered by Lord Acton that "power corrupts; absolute power corrupts absolutely" made originally in reference to abusive religious practices. These, and other explanations, reveal the complexity of what people believe constitutes corrupt behavior and how ingrained corruption may be in any society.

The difficulty in implementing anticorruption measures can be attributed to the fact that corruption takes on so many forms, literally hundreds of different manifestations that vary among societies. Furthermore, corruption is only one again of tens of bureaupathologies identifiable in any large-scale organization and it shades off into all kinds of conflicts of interest that border on corruption. No wonder there has yet to be a universally agreed definition that covers all instances, although several, such as those put forward by Nye (1967), Heidenheimer et al. (1989), and Khan (2006: Ch. 8) and used by Transparency International, the World Bank, and the United Nations Development Program, come close, simply because what might be considered corruption in one society might be considered just normal business (i.e. the way that things have always been done and are likely to continue, no matter what) in another society. These different societal views have long been accepted as localized norms into which people have been socialized and institutionalized in fairly rigid social arrangements. The wonder is not that corruption persists but that some societies have managed to free themselves of many of its forms.

Because corruption is deemed locally as being contrary or counter-productive to furthering a society's ideals and values, and for that reason hidden and obscured, its extent is virtually impossible to measure with any precision and then maybe long after its occurrence. Scandals, lawsuits, and public investigations can be counted, but these may be only a small fraction of what really prevails. Victimization surveys probably give a better picture but much of what victims allege cannot be verified without officially being recorded at the time of occurrence. Other sources are breaches of professional ethics and lapses in personal integrity as recorded by internal disciplinary bodies which tend to be soft on fellow members. Who can ever ascertain the truth in any society where private corruption tends to be ignored altogether in definitions of public corruption? In both sectors, much misconduct that comes to light is forgiven by successors who hope their indiscretions will be similarly forgiven or overlooked because their value to society is so much more important than relatively minor corrupt instances.

An example where public and private corruption cannot be separated may suffice. Private contractors gang together to share available public contracts so that none misses out and all reap huge profits at public expense. Where such collusion is known to public officials in the contracting agency or their political bosses, the awarders may have connections with the private contractors (through family, friendship, religion, schooling, military service, race, masonry and other secret associations). They may justify the practice of giving contracts to rigged bids as helping friends, creating employment locally, promoting wider development, and strengthening political links to influence public policy and determine actual legislation governing their business, without bribery and kickbacks being involved. Where such collusion is unknown, the blind officials carry on regardless, rewarding deceit and possible criminality and subjecting themselves to blackmail when the contractors leave their contracts unfinished and up their price to complete the work, knowing that they are in effect sole-source providers. By failing to do their duty on behalf of the trusting public that has to foot the bill, blind or perhaps blinded officials let the contractors get away with their ill-gotten gains, even though publicly the officials maintain that they act in good faith, follow the rules, and are blameless for outrageous favoritism, patronage, and exploitation of the public purse.

Anticorruption measures are too easily compromised, especially where the rule of law does not exist or when it is exercised selectively. Autocratic and totalitarian governments can ignore their own measures at will, particularly where corrupt practices entrench their position and reward them handsomely. This can also be true where one party dominates the political system and can exploit its position by rewarding loyal friends and supporters and depriving opponents and rivals. Any government so composed can change the rules of the game so that it is unlikely ever to be replaced without a popular uprising. Irrespective of regime, elites look out to co-opt anyone who might be useful to them or likely to challenge them, and if co-optation fails, intimidation gets their message over before they have to resort to terror to quell persistent critics. Normal governmental procedures enable those in authority to sabotage official investigations, turn them around into hunts for whistleblowers, frame the innocent while the real villains escape, and generally turn a blind eye to corrupt practices regardless, such are the privileges of office no matter what is publicly proclaimed.

All this is very disconcerting. But there are societies, mostly localized but sometimes national, that resist corrupt practices or overcome their previously dominant forms of corruption. They may not be able to rid themselves of all forms of corruption or every corrupt office holder. At least, they succeed in reducing, if not minimizing, the prevalence of corruption. They force corruption underground and hidden from public view. Even accusations of corruption end public careers and brand disgraced offenders for life. The loss of face in being exposed makes others think twice about committing a corrupt act and makes the guilty stand out. Honest people feel more confident that they can complain about possible corruption without fear or favor and that their complaints will be taken seriously and followed up. Should corruption be revealed, the honest feel justified and may even be rewarded for speaking out when others fear the consequences for being so brave.

But is social disgrace a powerful enough deterrent? Not if the guilty believe that the gains outweigh the risks of discovery. With the increased concentration of power at the apex of bureaucracy, the risks are diminished as street-level bureaucrats can hide what actually happens at their level from the ignorant elite, and a scheming elite can hide their nefarious acts from those below them in the hierarchy who remain unaware of their part in institutionalized corruption. The followers are innocent dupes in the wider scale of things, for they actually trust their bosses to be doing right even if they do not properly understand what is going on. Meantime, the potential rewards grow, especially in rich societies or in a society where the public sector dominates the economy and public agencies have a virtual monopoly in delivering public goods and services. It is not in anybody's interest to reveal corrupt practices: not the guilty, not their underlings, not even their victims.

Peers close ranks, obey their own self-imposed vow of silence, and prefer to handle incidents internally without publicity. In any event, they all have a job to do, they are all quite busy, and they have other things to worry about. There may be so many other public issues of greater importance and priority in this hectic and chaotic world that corruption and accusations of corruption get lost in the process of complex governance. Corruption is unlikely to get the attention it deserves unless it results in disaster and societal disgrace.

So, in time, societies develop their own distinctive patterns of corruption, some widespread, others very much localized, according to their own specific circumstances. Such patterns are deeply embedded in their culture. If anti-corruption measures are to work over the long haul, they must be directed at that culture and its underlying ideals and values resistant to change. What is most or more likely to convince people to change their attitudes and behavior? What can turn people against prevailing corrupt practices and get them to support effective anticorruption measures? What measures are more likely to work not just temporarily but over the long haul?

The culture of corruption

Forget ideology. Forget morality. Forget even family and lifelong friends. When people get to the pinnacle of their society, they are loath to leave it without a fight and without proper cause. They hang on as long as they can because they are privileged and admired. They enjoy a lifestyle envied by everybody else. They have inordinate authority and a range of choices far wider than anybody else. They can bestow favors or withdraw them without explanation. They can even enjoy themselves being in the public eye and admired as celebrities, as models for the young, as examples of what can be achieved. There are some drawbacks, like living in a glass bowl where every word, gesture, and decision is examined closely for hidden meaning and what impression they may make on the rest of society. But such drawbacks are far outweighed by their advantages. Even when all seems lost, they can always decamp to another society where they can live in comfort if not complete secrecy or fear of possible retribution by their aggrieved victims.

Indeed, life at the top is so attractive that individuals may do anything to get there and stay there, no matter what ruthlessness may be involved, no matter who they may destroy on their way up or in authority, no matter what harm they may cause their society and the globe. Life at the top is comfortable and sheltered; it gives access to immeasurable benefits; it presents opportunities to fulfill one's dreams and escape all the problems of being poor, discriminated against, and victimized. Where the apex is confined to few holders of authority (because of their overwhelming wealth or fortunate heredity or leadership of popular movements) the competition is fierce, especially in poor societies where there is little to go round and the gap between rich and poor may be vast. At least, richer societies can share more and allow more people to enjoy a level of comfort and security that compensates for exclusion from the apex and allows the apex to cream off potential rivals.

Corruption is in the eye of the beholder. People at the top do not see it in the same way as people at the bottom. Usually, people at the top deny they are corrupt or have corrupted anybody else. They have played according to the rules of the game in their society and they have been the most successful at them. Less fortunate folk are merely jealous and are fond of making all kinds of questionable accusations that they cannot back up. But, say their accusers, those at the top devise the rules of the game to their advantage and their very distance from the bottom, the victims of their corruption, shields them from the havoc that they create. Back comes the reply that successful folks are blameless, for they do not make the world as it is and they too would like to see things different from what they are. Indeed, that is exactly what they are trying to do, i.e. to make the world a better place. They know that if they utterly fail to improve the lot of others, they face protest, rebellion, violence, revolution, expulsion (if lucky) and death (if unlucky). They cannot rule entirely in their own self-interest because if they do, they cannot expect sympathy or obedience from others and their tenure would be cut short. They have to identify with the underprivileged and promote common ideals and values.

In contrast, the underprivileged see corruption differently because the privileged do not identify with common ideals and values. They, the privileged, do not really care about anybody else except their own. They take advantage of their authority to gain unjust benefits at everybody else's expense. They try to do this under cover because if their self-interested ways were revealed their corruption of public trust would be revealed. Sometimes the privileged are so uncaring and so confident of their tenure that they openly boast about their unjust (and presumably undeserved) privileges and show off their invincibility, thereby clearly demonstrating their motivation, their corrupt actions, and their indifference to the consequences on society. Totalitarians and autocrats do not care for public opinion which anyway they create and manipulate and use whatever it takes to eliminate protest. Democratic societies are less likely to ignore public opinion and disregard common ideals and values, but under certain conditions and pressures they too can act just as badly.

Just as there is not complete universal agreement over what constitutes corruption, so there is little consensus over what constitutes unacceptable corruption, abuse of authority, arbitrariness, ignorance, misuse of power, and unfair privilege. Opinion differs widely where corruption stops and other behaviors, such as incompetence, narrow-mindedness, communal loyalty, organized crime, improper management, nepotism, and patronage, begin. Conflicts of interest vary from one locale to another, from one organization to another, and one individual to another. What may be tolerated in one place may be considered off limits in another. Because corruption can be so beneficial to the corrupt, those excluded would like to join in if they could and obtain a share of the spoils. As so many forms of corruption have become traditional and institutionalized over the years and people so accustomed and socialized to them, they are no longer considered corruption at all and not really harmful to anybody uninvolved (i.e. the victimless crime). Hence, identification as corruption often relies on outsiders, strangers, idealists, and the radical young at heart.

Another troubling factor is that there are so many different forms of corruption that where they become habitual, excessive, and ubiquitous, corruption becomes a way of life to which people have to conform at a very early age. Otherwise, they find themselves always a loser, always taken advantage of, always seen as naïve or simpleminded. It is very difficult to free oneself from this accepted way of doing business and running one's personal affairs. After all, when one assumes a position of authority, it is expected that one will favor one's family (whether extended or reduced to one's closest kin) and lifelong friends, co-religionists, local community, and one's employer, for such bonds run deep. To do otherwise is to risk losing face among one's closest and dearest. To treat strangers better would be considered quite odd, as one really cannot trust strangers because when they get into positions of authority they may not return the favor but exclude oneself. In such an event, one cannot expect much sympathy from anyone since turned resentful, if not hostile, from being treated badly.

Even in fortunate societies where corruption is just an incidental fact of life, that fact has to be faced and dealt with. Complaining does not help much unless one's protests rally support from one's superiors willing to attack corruption head on. But they may be so busy with more important matters that they never get around to reform or enforcing reforms. Also, the superior authorities, unknown to oneself, may be getting their cut and may be the major beneficiaries of institutionalized corruption so that they have little incentive to reform. Superiors find it much easier to compensate complainers and shut them up so that the complainers do not go any further. This applies to any and all organizations which pay lip service to rooting out corruption but are guilty of corrupt practices themselves and are just as hypercritical, silence critics, and buy off complainants. The very organizations that are supposed to be clean and work on behalf of humanity, the powerless, the poor and the neglected are themselves guilty of fraud, deceit, mismanagement, and gross misconduct that they hide, condone, and perpetuate.

But why corruption in the first place? Simply because there is not enough to go round to satisfy everybody. If there were enough, there would be little sense being corrupt as one would find few takers. But there is always a scarcity of something that enables its possessors to exact an unfair price and for the dispossessed to gain unfair advantage by offering more than other unfortunates. So, one would expect that rich societies with greater abundance of everything should be less corrupt than their poorer brethren, and that the more a society develops, it would become less corrupt. But this economic analysis ignores the cultural roots of corruption and the fact of greed. Rich folks may never see themselves as rich enough, while poorer folks escaping dire poverty may be so obsessed by their fear of returning to such abject poverty that they too want more and more and are hard to satisfy no matter how well off they become. Indeed, the richer a society, the more pickings there are to be had, the higher the rewards, and the greater the means of attaining access to privilege. At the same time, the dysfunctions of corruption are less severe as rich societies can afford the cost and use palliatives to swamp complainants. In these more fortunate circumstances, corruption need not be so obvious and open but obscured by very sophisticated, legitimized, and nuanced practices. Corruption still exists but confined more to insiders. Rare scandals shake people's faith and reveal unsuspected hidden doings, but once the publicity dies away the same practices continue, if with a different cast of players.

Furthermore, the corrupt are not dumb. They know the risks they run. They can only rely on themselves and those they corrupt (and can be expected to protect them) but not even that should the authorities plant an informer amongst them. They test the lengths to which they can go without being exposed and try to keep safely within secure borders. They are smart enough to employ early warning systems and shift their operations accordingly. Within their ranks are clever individuals who invent new forms of undetectable corruption, keeping one step ahead of exposure, and who can find ways of corrupting anything if so minded. When discovered, they have long gone and vanished, taking their ill-gotten gains with them.

So all societies have to confront corruption of one kind or another. They can try to reduce scarcity. They can find effective ways of monitoring authority. They can employ effective laws, investigatory bodies, and enforcement agents. They can punish the guilty and make the price too high for disregarding common ideals and values. They can overhaul procedures and reorganize the way that public affairs are conducted. They can employ their smartest to uncover corrupt practices and head off possible corrupt opportunities. They can improve their governance, transparency, and public accountability and take steps to reduce conflicts of interest. They can stiffen popular resistance to corrupt practices. They can study what other societies do to combat corruption and obtain help from international bodies that recommend anticorruption measures. But they cannot guarantee personal integrity.

Honest folk know what is right or wrong in their society. They are not tempted by corrupt opportunities and they avoid conflicts of interest. They do not corrupt anyone. They may be scared to reveal corruption but amongst them are brave individuals who are not and turn whistleblower. Unfortunately, all too often, these are met with indifference and, worse still, they become victimized by offended authority and their peers who resent snitches, troublemakers, too righteous or too ideological for their own good. Since the offenders can destroy evidence that prove whistleblowers justified, the latter have difficulty showing they are not just spiteful or aggrieved by some disciplinary action taken against them. They find few listeners and often end up regretting their outspokenness. Their integrity comes too often at a heavy price.

The odds are stacked against whistleblowers because throughout the ages people have always suspected that the exercise of governance was a sordid affair in which few participants could remain unsullied and unsoiled. Just as everywhere else, life was full of intrigue, rivalry, skullduggery, ambition, self-aggrandizement, favoritism, and special consideration, as amplified in literature. It was best for insiders not to reveal too much about their doings lest they lose their credibility and open themselves to popular scorn. Only the most noble in character could rise above the fray and not fall foul of corruption. Such beliefs go deep in society and are not easily undone, not when daily people directly experience corruption or hear about it second-hand. Although they demand cleaner governance and they are increasingly aware of what needs to be done, the odds seem so heavily stacked against them.

Anticorruption measures

Why is it that the more we learn about the performance of governance, the more disappointed we become, the more suspicious of our public leaders, and the less credibility we give them to meet the problems of the day? Is it because our expectations are just too high, our leaders are not up to their job, and our faith in them has been misplaced? Or is it because the problems we face are more difficult than ever before to solve, our leaders are only too human, and governance cannot adjust in time to new situations? Probably, it is a combination of all these factors. But it seems too often that our leaders appear to be losing their moral compass and the governance arrangements they lead appear increasingly out of control and lack sufficient public accountability. The unfortunate outcome seems to be an upsurge in official misconduct due to lack of personal integrity and institutional failure to reveal all and take full accountability.

Regretfully, only within the past two or so decades has the international community come to realize how deep the rot has become, how unclean the hands of government leaders appear, and how fateful for their states and their peoples have been the outcomes of such official misconduct. But the international community is just as guilty, if not more so, when it preaches one thing and does the exact opposite, when it condemns some but turns a blind eye to worse offences by others. But all is not lost. We now know a lot more on what can and should be done to make, if not for entirely clean governance, at least cleaner governance than now exists around the globe. We have come a long way but we still fall far short of what needs to be done about dirty hands, while—alas—new forms and avenues have opened up that make further progress quite difficult. But at least one significant factor has changed, and that is that where once not so long ago the whole topic of dirty hands in governance was virtually taboo in polite society: now it is openly admitted and made that much easier to tackle.

The imperative of integrity

People either have integrity or they do not. They can or cannot be trusted. They do or do not have integrity. But how can anyone know without their being put to the test? Since the earliest days of civilization, moralists have never drawn back from condemning misconduct. If ever humankind was to progress from the state of nature, personal conduct was going to have to change from pursuing natural inclination, to discipline, educate and train people along different lines, and to set a better personal example for future generations. Most religious teachings included long discourses on how the Good Society could only come about if individuals could overcome their selfish genes and live by what came to be adopted as the Golden Rule: "Don't treat others as you would hate them to treat you." Behind all their dos and don'ts was the assertion that every person had a choice between doing good and doing bad as commonly accepted, and doing good was considered to be universal, from the youngest to the oldest with no exceptions.

These moralists were realistic enough to recognize that living up to such noble standards would be very difficult, given human frailties and that doing good required strict discipline so as not to be led astray and fall into temptation. So, every child had to be instructed into the right way, had to be shown the right way by example, and had to be disciplined to resist into falling into evil ways or wrongful conduct according to social norms. The best teachers were the family, religious authorities, the community at large, and government officials as exemplars of rectitude and correct behavior. Their role was to hold resolute and demonstrate how things could be different by doing good, working hard, maintaining self-discipline, and optimistically believing that the best was yet to come. A special obligation fell upon on all authority figures and leaders to set a model example for all others and to hold firm to moral precepts through thick and thin while adapting them to changing circumstances and conditions.

The upshot is that without individual integrity, nothing else really matters. People with integrity can be trusted to do the right thing and avoid being tempted to do wrong, thereby corrupting their position, public and private. They are honest and believable, abhorring misconduct and distancing themselves from the unworthy. So the key to cleaner, if not clean, governance is to staff all positions of authority with honorable persons of the highest possible integrity who have proven that they know right from wrong, and are creditable guardians of the public interest. Commensurably, anyone who is guilty of dishonesty, dishonorable conduct, and wrongdoing has to be hounded out of authority, disgraced, and prevented from profiteering from their misdeeds until they can prove without a shadow of a doubt that they have redeemed themselves in the public eye. Forgiveness has to be earned. Integrity tests are crucial at all levels, and even minor blemishes must be taken seriously as an indication of possible more serious misconduct to come should the opportunity arise. The higher people climb, so the more stringent should be the standard of integrity to which they are held.

Overcoming scarcity

Classical economists have a much simpler explanation for dirty hands than the moralists, namely that there is too much money chasing too few goods and services. Scarcity is the root cause of corruption simply because some people are prepared to pay whatever price is asked of them by exploitive suppliers. If supply could be increased to match excessive demand, the propensity for corruption would diminish considerably, for in circumstances of excessive supply, corruption could not occur. Unfortunately, not much can be done about natural scarcity which automatically puts the poor and powerless at a disadvantage outside non-monetary favors sought. So where dire scarcity exists, especially in access to basic needs, and engineered desires, corruption becomes virtually a way of life, and in the race for sheer survival, morality takes a beating. Without protectors and patrons in high places, the very weak suffer. Hence, if only supply could be increased or demand reduced, corruption would decline and oversupply would eliminate the economic causes of corruption. Since this is unlikely to happen in poor countries, the difference between rich and poor could be made up by some generous external providers who would have to ensure that their contribution would bypass corrupt channels and black markets as actually occurs during emergency relief operations, although much still flows through corrupt channels which are merely further enriched thereby.

Economists are more concerned where supply is artificially reduced by law and restrictive practices. For a host of reasons, governments outlaw certain goods and services and officially and publicly shut down all supply. This does not prevent trade in such illegal goods and services which find their way to eager consumers and customers through organized crime that is part and parcel of the underground or unofficial economy that orthodox economists largely ignore. These outcast entrepreneurs are quite willing to assume the risks involved for the possible excessive returns they expect to make, rewards that enable them to buy off law enforcement. Such mafias can become quite powerful and can institutionalize themselves so that in time their operations and corrupting influence can become quite safe and secure, they can buy themselves into good grace and respectability, and their stakeholders can come to protect them against exposure, investigation, and prosecution. In short, such criminals become virtually untouchable, above and beyond the law, and able to penetrate legitimate and legal business activities, expanding their empires and disguising their nefarious operations.

When such illegal enterprise reaches this point of dominance, even economists become squeamish. The tough-minded libertarians among them would legitimate their activities, throw open their now legal markets to all consumers, and take such business above ground into the officially recognized economy and have done with it. The more squeamish would not go this far and would pick and choose as to which activities should still remain illegal on moral grounds. Otherwise, they do recognize the wisdom of legitimization but under strict government regulation to ensure public safety and security and to see that fair competition takes place. Others would join the welfare economists who would convert such private enterprise into publicly controlled businesses, eliminating competition altogether so that the government could reap all the possible rewards for itself, use the proceeds to subsidize its other activities, particularly public welfare, and regulate its own public bodies just like everything else in the public sector. Thus, rent-seeking should be controlled, tax evasion minimized, kleptocracy eliminated, and economic crimes prosecuted.

Moving from particularism to universalism

An obvious characteristic of organized crime is its lawlessness. Nobody seems to be in charge to exercise sufficient control to standardize how things are done, and nobody seems to follow any consistent pattern of decision-making. Particularism rules, a particularism "that mirrors the vicious distribution of power within ... societies" where "anticorruption strategies are adopted and implemented in cooperation with the very predators who control the government, and, in some cases, the anticorruption instruments themselves" (Mungiu-Pippidi 2006: 87), where societies are "governed by convention rather than by law, where certain groups monopolize the powers of domination and sources of income" (ibid.: 88), where a "culture of privilege reigns ... making unequal treatment the accepted norm," where "individuals struggle to belong to the privileged group rather than to change the rules of the game," where "influence, not money, is the main currency," and where

> Favors are distributed or denied as part of a customary exchange with rules of its own, sometimes not involving direct personal gain for the "gatekeep." Bribery often occurs as a means of circumventing inequality; for many people with lower status, bribing an official may be the only way to secure equal treatment.
>
> (Mungiu-Pippidi 2006: 88)

Thus, the key to cleaner governance is universalism where individuals are treated and expect to be treated equally and fairly according to standardized rules of the game by all authority which is so constrained and is supposed to be no recognizer of status or networks of privilege: in brief, effective rule of law and accountable bureaucracy.

Wherever authority exercises discretionary and arbitrary power, it is liable to venture off course, compromise the public interest with its own self-interest, and hide its distortion from public view. To prevent or minimize this from happening, limits are placed on the exercise of authority to ensure that discretion is confined, deviations immediately detected, and checks and balances automatically operate to control any damage that might result from the abuse and misuse of position. This is the meaning of the modernization of governance through the rule of law, that discretion and arbitrariness do not exceed definite bounds and that governance be conducted with the utmost integrity and according to universal norms whose breach will result in disgrace and loss of office or exile out of all harm's way. This universalism does not entirely prevent dirty hands or corrupt practices among society's elite but it is designed to reduce opportunities to exploit position, power, and privilege. Law-abidingness is seen as a social virtue, curbing anarchy, chaos, disorder, and corruption. Ignorance of the law is no excuse. While justice may be tempered with mercy, breaking the law is taken seriously regardless. No individual is above or beyond the law.

Constitutionalism is considered the law's highest expression as it spells out in detail what governance can or cannot do, how it is supposed to operate at least formally, and what steps can be taken to challenge alleged wrongdoing by public office holders. A detailed written constitution provides a benchmark by which abuse and misuse of authority can be measured and dirty hands judged. For this reason, undemocratic regimes are almost by definition corrupt because the rule of law and its underlining assumption of universalism has little meaning when office holders do what they please and exempt themselves from their own laws whenever they choose. Nevertheless, even democratic polities may experience a general lawlessness when their peoples, once so used to autocratic rule, cannot adjust quickly enough to the new rules of the game or when they persist in sticking to some aspects of particularism which they are unable and unwilling to shed. Used to conniving against and denying overbearing authority or enjoying the fruits of particularism, people persist in finding ways and means around the laws and inducing public office holders to make exemption in their individual case, usually for a consideration. Superficially, bureaucratic and judicial enforcement work on the surface, but underneath little is assured as people go through the motions of obedience while conniving together to obtain the decision they want. Fixers and middlemen do well (for a fee) while organized crime operates outside the law and infiltrates both bureaucratic and judicial enforcement. Even independent agencies in governance may be suborned when subject or beholden to those who appoint them, staff them, finance them, and renew their jurisdiction, especially when they get too independent and threaten to challenge, override, and embarrass the powers-that-be. These independents may find themselves ignored, restricted, undermined, fired or replaced and made harmless and ineffective paper tigers.

Strengthening professionalism

Governance has long been far too complicated and complex to know instinctively what to do right off without prior study and initial learning, what is expected, and how to behave properly in public. Competition is stiff and mistakes tend to haunt one's progress up the ladder of success. Reputations have to be earned and they can be quickly destroyed by indiscretion. At all times, one is in the public eye and little can be hidden from prying eyes, not given the contemporary information revolution. Hiding corruption and dirty hands is getting more and more difficult as somebody somewhere will probably know. One slip and all can be undone. What makes things especially difficult is the professionalism that is taking over many occupations and public specialties. Not only do professional qualifications require each individual to perform to the level of established performance, but professionals are expected to live by a high code of public ethics jealously guarded by one's peers, who resent any member who disgraces them or lets them down through any malpractice and misbehavior. So, professional self-discipline should be sufficient to discourage the worst forms of corruption and official misconduct, although minor forms of indiscretion might be tolerated and forgiven as individual quirks so one must not be too harsh or unforgiving of peers who slip up.

But obviously professional self-discipline cannot prevent dirty hands when the level of professionalism is too low for public comfort, as happens too often in underdeveloped countries where professionals are scarce and the turnover high and where they have ample opportunity to emigrate. When professionals are intent on rent-seeking and taking advantage of their position, self-discipline collapses. This is particularly serious in the case of the military professions as they exercise legitimate authority and possess fearsome weapons which they do not hesitate to use against defenseless and unarmed peoples, prisoners of war, civilian captives, and anybody else that gets in their bloody-minded way. Likewise, the law-enforcement professions can terrorize the general populace, and all professionals can blackmail, short change, and cheat, and abuse the goodwill of their clients if they are so minded. Hence, maintaining and improving true professionalism is so important, and professional bodies have to take the lead on their own initiative and have to be buttressed from the outside in their quest for the highest standards of professional conduct. But some professions are more prone to corruption than others, while some are more lax when it comes to depriving members of their livelihood. The harshest punishments they leave instead to the courts and political authorities to determine.

Transparency

In governance, just how much secrecy can be justified? Clearly, office holders who operate in secret can hide far too much from the public and can deny any wrongdoing because they know that their dirty hands cannot be revealed. As with thieves, there is honor among miscreants, at least until they fall out. Even so, hardly anyone is willing to self-incriminate unless assured of protection, lesser charges, or lesser punishment. The silence of others can be purchased, incriminating evidence lost or destroyed, and witnesses can even be eliminated if the offense is so gross.

All too often, office holders get into the habit of stamping "secret" or "confidential" on too many documents and enforce a vow of secrecy on even routine business. To bring dirty hands into the light of day, office holders should not be given the benefit of the doubt in conducting public business, which ideally should be done according to the rights to freedom of information and as far as possible in the open, with minimum secrecy carefully defined in selected areas fairly easy to identify, such as military affairs, diplomatic relations, individual privacy, intellectual property, classified personnel records, and non-disclosure of health and financial information to unauthorized parties. Such selective secrecy should be maintained but only for good reason, where disclosure is likely to be harmful, distressing, and dangerous.

But transparency cannot work magic. It cannot deal with conflicts of interest enlarged by the fusing of public and private in governance. Where once the distinctions might have been fairly clear, today they are integrated. It is more and more tempting for those in authority to profit from the information that comes their way in the course of their public business. To require them to declare all their financial dealings entails invasions of their privacy and may even induce them to set aside or hide some assets or pass them on to trustworthy relatives and friends who conceal them. This is particularly true in relations between public officials and private contractors whose privacy is protected and their performance only indirectly publicly accountable and where a revolving door is common practice. Similarly, transparency does not really deal with internal relations between political careerists and bureaucratic careerists at the highest reaches of governance, particularly between those who come and go and those who stay behind. Even today, outsiders rarely get to know what really goes on between them, who covers up whose misconduct, what payoffs occur to maintain silence for all kinds of reasons from loyalty and patriotism to more sordid motives. The public get gleanings when the two camps do fall out but usually hear only after the event, by which time the damage has been done and the miscreants may have disappeared from sight. Obviously, there is more need for transparency almost everywhere in electioneering, political party financing, and contracting out the delivery of public goods and services

More accountability

Without transparency, who can be held truly accountable for what? Accountability bounds authority to ensure that office holders meet the expectations and standards of stakeholders regarding legality, financial discipline, operational efficiency, and effectiveness in achieving results and objectives: in short, how authority is appropriately exercised. Their ultimate boss is presumably the public in whose name they operate. But who is the real master? Is it really the overworked political overseers who may not be running the store at all, preferring a quiet life and just going along because they do not want to damage their political careers? Meantime, they and the public who rely on them are being deceived and corruption within is being overlooked and protected.

A sloppy job by political overseers is one thing. Deliberate self-seeking by organizations and individuals within them is another. Organizations have a vested interest in perpetuating their existence, growth, diversion of funds, and increased standing in the community, even when performing badly and outliving their contribution to society. This situation is possibly the worst form of corruption of all simply because what they do may no longer be needed or can be performed by other organizations. So, periodically, there ought to be a thorough reckoning of all public organizations, including contractors and their subcontractors and an ongoing and revolving administrative reform program to ensure greater accountability. Independent inspector general, general accounting and ombudsman offices that conduct investigations and audits, detect fraud and abuse, and keep governments and the public informed of problems and deficiencies in programs are valuable, although they have only mixed success (Anechiarico and Goldstock 2007). But at least they seem to be more reliable than self-policing in exposing fraud, waste, and corruption. Unfortunately, dotted all over the map of governance are rogue organizations, which, because of their power, position, and ability, are quite a sinister influence on other organizations. They are skilled, enterprising, sophisticated, and practiced at hiding their nefarious doings, playing just inside the rules, employing intermediaries to do their dirty work for them, and flooding mass media with such propaganda that few can believe that they are capable of the evil they do. Such bodies require the most monitoring.

Enforcing human rights

Fundamental to cleansing governance is not just respect for human rights but their enforcement and realization. If only the 1948 United Nations Charter of Human Rights had borne the fruit that its designers had intended. But from its very beginning, it has been ignored with impunity. The world has moved on since then and today the Charter is so dated that it badly needs revising. Nevertheless, it remains a beacon of enlightenment and its provisions if enforced would do much to cleanse governance. Every individual would be enthroned to hold all authority accountable for breaches of basic human rights governing the most important aspects of life. Most dirty hands entail breaches of individual rights, denials of fundamental liberties, mistreatment of the subject, and gross violations of dignity, reducing people to the status of sub-humans, playthings for their superiors.

Empowered individuals, fully conversant with their many different rights – legal, civil, political, economic, social, cultural – can take on wrongful authority, strive for justice, and demand rectification. Unfortunately, without universal agreement, what constitutes those rights differs from society to society, although there remains substantial agreement on which remain the most important: quoting the 1948 Charter, everyone has the right to life, liberty and security of person; freedom of speech and belief; freedom from fear and want, slavery and servitude, torture and cruel, inhuman or degrading treatment or punishment; freedom from arbitrary arrest, detention or exile and arbitrary interference with privacy, family, home or correspondence; and all have the right to marry and found a family. Whenever these rights and other rights are breached, so governance has dirty hands. And the remedies are aged and well known, some going back centuries. Crucial to reducing dirty hands is the political will to maintain the highest possible standards of integrity, to respect all these and many other universal human rights, to expose and prosecute the many different kinds of corruption that occur, particularly the most harmful and vulnerable, and to strengthen civil society (Quah 2003, 2007).

But today, dirty hands go well beyond the failure to respect human rights and the charges of dirty hands in governance now extend in world opinion to such things as the acquisition and deployment of weapons of mass destruction, the conduct of unjust wars and unjust military tactics, failure to prevent environmental degradation and undegradable pollution, mistreatment of enemies, conscripts, prisoners, refugees, children, spouses, and other protectionless groups, indifference to animal rights and the fate of unprotected species, and reckless and irresponsible research and development. Until there is greater universality and widespread consensus in dealing with these and other issues of the contemporary global society, governance is going to look bad regardless and public leaders are going to fall far short of cleansing public life. But that is no excuse not to persist, not to experiment, not to go on trying to restore credibility and confidence in public institutions that fail to satisfy.

The prize of restoring integrity is worth all the effort. As long as humans are imperfect and their systems imperfect, the unscrupulous befouling society will try to keep one step ahead and convince others to join them. The hope is that they will find the going harder and harder, as well it should be, until their misconduct is just not worthwhile and civilized behavior rules the day. Once, cleanliness was thought to be next to godliness, but surely it should be just normal behavior expected of everyone who commands authority, be that public or private. Global crises just strengthen the case.

References

Anderson, C. and Tverdova, Y. (2003) "Corruption, political allegiances, and attitudes toward government in contemporary democracies," *American Journal of Political Science*, 47(1): 91–109.

Anechiarico, F. and Goldstock, R. (2007) "Monitoring integrity and performance: an assessment of the Independent Private Sector Inspector General," *Public Integrity*, 9(2): 117–32.

Berkman, S. (2008) *The World Bank and the Gods of Lending*, Herndon, VA: Kumarian Press.

Campos, E. and Pradham, S. (eds) (2007) *The Many Faces of Corruption*, Washington, DC: World Bank.

Fischer, P.F. (2006) *Rent-Seeking, Institutions and Reforms in Africa: Theory and Empirical Evidence for Tanzania*, New York: Springer.

Girodo, M. (2007) "Corruption and indiscipline in the United Nations," in A. Banerjee and M. Sharma (eds) *Reinventing the United Nations*, New Delhi: Prentice-Hall of India.

Heidenheimer, A.J., Johnston, M., and LeVine, V.T. (eds) (1989) *Political Corruption: A Handbook*, New Brunswick, NJ: Transaction Publishers.

Khan, M. (2006) "Determinants of corruption in developing countries: the limits of conventional economics," in S. Rose-Ackerman (ed.) *International Handbook on the Economics of Corruption*, Cheltenham, UK: Edward Elgar.

Lambsdorff, J., Schramm, M., and Taube, M. (eds) (2004) *The New Institutional Economics of Corruption*, London: Routledge.

Mungiu-Pippidi, A. (2006) "Corruption: diagnosis and treatment," *Journal of Democracy*, 17(3): 86–99.

Nye, J. (1967) "Corruption and political development: a cost–benefit analysis," *American Political Science Review*, 61(2): 417–27.

Quah, J.S.T. (2003) *Curbing Corruption in Asia: A Comparative Study of Six Countries*, Singapore: Eastern Universities Press.

—— (2007) *Combating Corruption Singapore-Style: Lessons for Other Asian Countries*, Maryland Series in Contemporary Asian Studies No. 2 (189), Baltimore MD: School of Law, University of Maryland.

Spector, B. (ed.) (2005) *Fighting Corruption in Developing Countries: Strategies and Analysis*, Bloomfield, CT: Kumarian Press.

Index

Lightning Source UK Ltd.
Milton Keynes UK
08 March 2011

168913UK00002B/30/P

9 780415 665995